LOVE AND BETRAYAL
A CATULLUS READER

BRUCE ARNOLD
Mount Holyoke College

ANDREW ARONSON
Sidwell Friends School, Washington, DC

GILBERT LAWALL
The University of Massachusetts, Amherst

A Prentice Hall Latin Reader

Prentice
Hall

Glenview, Illinois
Needham, Massachusetts
Upper Saddle River, New Jersey

Photo Credits

Cover: ©Phoenix Art Group, Inc., Richard Franklin "To Go Beyond," Courtesy of Grand Image Ltd., Seattle, WA; **page 19:** Walters Art Gallery, Baltimore; **page 56:** Cabinet des Medailles, Paris, France; **pages 65, 115, 141, 142, 159, 205:** Alinari/Art Resource, NY; **page 69:** Mount Holyoke College Library/Photo courtesy Michael Flinn; **page 89:** Philadelphia Museum of Art, George W. Elkins Collection; **page 93:** Giraudon/Art Resource, NY; **page 162:** British Museum; **page 218:** National Museum, Athens

Acknowledgments

Grateful acknowledgment is made to the following for copyrighted material:
George Braziller, Inc. Excerpt from *Roman Culture: Weapons and the Man*, edited by Gary Wills. George Braziller, Inc. © 1966 by Gary Wills. **Cambridge University Press** Excerpt from *Theocritus*. Edited with Translation and Commentary, A.S.F. Gow. Cambridge: Cambridge University Press, 1952. **Gloria S. Duclos** Excerpt from "Catullus 11: Atque in perpetuum, Lesbia, ave atque vale" *Arethusa* 9, 1976, 78-79. **Faber & Faber Ltd.** Excerpt from *The Translations of Ezra Pound*. Faber & Faber Ltd. © 1954 by Ezra Pound. **Grove Press, Inc.** Excerpt from *The Poems of Catullus*. Translated and with an Introduction by Horace Gregory. New York: Grove Press, Inc. © 1956 by Horace Gregory. **Harcourt, Inc.** Excerpt from *The Waste Land*. From *The Complete Poems and Plays 1909-1950* by T.S. Eliot. Harcourt Brace & World, Inc., NY, © 1971 by Esme Valerie Eliot. **Harvard University Press** Excerpt from *Sappho and Alcaeus*. D.A. Campbell, ed., Loeb Classical Library. Cambridge, MA: Harvard University Press, 1982. Excerpt from *Appollonius Rhodius: Argonautica*, trans. R.C. Seaton. Loeb Classical Library. Cambridge, MA: Harvard University Press & London: William Heinemann, 1912-1988. Lines 3.282-98, 3.755-65, 3.961-65. Excerpt from *Lucretius: De Rerum Natura*, trans. W.H.D. Rouse and M.F. Smith. Loeb Classical Library. Cambridge, MA: Harvard University Press & London: William Heinemann, 1975. Lines 3.152-58. Excerpt from *Propertius: Elegies*, trans. G.P. Goold. Loeb Classical Library. Cambridge, MA: Harvard University Press & London: William Heinemann, 1990. Lines 3.8.3-4, 9-12, 27-28. **The Hudson Review, Inc.** Excerpt from *The Hudson Review*, Vol. V, No. 1 (Spring 1952)/ Copyright © 1952 by The Hudson Review, Inc. **Ives Street Press** Excerpt from *My Confidant, Catullus*. Ives Street Press. © 1983 by Thomas McAfee. **Macmillan Publishing** Excerpt from *Literature of the Western World* (vol.1), "Chaucer's Canterbury Tales," Translated by Theodore Morrison, © 1984 by Macmillan Publishing Co. **W. W. Norton & Company** Excerpt from *The Poems of Catullus*, Translated by Horace Gregory. W.W. Norton & Co., Inc. © 1956 by Horace Gregory. **Penguin Putnam, Inc.** Excerpt from *The Poems of Catullus*. Translated by Peter Whigham. Penguin Classics, 1966. © by Peter Whigham 1966. Pg. 197. **Phoenix** Excerpt from "Who Speaks the Final Lines? Catullus 62: Structure and Ritual," T. Goud, *Phoenix* 49, 1995, 30-31.

Note: Every effort has been made to locate the copyright owner of material reprinted in this book. Omissions brought to our attention will be corrected in subsequent editions.

ISBN: 0-13-043345-4
9 10 11 12   09 08 07

CREDITS

The authors are grateful to the following and to their students for corrections and suggestions that they made after piloting this book and its teacher's guide in 1998/1999:

Andrew Aronson
The Sidwell Friends School
Washington, District of Columbia

Karl Hayes
Elgin Academy
Elgin, Illinois

Herbert Holland
Gloversville High School
Gloversville, New York

Helene Lerner
Wayland High School
Wayland, Massachusetts

Brian McCarthy
Mt. Greylock Regional High School
Williamstown, Massachusetts

Sally Murphy
The Winsor School
Boston, Massachusetts

David Perry
Rye High School
Rye, New York

The authors are grateful to the following for numerous excellent suggestions in the final stages of preparing this material for publication:

Sean Smith
Amherst Regional High School
Amherst, Massachusetts

CONTENTS

INTRODUCTION

Catullus has commonly proved to be a potent resource against boredom for those students who otherwise may think of Roman authors as old fuddy-duddies. The youthful hero who tells his elders exactly what he thinks of them and then begs his girlfriend to give him hundreds and thousands of kisses right now before it's too late grips the interest of most young people who are in their early years of studying Latin. Catullus has been Western civilization's poster child for youthful alienation, and thus his life elicits ready sympathy on the part of the casual reader. What students should know, therefore, about the poet's life and poetry may not always seem entirely useful when first coming to grips with this author, but it may serve to help them, on further reflection, to understand the many portions of the Catullan corpus that do not immediately bubble up on the page with gushing romantic sentiment.

It might strike the modern student of Catullus as odd that the Latin love poets, who in subsequent generations looked back to him as a model for their own work, described him as **doctus Catullus**. His designation as "learned" derives primarily from the fact that he belonged to the first generation of Latin poets to be significantly instructed in and shaped by the aesthetic sensibilities and literary practices of Greek poets of the third century B.C., several hundred years before his own day and age (Catullus' dates are usually given as 84–54 B.C.). Alexander the Great had founded Alexandria in 331 B.C. as the administrative center of Greek rule in Egypt, and his successors, the Ptolemies, built and cultivated a great library there, which became the most important center of Greek literature and learning during the Hellenistic era (323–31 B.C.). The most notable of the third century Alexandrian or Hellenistic Greek poets was Callimachus, who espoused a critical awareness of literary form, scrupulous attention to refinement in composition, and elegant erudition. He made fun of long, continuous narrative poems that were still being written in imitation of Homer, comparing them to the muddy Euphrates River. He himself experimented with short poems, such as epigrams, hymns, and personal invective, books of discontinuous, episodic narratives, and a miniature epic or "epyllion"; in his treatment of myth he gave some attention, as did other Alexandrians poets, to exploring the feelings of lovers. He attached more importance to themes of personal and scholarly interest than to the communal and moralistic values common to the traditional epic and dramatic poetry of archaic and classical Greece. Many of the features of Callimachus' innovative poetic program were deliberately taken up in the poetry of Catullus and presumably in the poetry, no longer extant, of other Latin poets of that period who are associated loosely with Catullus. These are the very ones whom Catullus' older contemporary Cicero called

poētae novī and *neoteroi* (a Greek word meaning "newer" or "rather new"), terms that expressed his disdain for what he regarded as their "modern" tendencies. As we have seen, these tendencies had been around for several hundred years in the Greek world, but they seemed revolutionary to many in the Roman world who still preferred the traditional epic and dramatic poetry of the early Latin writers Naevius (late third century B.C.) and Ennius (239–169 B.C.), with their patriotic and nationalistic themes.

Some of the Latin poets who shaped the neoteric revolution in Italy, such as C. Helvius Cinna and Licinius Calvus, were close friends of Catullus and are warmly acknowledged in his poetry; many of them came from Cisalpine Gaul, as did Catullus himself, who was a native of Verona. Prominent among them was Valerius Cato, who settled at Rome as a grammarian and teacher of poetry in the Alexandrian tradition. We also hear of a Greek poet, Parthenius of Nicaea, who was brought to Rome from Bithynia by Cinna and whose presence in Rome stimulated interest in Alexandrian literature and especially in the poetry of Callimachus. There can be little doubt that such friendships and associations with poets who were engaged in experimenting with new styles of thinking, writing, and living during the mid seventies and the sixties B.C. had a profound influence on the youthful Catullus' own destiny as a poet.

According to Jerome (c. A.D. 347–420), who relied on Suetonius (c. A.D. 70–130), our poet lived only thirty years. Thus, if we assume that the last datable allusions in his poetry fall in the final year of his life, we may speculate that he lived from approximately 84 to 54 B.C. (Jerome himself gives the dates as 87–57 B.C., which cannot be right.) At some time in his life Catullus took up residence in Rome, where he came into contact with many of the men prominent in politics and literature who are known to us through historical sources. He is antagonistic toward a great many of the influential politicians of the time, such as Caesar, Pompey, Memmius, Clodius, Calpurnius Piso, and Vatinius, as well as lesser satellites such as Gellius and Mamurra, Caesar's chief engineer in his Gallic campaigns. In addition, poets like Volusius and Suffenus, who were apparently working in the tradition of Latin epic going back to the *Annals* of Ennius over a century before, come in for harsh criticism. The great city of Rome certainly opened unparalleled opportunities for enjoying the urbane intellectual, social, and poetic life that engaged Catullus so deeply, yet on the other hand he was outraged by much of what passed for culture, literature, and politics in the capital. He was always an outsider to some extent, and this allowed him to view the Roman élite from the perspective of his own discomfort, perhaps something like that of a Midwesterner living in New York City, unclouded by the prevailing political ideologies and social practices of the day—mostly corrupt from his perspective.

The most notable topic that extends its influence throughout Catullus' brief poetic career is a love affair with a woman he calls Lesbia, a name that alludes to Sappho, the famous Greek love poetess of the island of Lesbos (seventh to sixth centuries B.C.). The Lesbia of Catullus' poetry is thus at least in part a literary creation who is meant to recall the emotion and the artistry of Sappho. Two of Catullus' most important poems, which describe critical moments in his turbulent affair with the woman he calls Lesbia, are written in a meter reminiscent of Sappho, and both contain allusions to her poetry as the poet describes his own feelings. In part, then, a literary creation, Catullus' affair with Lesbia is usually regarded also as reflecting an affair that he had in real life with a beautiful, captivating, and talented woman named Clodia, who was most likely the wife of Q. Caecilius Metellus Celer, governor of Cisalpine Gaul in 62–61 B.C. and consul in 60 (died 59 B.C.). Nothing that Catullus' poetry says about his relationship with Lesbia/Clodia can be corroborated by other sources, and much that he relates seems more appropriate to a literary fiction than a literary autobiography. His poems offer the first example we have from ancient literature of the poetic record of an affair (imaginary, real, or a combination of the two) extending over time with a beginning, middle, and end. Catullus is also the first poet of whom we have any record who wrote in a subjective manner about his own (or what purports to be his own) love affair as it developed over the course of time.

In the first eleven poems there is an interesting array of pieces that treat Catullus' love affair with a **puella**, who is sometimes explicitly named as Lesbia. These poems appear to offer the outlines of an affair: first the poet's attraction to the **puella** (poems 2 and 3), then his courting of her love (poems 5 and 7), then a realization that she is no longer interested (poem 8), and finally the dissolution of the affair in bitter acrimony as the poet finds himself betrayed by a mistress whom he has discovered to be wildly promiscuous (poem 11).

The theme of betrayal recurs throughout Catullus' poems—sometimes betrayal by his **puella** and sometimes betrayal by his male friends and associates: hence the title of this book. As you read the poems relating to the "affair" with "Lesbia," you will want to think about the extent to which these poems may have been prompted by actual events in the poet's affair with a real woman and the extent to which they are fictional, literary creations. Whether you regard them as more biographical or more fictional, you will likely find yourself wanting to locate and rearrange all of the "Lesbia" poems into a cycle that makes emotional and psychological sense of the ups and downs of the love affair. Two things that you will certainly find are that the poems often allude to Greek models (Sappho, Callimachus, and other Hellenistic poets) and that they are works of supreme poetic artistry that repay very careful attention to their poetic craftsmanship, something on which the neoteric poets all prided themselves. While possibly inspired by actual moments in a real-life affair with Clodia the wife of Metellus (known as **Clōdia Metellī**), Catullus' poems are also creations that he prayed would "endure through the years for more than one century" (1.10) because of what they have to say to readers of all generations, our own no less than any other.

One other significant event in the biography of the poet is clearly marked for the reader as a major contributor to his embitterment: his year-long tenure of service on the provincial staff of Gaius Memmius in Bithynia, which can be dated with all probability to 57–56 B.C. Memmius was considered an expert in literary matters and was a patron of the Roman poet Lucretius. This powerful man's involvement in the literary scene at Rome may have been a factor in Catullus' acquaintance with him and his being appointed to his personal staff. Things did not work out, however, as Catullus planned, and he levels some nasty vituperation at Memmius in poems 10 and 28.

In Rome Catullus depended upon the sympathy of a few close friends such as Veranius and Fabullus and of fellow neoterics such as Licinius Calvus and Cinna. Among these close friends Catullus cultivated a life style based on **ōtium**, *leisure*, and devoted to friendship, love, and poetry. The key term describing the ideal relationships among the people in this circle of friends is **urbanitās** (its opposite is **rūsticitās**), and readers of Catullus soon discover a range of other words that the poet repeatedly uses when writing about the sophisticated urbane values and interactions among the members of his social and literary coterie.

By Catullus' own testimony there were few in the élite circles with whom he was on good terms. This was the age of the so-called First Triumvirate, an agreement made in 60 B.C. between Julius Caesar, Pompey the Great, and Marcus Crassus with the design of controlling political affairs at Rome and reserving the choicest political offices for themselves and their followers. The pact was symptomatic of the destructive ambitions and illegal maneuvering that undermined political life during the fifties and led ultimately to its cataclysmic collapse in civil war at the end of the decade. Many of Catullus' poems raise what is almost a "voice in the wilderness," protesting against the unrestricted greed and social crassness that were so prevalent at the time. In particular, Catullus singles out Caesar and Pompey and their underlings for scathing criticism.

Another disheartening event in Catullus' life was the death of his brother, whose grave in the vicinity of Troy Catullus visited and commemorated with the justly famous and moving poem 101. There seems to have been deep affection between the brothers, and Catullus' tragic sense of loss over at his brother's death appears also in poems 65 and 68.

Catullus seems to have admired the traditional value set upon the Roman family, as the hymn to Diana (34) and the two wedding poems (61 and 62) indicate. Suetonius reports (*Life of Julius Caesar* 73) that Catullus' father enjoyed Caesar's friendship and that the son on one occasion apologized to Caesar for the libelous verses he had written against him. While it is difficult to imagine Catullus abandoning his deep-seated hatred toward the budding dictator and his minions, there is no difficulty in supposing that the poet undertook such a reconciliation in deference to his father's ties of hospitality, which may have been important for the family's influence and business contacts.

The problems of understanding Catullus' poetry extend beyond the mysteries of his personal life. The text itself of the poems has spawned many questions and insoluble conundrums. Our modern editions of the text descend from three manuscripts copied in the fourteenth century, all of which are derived from a single version, now lost, that managed to make it through the Middle Ages. That single copy had many errors, for which much scholarly work has produced some plausible corrections, and some fragmentary parts that have never been adequately explained or integrated with their surrounding poems. You will encounter some of these textual problems in the poems contained in this book, and there will be some discussion of them in the notes. This should help you to understand how fragile is much of our literary heritage from the classical world and how difficult it is to restore our damaged texts to readings in which we can have confidence.

There is another thorny problem presented by the text that has prompted much scholarly debate. Did Catullus arrange part or all of the poems in his corpus in the order in which we now have them, or is the collection a miscellany gathered together by a posthumous editor? The first poem in the corpus as we have it is a piece dedicating a **novus libellus**, *a new little papyrus roll*, to a certain Cornelius. The problem is that the word **libellus** seems to imply a single, short papyrus roll, but the 2,289 lines of poetry in the present corpus exceed what would have comfortably fit on the literary papyrus rolls of which we have knowledge. Many scholars, therefore, assume a threefold division of Catullus' poetry, which would have originally been transmitted on three separate rolls: poems 1–60 (848 lines), poems 61–64 (795 lines), and poems 65–116 (646 lines). These divisions are not arbitrary but coincide with major breaks in the grouping of poems by genre or meter. The first 60 poems are short, personal compositions, often addressed to a specific recipient, written in a variety of meters (and thus called "polymetric"), the most common of which is the hendecasyllabic meter. The second group of four long poems may all be said to treat marriage in one form or another, including the two epithalamia, which recall one of the favorite genres of poetry that Sappho worked in. This group also includes a highly polished short epic or epyllion on the wedding of Peleus and Thetis. The poems of the final group are all written in the elegiac meter, a common meter for writing love poetry. Most of these poems are short epigrams, a literary type recalling one of the favorite genres of Hellenistic poets such as Callimachus, who loved the brief compass and compressed expression of this poetic form. Other scholars have produced other divisions of the poems, and some hold that the **novus libellus** dedicated to Cornelius may have included only poems 2–11 or 2–14. However this may be, Catullus' poetry from one end of the corpus to the other features recurrent themes, such as love, friendship, betrayal, social commentary, and discussions of literary practice, and the range of different genres in which he writes is truly impressive. He appears to have given examples in Latin of the most important kinds of short poetry that were written by the Greeks before him, including both the Hellenistic poets and earlier lyric poets such as Sappho.

TIME LINE

84 A plausible date for the birth of Catullus (see Introduction).
81 Sulla dictator after returning from campaign in Asia against
   Mithradates and civil war against Marians in Italy.
78 Death of Sulla.
75 Beginning of Cicero's career as quaestor in Sicily.
70 First consulship of Pompey and Crassus.
   Birth of Vergil.
66 Cicero as praetor delivers speech *De imperio Pompei*.
65 Birth of Horace.
63 Consulship of Cicero and suppression of the Catilinarian conspiracy.
62 After campaigning in the East, Pompey settles affairs there and
   returns to Rome, disbanding his army.
62–60 Approximate period of Catullus' move to Rome.
61 Governorship of Metellus Celer in Cisalpine Gaul.
60 Caesar returns from a provincial command in Spain and forms the so-
   called First Triumvirate, an illegal agreement for sharing power
   with Pompey and Crassus.
59 Caesar's consulship, during which he receives Cisalpine Gaul and
   Illyricum under the *lex Vatinia*.
58 P. Clodius is tribune and brings about the exile of Cicero.
57 Rioting in Rome between Clodius and Milo.
   Cicero returns from exile.
   Catullus spends the year on the staff of C. Memmius in Bithynia.
56 Cicero delivers the *Pro Caelio*.
   Renewal of the so-called First Triumvirate at Luca.
   Catullus returns to Italy.
55 Second consulship of Pompey and Crassus.
   Caesar bridges the Rhine and later invades Britain.
54 Pompey governs Spain while remaining near Rome.
   Caesar makes a second invasion of Britain.
   Crassus prepares in Syria for a campaign against the Parthians.
   Last datable allusions in the poetry of Catullus (to the campaigns in
   Britain and Parthia), probably indicating that he died about this
   time or in the next couple of years.
53 Crassus defeated and killed in the military disaster at Carrhae.
52 Caesar finally subdues powerful rebellion in Gaul.
50 Caesar crosses the Rubicon into Italy, beginning civil war with
   Pompey and the Senate.
48 Caesar defeats Pompey at Pharsalus.
44 Caesar becomes dictator for life and is assassinated on the Ides of
   March.

USING THIS BOOK

The running vocabularies facing the Latin passages contain most of the words that are not in *ECCE ROMANI*, Books I and II, published by Prentice Hall. Words the meaning of which can be easily deduced are not given in the running vocabularies. A word that is in *ECCE ROMANI*, Books I and II, is included in the facing vocabulary if it is being used in a sense different from the sense in which it is used in that series. Words not given on the facing pages will be found in the vocabulary at the end of the book, thus allowing this book to be used after completion of any standard Latin program. When words that appear in the facing vocabularies reappear in later poems, they are glossed again on the facing page. This facilitates reading of the poems in any order; the vocabulary aids will always be there no matter in what order the poems are read. Note that a word that is glossed on the facing page and then reappears later in the same poem is not normally glossed at this later reappearance and may not appear in the end vocabulary. Look for the word in the earlier glosses for the poem.

The format of vocabulary entries is similar to that in the *ECCE ROMANI* series, with two major modifications. First, information about the Latin words themselves—in particular, information about the individual parts of compound verbs, adjectives, and nouns—is given in brackets. Second, cross references to uses of the same or similar words in other poems are given in parentheses after the Latin word in question. Tracking down these cross references helps the reader build up an awareness of some of the distinctive features of Catullus' diction and expression.

Several definitions are usually given for the Latin words, with the most basic meaning of the word coming first and an appropriate meaning for the context coming last. Definitions and translations are given in italics. Words or phrases that help round out a definition but are not part of the definition itself are enclosed in parentheses. Words or phrases that fill out a suggested translation to make it more complete or to make it better English are placed in square brackets.

When reading a poem of Catullus from this book for the first time, one should not look at the facing vocabulary and notes at all but should read through the Latin of the poem, making as much sense of it as possible. When reading it a second or third time, one usually goes from the right-hand page to the vocabulary on the left-hand page, noting the italicized meanings, especially the last one given, for any unfamiliar words, and back again to the right-hand page. Only after one has grasped the sense of the poem should one look more closely at the vocabulary entries, the grammatical notes, and the other information on the left-hand page.

The Latin texts of the poems of Catullus as printed in this book are for the most part those that appear in the Oxford Classical Text edition of the poems of Catullus, edited by R. A. B. Mynors and published in 1958. Much scholarly attention has been directed to the text of the poems of Catullus since Mynors' edition; the most recent comprehensive edition of the poems produced in the English-speaking world is that of D. S. F. Thomson, *Catullus: Edited with a Textual and Interpretative Commentary*, University of Toronto Press, 1997. At a number of points Thomson and other modern editors have supplied readings that seem to be preferable to those of Mynors. In the present book we have often made note of these in special sections labeled **Text** appearing beneath the notes on the left-hand pages. Rarely we have incorporated readings different from those of Mynors in the poems as printed on the right-hand pages, and we have then given the Oxford Classical Text version in a section labeled **Text** on the left-hand page.

The Latin texts of the poems on the right-hand pages of this book are followed by study questions. Usually these are of two sorts, labeled **Initial Explorations** and **Discussion**. Beginning with poem 62, we provide only one set of questions, labeled **Explorations**. Detailed comparison with other poems is frequently invited in sections labeled **Comparison**.

The poems as presented in this book are often divided into segments printed on successive pages so that the facing vocabularies and notes and the questions will always be on the same page-spread as the related segments of the poems. It is very important, however, to see the poem in its entirety and to be able to mark it in various ways as one studies its structure, its poetic devices, and so forth. We accordingly provide for the teacher large-print versions of the poems with each poem intact (except for Catullus 62, which is too long to fit on one page). Teachers may use these as masters for making overhead transparencies, and they may photocopy them and distribute them to students for their use.

In preparing the vocabularies and notes on the left-hand pages and the questions accompanying the poems, the following reference books were heavily used, and the authors wish to acknowledge their profound debt to them:

Grammar:
> Greenough, J. B., and G. L. Kittredge, A. A. Howard, and Benjamin L. D'Ooge, eds. *Allen and Greenough's New Latin Grammar for Schools and Colleges*. Boston MA: Ginn and Company, 1931.

Dictionaries:
> Glare, P. G. W., ed. *Oxford Latin Dictionary*. Oxford ENG: Clarendon Press, 1982.
> Hornblower, Simon, and Antony Spawforth, eds. *Oxford Classical Dic-*

tionary. 3rd ed. Oxford ENG: Oxford University Press, 1996.

Smith, Sir William, and Sir John Lockwood, eds. *Chambers Murray Latin-English Dictionary.* Cambridge ENG: Cambridge University Press, 1933.

Commentaries:

Fordyce, C. J., ed. *Catullus: A Commentary.* Oxford ENG: Oxford University Press, 1961, 1965, 1966.

Merrill, Elmer Truesdell, ed. *Catullus.* Cambridge: Harvard University Press, 1893.

Quinn, Kenneth, ed. *Catullus: The Poems.* New York: Macmillan, 1970, 1973.

Thomson, D. F. S., ed. *Catullus: Edited with a Textual and Interpretative Commentary.* Toronto CAN: University of Toronto Press, 1997.

POETIC AND RHETORICAL DEVICES AND FIGURES OF SPEECH

The following poetic and rhetorical devices and figures of speech occur in the selections from Catullus' poetry included in this book. Those included in the *Teacher's Guide to Advanced Placement Courses in Latin* are marked with asterisks. Definitions are followed by representative examples (some of the definitions in this section and the section on metrical terms are formulated to be consistent with those in *Love and Transformation: An Ovid Reader*, edited by Richard A. Lafleur and published by Scott Foresman-Addison Wesley, 2nd ed., 1999).

***Allegory**: Gr., "speaking differently," a prolonged metaphor, i.e., a type of imagery involving the extended use of a person or object to represent some concept outside the literal narrative of a text, e.g., the extended simile of the flower in the garden to represent the desirability of virginity in 62.39–44.

***Alliteration**: deliberate repetition of sounds, usually of initial consonants but also of initial stressed vowels, in successive words, for emphasis and for musical and occasionally onomatopoetic effect, e.g.: **Cui dōnō lepidum novum libellum** (1.1, with consonance and assonance as well as alliteration); cf. assonance and consonance.

***Anaphora**: Gr., "carrying back," repetition of words or phrases at the beginning of successive clauses, often with asyndeton, for emphasis and emotional effect, e.g., **Ō factum male! Ō miselle passer!** (3.16)

Anastrophe: Gr., "turning back," the reversal of normal word order, as with a preposition following its object, often with the effect of emphasizing the word(s) placed earlier, e.g., **ōrāclum Iovis inter aestuōsī** (7.5).

Antithesis: Gr., "set against, in opposition," sharp contrast of juxta-posed ideas, e.g., **amant amantur** (45.20).

*Apostrophe: Gr., "turning away," a break in a narrative to address some person or personified thing present or absent, sometimes for emotional effect, sometimes to evoke a witness to a statement being made, e.g., **Amastri Pontica et Cytōre buxifer** (4.13).

*Ascending Tricolon: see Tricolon Crescens.

*Assonance: repetition of internal or final vowel or syllable sounds in successive words, for musical and sometimes onomatopoetic effect, e.g.: **cui dōnō lepid<u>um</u> nov<u>um</u> libell<u>um</u> / āridā modo pūmice expolīt<u>um</u>?** (1.1–2); cf. homoioteleuton.

*Asyndeton: Gr., "without connectives," omission of conjunctions where one or more would ordinarily be expected in a series of words, phrases, or clauses, underscoring the words in the series, e.g., **perfer, obdūrā** (8.11); cf. polysyndeton.

*Chiasmus: Gr., "crossing," arrangement of words, phrases, or clauses in an oppositional, ABBA order, often to emphasize some opposition or to draw the elements of the chiasmus closer together, e.g., **frātrēsque ūnanimōs anumque mātrem** (9.4) (noun A, adjective B, adjective B, noun A).

Conduplicatio: "repetition," for emphasis and emotional effect, e.g., <u>**passer**</u> mortuus est <u>meae puellae</u>, / <u>**passer**</u>, dēliciae <u>meae puellae</u> (3.3–4).

Consonance: repetition of consonants at the beginning, middle, or end of words (thus overlapping with the term *alliteration*), e.g., **quae tū vo<u>l</u>ēbās nec pue<u>ll</u>a nō<u>l</u>ēbat** (8.7); cf. alliteration.

*Ellipsis: Gr., "a falling short," omission of one or more words necessary to the sense of a clause but easily understood from the context; often a form of the verb **sum**, e.g., **salapūtium [est] disertum** (53.5); **Chommoda dīcēbat, sī quandō commoda vellet / dīcere, et īnsidiās Arrius hīnsidiās** (84.1–2; see note on passage).

*Enjambement or **Enjambment**: "a straddling," delay of the final word or phrase of a sentence (or clause) to the beginning of the following verse, to create suspense or emphasize an idea or image, e.g., **sed identidem omnium / īlia rumpēns** (11.19–20).

*Hendiadys: Gr., "one through two," use of two nouns connected by a conjunction to express a single complex idea, instead of having one noun modified by an adjective; the usual effect is to give equal prominence to an image that would ordinarily be subordinated, especially some quality of a person or thing, e.g., **pestem perniciemque** (76.20), literally *plague and ruin = ruinous plague*.

Homoioteleuton: Gr., "like ending," a recurrence of similar endings in successive words, e.g., **Cui dōnō lepid<u>um</u> nov<u>um</u> libell<u>um</u> / āridā**

modo pūmice expolītum (1.1–2); cf. assonance and polyptoton.

Hyperbaton: Gr., "a stepping across, transposition," a violation of usual word order for special effect, e.g., **nōn inmerentī quam mihī meus venter,** / **dum sūmptuōsās appetō, dedit,** cēnās (44.8–9), where **dedit,** the verb of the relative clause in line 8, is delayed and interrupts the **dum** clause in line 9. Also here the relative pronoun **quam** does not stand at the beginning of its clause as is usual but comes as the third word in its clause (delayed relative).

*Hyperbole: Gr., "a throwing beyond, exaggeration," self-conscious exaggeration for rhetorical effect, e.g., **Vērānī, omnibus ē meīs amīcīs/ antistāns mihi mīlibus trecentīs** (9.1–2).

Hysteron Proteron: Gr., "the latter put as the former," a reversal of the natural, logical, or chronological order of terms or ideas, e.g., **ut tēcum loquerer simulque ut essem** (50.13), where the idea of conversing is placed before the idea of being together, which would be prerequisite to any conversation; the more important idea is put first for emphasis, out of chronological order.

*Interlocking Order or **Synchysis:** Gr., "a pouring together," an interlocking arrangement of related pairs of words in an ABAB pattern, often emphasizing the close connection between two thoughts or images, e.g., **Vatīniāna** / **meus crīmina Calvus** (53.2–3).

*Irony: Gr., "pretended ignorance," the use of language with a meaning opposite its literal meaning, e.g., Catullus' reference to himself as **pessimus omnium poēta** in 49.6 is often interpreted as ironic.

*Litotes: Gr., "plainness," a form of deliberate understatement in which a quality is described by denying its opposite, usually intensifying the statement, e.g., **nōn sānē illepidum neque invenustum** (10.4).

*Metaphor: Gr., "carrying across, transference," an implied comparison, using one word for another that it suggests, usually with a visual effect, e.g., **palmulīs** (4.5), *little palms* (of hands) = *blades* (of oars); cf. simile.

*Metonymy: Gr., "change of name," a type of imagery in which one word, generally a noun, is employed to suggest another with which it is closely related, e.g., **neque ūllius natantis impetum trabis** (4.3), where **trabis,** *timber,* is used in place of **nāvis,** *ship;* this figure is a hallmark of high poetic or epic style and allows the poet to avoid prosaic, commonplace words (such as **nāvis**); this example of metonymy is also an example of synecdoche (see below).

*Onomatopoeia: Gr., "the making of words" (adjective, *onomatopoetic* or *onomatopoeic*), use of words the sounds of which suggest their meaning or the general meaning of their immediate context, e.g., **pīpiābat** (3.10), *used to chirp.*

*Oxymoron: Gr., "pointedly foolish," the juxtaposition of incongruous or contradictory terms, e.g., **tacitum cubīle clāmat** (6.7).

*Personification: "person making," a type of imagery by which human traits are attributed to plants, animals, inanimate objects, or abstract ideas, which are then addressed and which may speak as if they were human, e.g., **Phasēlus ille, quem vidētis, hospitēs, / ait fuisse nāvium celerrimus** (4.1–2).

*Pleonasm: Gr., "excess," use of more words than necessary, repetition of the same idea in different words, e.g., **quam tē libenter quamque laetus invīsō** (31.4).

Polyptoton: Gr., "many case endings," repetition of the same word or of words from the same root but with different endings, e.g., **quīcum lūdere, quem in sinū tenēre, / cui prīmum digitum dare appetentī** (2.2–3); cf. homoioteleuton.

*Polysyndeton: Gr., "using many connectives," use of a greater number of conjunctions than usual or necessary, often to emphasize the elements in a series, e.g., **ōtiōque et urtīcā** (44.15).

*Prolepsis: Gr., "taking beforehand, anticipation," attribution of some characteristic to a person or thing before it is logically appropriate, especially application of a quality to a noun before the action of the verb has created that quality, e.g., **miserō quod omnīs/ ēripit sēnsūs mihi** (51.5–6), not *from miserable me* but *from me [and makes me] miserable.*

*Simile: "like," an explicit comparison (often introduced by **ut**, **velut**, **quālis**, or **similis***)* between one person or thing and another, the latter generally something more familiar to the reader (frequently a scene from nature) and thus more easily visualized, e.g., **amōrem, / quī illius culpā cecidit velut prātī/ ultimī flōs** (11.22–23), cf. metaphor.

*Synchysis: see Interlocking Order above.

*Synecdoche: Gr., "understanding one thing with another," a type of metonymy in which a part is named in place of an entire object, or a material for a thing made of that material, or an individual in place of a class, e.g., **vēnimus larem ad nostrum** (31.9), where **larem . . . nostrum** is named in place of **domum nostram** to focus attention on a key element of the concept of home and to avoid the commonplace word **domum;** cf. metonymy.

*Tmesis: "cutting," separation of a compound word into its constituent parts, generally for metrical convenience, e.g., **mala . . . dīcit** (83.1) = **maledīcit.**

*Transferred Epithet: application of an adjective to one noun when it properly applies to another, often involving personification and focusing special attention on the modified noun, e.g., **Nam tē nōn viduās iacēre noctēs** (6.6), where **viduās** logically describes the person referred to with the pronoun **tē** but modifies **noctēs** grammatically.

*Tricolon Crescens or **Ascending Tricolon**: Gr., "having three members," a climactic series of three (or more) examples, illustrations, phrases, or clauses, each (or at least the last) more fully developed or more intense than the preceding, e.g., **quīcum lūdere, quem in sinū tenēre, / cui prīmum digitum dare appetentī / et ācrīs solet incitāre morsūs** (2.2–4).

Word-Picture: a type of imagery in which the words of a phrase are arranged in an order that suggests the visual image being described, e.g., **manūsque collō / ambās iniciēns** (35.9–10), where the words **manūs . . . ambās** surround the word **collō** just as the girl embraces the man's neck.

Zeugma: Gr., "yoking," use of a single word with a pair of others (e.g., a verb with two adverbial modifiers), when it logically applies to only one of them or applies to them both, but in two quite different ways, e.g., **mē recūrāvī ōtiōque et urtīcā** (44.15; see note on passage).

THE METERS OF CATULLUS' VERSE

Hendecasyllabic or Phalaecean (first found in Catullus 1):

Traditionally this meter is divided into feet as follows:

$$\breve{\times}\ \breve{\times}\ |\ -\ \cup\ \cup\ |\ -\ \cup\ |\ -\ \cup\ |\ -\ \breve{\times}$$

It is now regarded as preferable not to divide the line into feet as above but to give the scheme as follows:

$$\breve{\times}\ \breve{\times}\ -\ \cup\ \cup\ -\ \cup\ -\ \cup\ -\ \breve{\times}$$

This allows the third, fourth, fifth, and sixth syllables to be regarded as a choriamb (- ⌣ ⌣ -), which was one of the basic metrical patterns in lyric meters.

Pure Iambic Trimeter (found in Catullus 4 and used by Catullus elsewhere only in poem 29, which is not in this book):

$$\cup\ -\ \cup\ -\ |\ \cup\ \|\ -\ \cup\ -\ |\ \cup\ -\ \cup\ \breve{\times}$$

The meter consists of three pairs of iambic feet, divided here by the two single vertical lines. The double vertical lines mark the caesura. The pattern is invariable, except that the final syllable may be either long or short.

Choliambic (first found in Catullus 8):

The choliambic meter is based on the iambic trimeter (three pairs of iambic feet):

$$\times - \cup \times \mid \times \parallel - \cup - \mid \cup - - \times$$

In the choliambic (Gr., "limping iambic") meter, the next to the last syllable is long instead of short, thus producing the limping effect. Note where substitutions are possible.

Sapphic Strophe (used by Catullus only in poems 11 and 51):

Traditionally this meter is divided into feet as follows:

Three lines (Lesser Sapphic) $- \cup \mid - \times \mid - \parallel \cup \cup \mid - \cup \mid - \times$

One line (Adonic) $\qquad\qquad - \cup \cup \mid - \times$

It is now regarded as preferable not to divide the line into feet as above but to give the scheme as follows:

Three lines (Lesser Sapphic) $- \cup - \times - \parallel \cup \cup - \cup - \times$

One line (Adonic) $\qquad\qquad - \cup \cup - \times$

This allows one to recognize choriambs ($- \cup \cup -$) as basic constituents of this lyric meter.

Catullus 34

Three lines (Glyconic) $\quad \times \times - \cup \cup - \cup \times$
One line (Pherecratean) $\quad \times \times - \cup \cup - \times$

Dactylic Hexameter (Catullus 62):

$$- \overset{\smile\smile}{} \mid - \overset{\smile\smile}{} \mid - \parallel \overset{\smile\smile}{} \mid - \overset{\smile\smile}{} \mid - \overset{\smile\smile}{} \mid - \times$$

$$- \overset{\smile\smile}{} \mid - \overset{\smile\smile}{} \mid - \cup \parallel \cup \mid - \overset{\smile\smile}{} \mid - \overset{\smile\smile}{} \mid - \times$$

$$- \overset{\smile\smile}{} \mid - \parallel \overset{\smile\smile}{} \mid - \overset{\smile\smile}{} \mid - \parallel \overset{\smile\smile}{} \mid - \overset{\smile\smile}{} \mid - \times$$

$$- \overset{\smile\smile}{} \mid - \parallel \overset{\smile\smile}{} \mid - \times \mid - \cup \parallel \cup \mid - \overset{\smile\smile}{} \mid - \times$$

Spondees may be substituted for dactyls in the first five feet, but the substitution of a spondee in the fifth foot is rare. Double vertical lines indicate where caesuras may occur.

Elegiac Couplet (first found in Catullus 70):

Hexameter: – ⏕ | – ⏕ | – ⏕ | – ⏕ | – ⏕ | – ⏒

Pentameter: – ⏕ | – ⏕ | – | / – ⏑ ⏑ | – ⏑ ⏑ | ⏒

For caesuras in the hexameter, see above under **Dactylic Hexameter**. In the pentameter, the second half of the third foot and the second half of the sixth foot of a hexameter have been truncated, thus giving two sets of two and a half feet (= five feet or a pentameter). A diaeresis (here frequently coinciding with a pause in the sense) normally occurs after the third foot of the pentameter (marked here with a forward slash).

METRICAL TERMS

The following metrical terms will be fond to be useful. Those included in the *Teacher's Guide to Advanced Placement Courses in Latin* are marked with asterisks.

*Caesura: a pause between words occurring within a metrical foot; the effect is to emphasize the word immediately preceding or, less often, following; cf. diaeresis.

Consonantal i and u: the vowels *i* and *u* become consonants before vowels.

 Coriamb: a metrical foot with the pattern – ⏑ ⏑ – .

*Dactyl: a metrical foot with the pattern – ⏑ ⏑ .

*Diaeresis: a pause between words coinciding with the end of a metrical foot, less common than caesura and sometimes employed to emphasize the word immediately preceding or, less often, following.

*Diastole: lengthening of an ordinarily short vowel (and hence the syllable containing it), usually when it occurs under the ictus and before a caesura; sometimes reflecting an archaic pronunciation; for an example, see poem 62.4.

*Elision: Lat., "bruising," the partial suppression of a vowel or diphthong at the end of a word when the following word begins with a vowel or with *h*. A final *m* does not block elision, and thus the letters *um* of **cum** are elided in poem 1.5: **iam tum, cum‿ausus es ūnus Ītalōrum**.

*Hexameter: a line of poetry consisting of six metrical feet.

*Hiatus: Lat., "gaping," omission of elision; this is generally avoided, but when it does occur it emphasizes the word that is not elided or coincides with a pause in the sense, e.g., Ō **factum male!** Ō **miselle passer!** (3.16; **male!** and Ō do not elide).

*Hypermetric Line: a line containing an extra syllable, which elides with the word at the beginning of the next line, e.g., **prātī / ultimī** 11.22–23). Elision of this sort is called *synapheia* (see below).

Iambic Shortening: words with a metrical pattern of a short syllable followed by a long syllable, e.g., **sciō**, could be pronounced as two short syllables in ordinary speech. In Catullus 2.6 this carries over into **nescio**. A number of examples will be found in Catullus, e.g., **volo** for **volō** (6.16).

*Iambus (Iamb): a metrical foot with the pattern ˘ – .

*Ictus: Lat., "stroke," the verse accent or beat, falling on the first long syllable in each foot.

*Pentameter: the second line of an elegiac couplet.

Spondaic line: a dactylic hexameter with a spondee in the fifth foot, e.g., **ūna salūs haec est, hōc est tibi pervincendum** (76.15).

*Spondee: a metrical foot with the pattern – – .

Synaeresis: Gr., "taking together," occasional pronunciation of the vowel *i* as a consonant *y* before a vowel, e.g., **cōnūbium** (62.57), normally four syllables, pronounced as *cōnūbyum*, three syllables. So, perhaps also **omnium** (11.19).

Synapheia or **Synaphaea**: Gr., "binding," elision at the end of one line with a word at the beginning of the next, e.g., **prātī / ultimī** (11.22–23); **prātī** elides with **ultimī**.

*Syncope or **syncopation**: Gr., "striking together, cutting short," omission of a letter or a syllable from the middle of a word, e.g., **saeclō** (1.10) = **saeculō**; **nōrat** (3.6) = **nōverat**.

*Synizesis: Gr., "settling together, collapsing," the pronunciation of two vowels as one syllable without forming a diphthong, e.g., **deinde**.

*Systole: shortening of a vowel that was ordinarily long, e.g., **illius** (3.8) for **illīus**.

*Trochee: a metrical foot with the pattern – ˘ .

LEXICAL AND GRAMMATICAL TERMS

Archaism: deliberate use of old-fashioned words or forms no longer in common currency.

Asterisks: e.g., ***stanō** (8.11), indication of a hypothetical form not actually found in surviving written documents.

Diminutives: the suffixes **-ulus, -olus** (after a vowel), **-culus, -ellus**, and **-illus** form diminutive adjectives and nouns, often expressing endearment and affection, sometimes pity, e.g., **Cui dōnō lepidum novum <u>libellum</u>** (1.1), *[my] dear little papyrus roll.*

Inceptive Verbs: verbs with an **-sc-** infix such as **cognōscō** are called inceptive verbs and often denote the beginning (cf. Lat. **incipiō**, *to begin*) of an action. Thus, **cognōscō** means *to get to know, learn, become acquainted with.* The inceptive infix **-sc-** appears only in the present stem of inceptive verbs, and forms of these verbs derived from the perfect stem are not translated as inceptive. The perfect tense of **cognōscō**, for example, **cognōvī**, means *to have come to understand, to know* and may often best be translated in context as a present tense, *I know.* The pluperfect of inceptive verbs may often best be translated as an imperfect.

Impersonal Verbs: impersonal verbs such as **libet (lubet)** + dat., *(it) is pleasing* (to), do not appear in the first or second persons and do not have personal subjects. In dictionaries the subject is given as the impersonal *it*, and this word may be used in your translation. There will often, however, be an infinitive, a phrase, or a clause introduced by **ut** and with its verb in the subjunctive that serves as the actual grammatical subject of the impersonal verb. Thus, in Catullus 2.6, the words **lubet iocārī** may be translated *it pleases [her] to play*, with the infinitive filling out the meaning of the impersonal verb, or we may translate *to play pleases [her]*, with the infinitive serving as the subject of the impersonal verb. You may translate either way, but in the notes in this book the actual grammatical subjects of impersonal verbs will usually be pointed out and used as subjects in translations.

LOVE AND BETRAYAL
SELECTIONS FROM CATULLUS

Vīvāmus, mea Lesbia, atque amēmus!

"Sappho and Alcaeus"
Sir Lawrence Alma-Tadema, British, 1836–1912
The Walters Art Gallery
Baltimore, Maryland

Meter: hendecasyllabic

1   **lepidus, -a, -um** [colloquial word, common in Plautus and Terence], *charming, delightful, nice; witty, amusing.*
    libellus, -ī, m. [dim. of **liber, librī,** m., *papyrus roll* (the ancient form of what we think of as a book)], *little papyrus roll.*

2   **āridus, -a, -um,** *dry.*
    modo, adv., *only; recently, just now.*
    pūmex, pūmicis, f. here, though usually m., *pumice-stone* (used like sandpaper to smooth the ends of a papyrus roll).
    expoliō [**ex-,** *thoroughly* + **poliō, -īre, -īvī, -ītus,** *to polish*], **-īre, -īvī, -ītus,** *to smooth, polish.*

3   **Cornēlius, -ī, m.,** *Cornelius* (Cornelius Nepos, c. 110–24 B.C., historian, biographer, and minor poet; Nepos, like Catullus, was a Transpadane; he was considerably older than Catullus, and he had important connections in Rome, being a friend of Atticus and Cicero).
    namque, conj., *for.*

4   **esse aliquid:** colloquial, *[they] were [worth] something, were of some value.*
    nūgae, -ārum, f. pl., *nonsense; trifles, frivolities.*

5   **iam tum, cum:** *already at that time, when.*
    ausus es: from the semi-deponent verb **audēre.**
    ūnus Ītalōrum: *the [only] one of the Italians, alone of Italians.*

6   **aevum, -ī,** n., *age, generation; time.*
    omne aevum: *all recorded history.* The work of Cornelius Nepos referred to here was entitled *Chronica* (= *Annals*) and was a universal history of the Greco-Roman world in three papyrus rolls.
    explicō [**ex-,** *out* + **plicō, -āre, -āvī, -ātus,** *to fold; to roll*], **-āre, -āvī, -ātus,** *to unfold, unroll; to make known, explain, give an account of.*
    carta, -ae, f., *sheet of papyrus;* by extension, *papyrus roll* (i.e., sheets of papyrus glued together), *volume* (of written work).

7   **doctus, -a, -um,** *learned, full of learning.*
    Iuppiter: *by Jupiter!* = *I swear it!*
    labōriōsus, -a, -um, *involving much work; laborious, painstaking.*

8   **habē tibi:** a legal phrase used when transferring property from one person to another, *take for yourself!* Used colloquially, it implies indifference, as if one were to say, *it's yours, you may have it.*
    quisquis, quisquis, quidquid, indefinite pronoun/adjective, *whoever, whatever.*
       quidquid hoc libellī: supply **est,** a depreciatory phrase, *whatever this [is] of a little papyrus roll.*

CATULLUS 1

Dedication

Catullus dedicates his new papyrus roll of verse to Cornelius Nepos.

1 Cui dōnō lepidum novum libellum
2 āridā modo pūmice expolītum?
3 Cornēlī, tibi: namque tū solēbās
4 meās esse aliquid putāre nūgās
5 iam tum, cum ausus es ūnus Ītalōrum
6 omne aevum tribus explicāre cartīs
7 doctīs, Iuppiter, et labōriōsīs.
8 Quārē habē tibi quidquid hoc libellī

continued

Initial Explorations

1. What qualities does Catullus ascribe to his **libellus**? (1–2)
2. Examine each word that Catullus uses to describe his **libellus** in the first two lines. How could each word simultaneously describe both the physical appearance of the **libellus** and also the quality of the poetry within it?
3. Why does Catullus use the diminutive form **libellum**? (1)
4. Identify examples of alliteration, assonance, and homoioteleuton in the first two lines. What effects are produced by these features of the verse?
5. How is **modo** in line 2 related to **novum** in line 1? How is **expolītum** in line 2 related to **lepidum** in line 1? How do these words form a chiasmus?
6. Identify the rhetorical figure involved in the words **solēbās / meās . . . nūgās** (3–4). What is its effect?
7. Why has Catullus chosen Cornelius as the recipient of his **libellus**? (3–4)
8. How by word choice and word order has Catullus drawn an effective contrast between Cornelius' estimation of the poet's work and Catullus' own estimation of it? (3–4)
9. In line 5 Catullus commends Cornelius for being a bold writer. What did Cornelius dare to produce? (5–6)
10. What are the characteristics of Cornelius as a writer and of his literary production? (5–7) What stylistic devices does Catullus employ in describing Cornelius' literary achievement? What are some of the implications of Catullus' use of the two adjectives **doctīs** and **labōriōsīs** (7)?
11. Compare line 6 with line 1, and line 7 with line 2. How do Catullus' and Cornelius' respective works of poetry and history differ? Does Catullus express unqualified admiration of Cornelius' work?

9   **quāliscumque, quāliscumque, quālecumque**, indefinite adjective, *of whatever sort.*

         quālecumque: idiomatically, *such as it is* or *for what it's worth.*

     quod: connecting relative and subject of the jussive subjunctive **maneat** (10), *and may it. . . .*

     <ō>: not found in the manuscripts, but supplied by modern editors.

     patrōna, -ae, f., *patroness.*

10   **perennis, -is, -e** [**per-**, *through* + **annus, -ī**, m., *year*], *lasting through the years; enduring.*

         perenne: predicate adjective, modifying **quod** (9).

     saeclum, -ī, n. [syncope for **saeculum**], *age; lifetime; generation; century.*

Text

8   **quālecumque; quod**: Thomson puts a comma at the end of line 8 and deletes the semicolon here, giving:

        8   Quārē habē tibi quidquid hoc libellī,

        9   quālecumque quod, <ō> patrōna virgō,

       10   plūs ūnō maneat perenne saeclō.

     quālecumque quod: **quod** is now a delayed relative pronoun, and the phrase = **quod quālecumque**. . . . , *which, such as it is.* . . . Such delaying of relative pronouns is an example of hyperbaton and is found elsewhere in Catullus.

Comparison

Compare the following English rendering of Catullus 1 by Andrew Lang (1888). To what extent has Lang succeeded in his rendering of Catullus' poem? In what ways has he failed? What changes has he deliberately made? Which is the better poem? Why?

My little book, that's neat and new,
Fresh polished with dry pumice stone,
To whom, Cornelius, but to you,
Shall *this* be sent, for you alone—
(Who used to praise my lines, my own)—
Have dared, in weighty volumes three,
(What labors, Jove, what learning thine!)
To tell the Tale of Italy,
And all the legend of our line.

So take, whate'er its worth may be,
My Book,—but, Lady and Queen of Song,
This one kind gift I crave of thee,
That it may live for ages long!

9   quālecumque; quod, <ō> patrōna virgō,
10 plūs ūnō maneat perenne saeclō.

Initial Explorations

12. What attitude toward his own work does Catullus seem to reveal in his choice of the phrases **habē tibi** and **quidquid hoc libellī** and in the word **quālecumque**? (8–9) What words earlier in the poem express a similar attitude?

13. To whom do you suppose the word **virgō** (9) refers?

14. What prayer does Catullus make to the **virgō**? (9–10)

15. Explain the tension that exists between the content of the wish in the final two lines and the poet's earlier assessment of his work.

16. Read the poem aloud in meter and comment on your reading. Recall the effects produced by alliteration, assonance, and homoioteleuton in lines 1–2, and comment on (a) the effect of homoioteleuton in lines 1–2, 3–4, 6–7, and 9–10, (b) the elisions in lines 5–6, and (c) the strong alliteration or consonance in lines 8–9.

Discussion

1. What does the poem say about Catullus' **libellus** and about what Catullus valued in his poetry and thought noteworthy about it?

2. Is Catullus' admiration of Cornelius' *Chronica* sincere or is it tinged with sly humor?

3. What is the role of the **patrōna virgō** in the final two lines?

4. Consider the underlying paradox of the whole poem. Although the poet seems to downplay the significance of his poetry and to elevate the importance of Cornelius' history, the emphasis in lines 1–2 on the charm and polish of Catullus' poetry and the emphasis in line 7 on the choppy and double-edged description of Cornelius' volumes of history seem to suggest the opposite. With what final impression of the quality of the two writers' works are you left after reading the whole poem?

Comparison

The Greek poet Callimachus, who inspired Catullus in a number of ways, made a prayer to the Graces that Catullus may have had in mind when formulating his prayer to the **patrōna virgō**:

Come now and wipe your anointed hands
　　on my elegies so that they may last for many a year.

—*Aetia* I, fragment 7, lines 13–14

Meter: hendecasyllabic

1   **passer, passeris**, m., *small bird* (usually thought to be a *sparrow*, but taken by some to be a *blue thrush*; the word and its diminutive, **passerculus**, were used as terms of endearment).

        passer: vocative, picked up by **tēcum** in line 9.

    dēliciae, -ārum, f. pl. [usually pl. in form, sing. in meaning], *pleasure, delight; pet; darling, sweetheart.*

    puella, -ae, f., *girl; girlfriend, sweetheart.*

2   **quīcum**: = **quōcum**.

        quīcum lūdere: all the infinitives in lines 2–4 are dependent on **solet** (4); the subject (*she*) is the **puella** (1).

    sinus, -ūs, m., *fold of a toga; lap; bosom.*

3   **prīmum digitum**: *fingertip.*

    appetō [**ad-**, *toward, against* + **petō, petere, petīvī, petītus**, *to look for, seek*], **appetere, appetīvī, appetītus**, *to try to reach; to seek instinctively; to desire; to attack, assail.*

        cui . . . appetentī: the participle, completing the line framing, may be translated with **cui** as a substantive, *to whose eager attack.*

        quīcum (2) **. . . quem . . . / cui** (3): polyptoton and anaphora.

4   **ācer, ācris, ācre**, *keen, sharp.*

    ācrīs: = **ācrēs**, *i*-stem nouns and adjectives commonly retain their original spelling in the accusative plural.

    incitō [**in-**, *in, into* + **citō, -āre, -āvī, -ātus**, *to set in motion, rouse*], **-āre, -āvī, -ātus**, *to urge on, arouse, provoke.*

    morsus, -ūs, m., *nibble, bite, peck* (of a bird).

CATULLUS 2

A Pet Bird

*Catullus wishes that the pet bird of his **puella** could satisfy his needs as well as it appears to satisfy hers.*

1   Passer, dēliciae meae puellae,
2   quīcum lūdere, quem in sinū tenēre,
3   cui prīmum digitum dare appetentī
4   et ācrīs solet incitāre morsūs,

continued

Initial Explorations

1. The words **passer, meae,** and **puellae** in line 1 inform us of a triangle of relationships that this poem will explore. Identify the members of the triangle.
2. What does the word **dēliciae** with its range of meanings tell us about how the poet views the relationship between the **puella** and the **passer**?
3. Describe each of the interactions between the **puella** and the **passer** in lines 2–4.
4. Identify the clauses of an ascending tricolon in lines 2–4.
5. In addition to its literal meaning, what suggestive meaning does the infinitive **lūdere** carry in this context? (2)
6. Of the words **quem in sinū tenēre**, which one adds an erotic coloring to the scene? (2)
7. What is the relationship between the actions of the **puella** in line 3 and in line 4? Can something more than innocent play be seen here?
8. What meaning of the verb **appetere** is most appropriate in translating the participle **appetentī** (3)? How does this word contribute an amorous overtone to the scene?
9. Why is the verb **solet** (4) important? What does it add to the description of the behavior of the **puella**?
10. Discuss the words **ācrīs . . . morsūs** (4). In what direction do these two words take the poet's description of the scene? Elsewhere Catullus uses similar language of lovers' kisses: e.g., Catullus 8.18, **Quem basiābis? Cui labella mordēbis?** *Whom will you kiss? Whose little lips will you <u>bite</u>?* and 68b.86–88, *the dove is said to snatch kisses with her <u>biting</u> beak* (**mordentī . . . rōstrō**) *more wantonly than even an especially passionate woman.* How does this affect your understanding of the scene here?

5   **cum**: *whenever*; **cum** may introduce a general temporal clause with its verb
     in the indicative describing repeated action.
     dēsīderium, -ī, n., *desire, longing; something longed for, object of desire; sweet-
     heart.*
     niteō, nitēre, *to shine; to be beautiful, be radiant.*
       dēsideriō meō nitentī: usually interpreted as dative with **lubet** (6), *to the
         radiant object of my desire*, but some, including Thomson, regard
         dēsideriō meō as ablative and translate *to [her] radiant with desire for me.*
6   **nesciō quis, nesciō quid**, indefinite pronoun [only the **quis, quid** part
     changes form; lit., *I don't know who, I don't know what*], *someone or other, some-
     thing or other.*
       nescio: iambic shortening carries over here into the compound **ne-scio**.
     lubet: archaic for **libet**, impersonal + dat., *(it) is pleasing* (to).
       lubet: the subject is the infinitive **iocārī**.
     iocor, -ārī, -ātus sum, *to jest, joke; to play a game.*
       iocārī: governing **cārum nescio quid** as internal or cognate accusative, *to
         play some dear game or other* or *to engage in some endearing play.*
7   **sōlāciolum, -ī**, n. [dim., probably coined by Catullus] + gen., *slight relief*
     (from), *small comfort* (for).
       et sōlāciolum: a second internal or cognate accusative with **iocārī**, *and to
         play at a small comfort* (for her. . . .). The Renaissance scholar Guarinus
         suggested reading **ut** instead of **et**. He is followed by Thomson. This
         ut would be translated *as*. Line 7 would then clarify the vague **cārum
         nescio quid** in line 6; the **puella** plays with the **passer** *as a small com-
         fort for her heartache.*
     dolor, dolōris, m., *pain, smart, heartache.*
8   **acquiēscō** [**ad-**, intensive prefix + **quiēscō, quiēscere, quiēvī, quiētūrus**, *to
     fall asleep; to rest*], inceptive, **acquiēscere, acquiēvī**, *to quiet down, find rest.*
       ut . . . acquiēscat: either a result or more likely a purpose clause.
     ārdor, ārdōris, m., *fire; heat; passionate desire.*
9   **sīcut**, adv., *just as.*
     ipsa: literally, *[she] herself*; here perhaps, *your mistress*, in the sense that **ipse**
       and **ipsa** often refer to the master and mistress of the household and owner
       and overseer of household slaves and workers.
     possem: *would that I could, if only I could*; the imperfect subjunctive here ex-
       presses an unrealized wish in present time.
         tēcum . . . possem: note the strict correspondence between the meter
           and the individual words in the line.
10   **trīstīs**: for the ending, see the note on **ācrīs** in line 4.
     levō, -āre, -āvī, -ātus, *to lighten, alleviate.*
     cūra, -ae, f., *worry, care, distress* (here, the cares or distress felt by a lover).

5   cum dēsīderiō meō nitentī
6   cārum nescio quid lubet iocārī,
7   et sōlāciolum suī dolōris,
8   crēdō, ut tum gravis acquiēscat ārdor;
9   tēcum lūdere sīcut ipsa possem
10   et trīstīs animī levāre cūrās!

Initial Explorations

11. The words **dēsīderiō meō nitentī** (5) may be translated *to the radiant object of my desire* or *to [her] shining with longing for me*. Does one translation seem to be more appropriate than the other? Need one choose?

12. Why, according to the poet, is the **puella** playing with the **passer**? (5–8) Include in your answer reference to the three line-ending words, **iocārī**, **dolōris**, and **ārdor**. To what extent is the **passer** described as a surrogate lover?

13. How does the presence of the parenthetical word **crēdō** qualify the statements in lines 7 and 8? What level of knowledge of the true intentions of the **puella** does this word suggest on the part of the poet?

14. Is the **puella** or the **passer** the center of the poet's interest in lines 1–8?

15. What is the poet's wish in line 9? in line 10?

16. What is implied in the use of the imperfect subjunctive (**possem**, 9) for the poet's wish?

Discussion

1. What is the relationship between Catullus and the **puella**?

2. How satisfactory is this poem as an introduction to a cycle of poems devoted to the love affair between Catullus and the **puella**?

Meter: hendecasyllabic

1   **tam ... quam**: *as ... as.*
     grātus, -a, -um + dat., *welcome* (to), *pleasing* (to).
        Tam grātum est: *It is as pleasing.* The three lines printed here as Catullus
        2b are joined together with poem 2 in the manuscripts, but most editors
        separate them as a fragment of a poem the remainder of which is now
        lost (similar things happen elsewhere in the Catullan corpus). If they
        were to be joined after line 10 of poem 2, that line would end with a
        comma and the lines of 2b would complete the sentence. The main rea-
        son editors usually print 2b as a fragment of a separate poem is the
        change in the mood of the verbs. Catullus says in 2.9 *if only I could sport
        with you*, using the imperfect subjunctive **possem**. If fragment 2b is to be
        joined to that statement, it is odd that Catullus continues with the indica-
        tive **est**, *it is as pleasing as*, when we would naturally expect the subjunc-
        tive, *it would be as pleasing as*. Furthermore, the comparison to Atalanta,
        the swift girl who refused to marry anyone who could not defeat her in a
        race and who was finally defeated by the stratagem of the golden apple,
        does not appear to illuminate or fit easily with any of the themes of Ca-
        tullus 2.
     ferunt: *they say.*
     puellae: Atalanta, the swift huntress, whose hand in marriage Hippomenes
        (or Milanion; the name of her successful suitor differs in the sources) won
        by throwing three golden apples given him by Venus aside off the race
        course at intervals during his race with Atalanta, the prize of which would
        be marriage with her. Atalanta stopped to pick up the apples and so lost
        the race. According to one version of the story she deliberately wasted
        time in retrieving the last apple because she had fallen in love with Hip-
        pomenes (or Milanion) and wanted to lose the race so that he would marry
        her (see Ovid, *Metamorphoses* 10.560–704).
2   **pernīx, pernīcis**, *swift, nimble, agile.*
     aureolus, -a, -um [dim. of **aureus, -a, -um**, *golden*], *golden.*
     mālum: note the macron; do not confuse with **malus, -a, -um**.
3   **quod**: relative pronoun.
     zōna, -ae, f. [Greek loan word], *girdle* (worn by unmarried girls).
     soluit: pronounce as three syllables here (usually spelled **solvit**).

CATULLUS 2b

Atalanta

The poet compares a personal pleasure to Atalanta's delight with the golden apple.

1 Tam grātum est mihi quam ferunt puellae
2 pernīcī aureolum fuisse mālum,
3 quod zōnam soluit diū ligātam.

Discussion

Could these lines make sense as an ending to Catullus 2?

Meter: hendecasyllabic

1   **lūgeō, lūgēre, lūxī, lūctus**, *to mourn, grieve.*
     Venus, Veneris, f., *Venus* (goddess of love); *charm.*
     Cupīdō, Cupīdinis, m., *Cupid* (son of Venus and god of love); *desire.*
       Venerēs Cupīdinēsque: Catullus is calling upon all the Venuses and Cupids in the world, i.e., all the manifestations of charm and desire.
2   **quantum, -ī**, n., pronoun, *whatever amount.*
       quantum est: the third vocative with **lūgēte**: *whatever amount [of] . . . there is* = *however many [of] . . . there are*, a colloquial expression.
     venustus, -a, -um, *endowed/involved with Venus; attractive, charming.*
       venustiōrum: the comparative adjective may be translated *rather/quite. . . .*
         hominum venustiōrum: perhaps, *of men who are quite caught up in the bonds of Venus herself*, i.e., *who are deeply in love.*
4   **passer . . . meae puellae**: = line 3; conduplicatio, as often in dirges.
     dēliciae: see note to line 1 of Catullus 2.
       passer, dēliciae meae puellae: = Catullus 2.1, vocative there, nominative here.
6   **mellītus, -a, -um** [**mel, mellis**, n., *honey*], *honey-sweet, as sweet as honey.*
     erat: the subject is **passer**.
     nōscō, nōscere, nōvī, nōtus, inceptive, *to get to know, learn;* perfect, *to know* (a person or thing).
       nōrat: syncope for **nōverat**; the pluperfect translates into English as an imperfect with the meaning *used to know.*
7   **ipsam**: = **dominam**, *his mistress* (modified by **suam** in line 6), compare **ipsa** in Catullus 2.9.
     puella mātrem: supply **nōvit**.
8   **sēsē**: an alternate form of **sē**. The form **sēsē** may originally have conveyed greater emphasis, but often it is indistinguishable in sense from the simple **sē**.
     gremium, -ī, n., *bosom, lap.*
     illius: = **illīus**, with short *i* for the sake of the meter.
9   **circumsiliō** [**circum-**, *around* + **saliō, salīre, saluī, salitus**, *to jump, leap*], **circumsilīre**, *to jump/leap/hop around.*
     modo . . . modo: *now . . . now.*
10   **domina, -ae**, f., *mistress* (female head of a household); *owner; female ruler; mistress* (a woman loved by a man but not married to him).
     usque, adv., *continuously, all the time.*
     pīpiō, -āre [onomatopoetic], *to chirp.*

CATULLUS 3

Death of the Pet Bird

Catullus eulogizes the pet bird.

1   Lūgēte, ō Venerēs Cupīdinēsque
2   et quantum est hominum venustiōrum:
3   passer mortuus est meae puellae,
4   passer, dēliciae meae puellae,
5   quem plūs illa oculīs suīs amābat.
6   Nam mellītus erat suamque nōrat
7   ipsam tam bene quam puella mātrem,
8   nec sēsē ā gremiō illius movēbat,
9   sed circumsiliēns modo hūc modo illūc
10   ad sōlam dominam usque pīpiābat;

continued

Initial Explorations

1. Whom does the poet call upon to grieve? Why does he invoke these gods and men? (1–2)
2. Locate and analyze two ascending tricola in lines 1–2 and 4–5.
3. Lines 4–10 recall Catullus 2. Compare the relationship of the **passer** and the **puella** in these lines with lines 1–4 of Catullus 2. What are the similarities and differences?
4. With what word earlier in the poem does **mellītus** (6) correspond? How does the word **mellītus** contribute to our understanding of the relationship between the **puella** and the **passer** as expressed in this poem?
5. The verb **nōrat** (6) may connote a knowing in carnal or sexual as well as mental terms. What limitation does line 7 place on the dual meaning of **nōrat** in this context? Why is that significant?
6. The word **gremiō** (8) reminds the reader of **sinū** in Catullus 2.2. How has the bird's behavior at the bosom or on the lap of the **puella** changed between poems?
7. Comment on the impression produced by the polysyllabic participle placed next to four choppy and elided adverbs in line 9.
8. What do the words **ad sōlam dominam usque pīpiābat** (10) say about the relationship of the bird to the **puella**? Which meaning of the word **domina** is most appropriate? In the context of the scene described in lines 4–10, is more than one meaning of the word applicable?

11   **tenebricōsus, -a, -um** [a colloquial formation from **tenebrae, -ārum,** f. pl., *darkness, gloom*], *dark, gloomy.*

12   **quisquam, quisquam, quicquam,** indefinite pronoun, *anyone, anything.* **negant ... quemquam:** *they say that no one. ...*

13   **male sit:** colloquial, + dat., *may it go badly* (for), *curses* (on). **tenebrae, -ārum,** f. pl., *darkness, gloom.*

14   **Orcus, -ī,** m., *Orcus* (god of the underworld); *death; the underworld.* **quae ... dēvorātis:** *you who. ...* **bellus, -a, -um** [colloquial, cf. the more formal **pulcher, pulchra, pulchrum,** *beautiful, handsome, lovely*], *handsome, pretty, charming.*

15   **mihi:** *from me,* dative of separation with **abstulistis.**

16   **Ō factum male!:** *O misfortune!* (literally, *[thing] done badly*). **misellus, -a, -um** [dim. of **miser, misera, miserum,** *wretched*], *poor little, wretched.*

17   **opera, -ae,** f., *effort; deed.* **tuā ... operā:** idiomatic, *because of your doing, due to you.* **meae puellae:** genitive, with **ocellī** (18).

18   **flendō:** *from. ... ,* gerund, ablative of cause. **turgidulus, -a, -um** [dim. of **turgidus, -a, -um,** *swollen*], *slightly swollen, puffed.* **rubeō, rebēre,** *to be red.* **ocellus, -ī,** m. [dim. of **oculus, -ī,** m., *eye*], *little eye, dear eye.* **turgidulī ... ocellī:** colloquial diminutives expressing endearment or compassion.

Text

16   **male! Ō:** hiatus emphasizes the pathos of the exclamations. Goold, however, emends as follows, eliminating the hiatus:
> 16   Ō factum male, quod, miselle passer,
> 17   tuā nunc operā meae puellae
> 18   flendō turgidulī rubent ocellī!

17   Instead of **tuā,** Thomson prints **vestrā,** referring to the **malae tenebrae / Orcī** (13–14), whereas **tuā** would refer to the **passer** (16). Thomson gives lines 15–17 as follows (note the different punctuation):
> 15   tam bellum mihi passerem abstulistis
> 16   (ō factum male! ō miselle passer!);
> 17   vestrā nunc operā meae puellae

11   quī nunc it per iter tenebricōsum
12   illūc, unde negant redīre quemquam.
13   At vōbīs male sit, malae tenebrae
14   Orcī, quae omnia bella dēvorātis:
15   tam bellum mihi passerem abstulistis.
16   Ō factum male! Ō miselle passer!
17   Tuā nunc operā meae puellae
18   flendō turgidulī rubent ocellī.

Initial Explorations

9. What journey must the bird now make? (11–12) How is it portrayed? What is its mythological background? Do the word **tenebricōsus** and the sentiment expressed in line 12 reinforce or undercut the gravity of the loss? Is there an element of parody here?

10. Whom does the poet curse? (13–14) What specific reason does the poet give for uttering the curse?

11. In a surprising conclusion, what is the bird (or the shades of Orcus if Thomson's reading is accepted) blamed for? (17–18) Does the traditional text or Thomson's emendation make better sense?

12. What feelings does the poet express in the final line? How does he express them?

13. Where in the poem do you find shifts in sentiment and tone? Describe the sentiment and tone of each section of the poem.

14. Read the poem aloud and in meter. Describe the effects of the various sound and metrical patterns in the poem, such as (a) the repetition of double *l*s and the resulting linkage among words, (b) the resonance of *m*s in lines 6–7, (c) the multiple elisions and onomatopoeia in lines 9–10, (d) the contrast between mono- or disyllabic words in the first half of line 11 and the polysyllabic word at the end of the line, (e) the repetitions in lines 13–15 (**malae . . . male; bella . . . bellum**), (f) the anaphora and exclamations in line 16, and (g) the soft liquid sounds of line 18.

Discussion

1. How is the **passer** given human qualities in the image of a lover?
2. How does the portrayal of the **passer** with the **puella** in Catullus 3 complement that in Catullus 2?
3. How does the death of the **passer** open the way for future developments in Catullus' love for the **puella**?

Meter: iambic trimeter

1   **phasēlus, -ī**, m. [Greek loan word meaning *bean*], *small boat, yacht* (named **phasēlus** from its resemblance to a bean-pod).

    hospes, hospitis, m., *guest; visitor; stranger.*

2   **ait**: pronounce as two syllables.

        ait fuisse . . . celerrimus: *says that it was the swiftest. . . .* The **phasēlus** uses Greek grammar, for, unlike Latin, Greek uses the nominative case in indirect statement and does not express the subject of the indirect statement when that subject is the same as the subject of the verb of saying; normal Latin would be **ait sē fuisse . . . celerrimum**.

            ait . . . neque (3) **. . . nequīsse** (4): *and [it] says that it was not unable*; either litotes = *and [it] says that it* <u>was</u> *able* or a denial of a denial = *and [it] denies that it was* <u>not</u> *able* (as if someone had said that it was not able, and it now denies that anyone ever said such a thing).

3   **natō, -āre, -āvī, -ātūrus**, *to swim; to float; to sail.*

    impetus, -ūs, m. [a word associated with epic poetry], *strong forward movement, speed.*

    trabs, trabis, f., *tree trunk; wooden beam, timber;* by metonymy in poetry, *boat.*

4   **nequeō, nequīre, nequīvī/nequiī** (perfect infinitive, **nequīsse**), *to be unable.*

    praetereō [praeter-, *past, by* + **eō, īre, iī, itūrus**, *to go*], **praeterīre, praeterīvī/praeteriī, praeteritus**, *to go past; to surpass.*

    sīve . . . sīve (5), conj., *whether . . . or if* or *or whether.*

    palmula, -ae, f. [dim. of **palma, -ae**, f., *palm* (of the hand)], *palm* (of the hand); metaphorically, *blade of an oar; oar.*

5   **opus est**, impersonal idiom, *(it) is necessary.*

        opus foret (= **esset**): *was necessary;* the subject is **volāre**. Dependent clauses in indirect statement have their verbs in the subjunctive.

    volō, -āre, -āvī, -ātūrus, *to fly, speed, go quickly.*

    linteum, -ī, n., *linen; towel, napkin; sail.*

6   **Et hoc negat . . . negāre lītus** (7): *And it denies that the shore . . . denies this [claim]*, i.e., that it was the swiftest ship. In addition to **lītus**, the infinitive **negāre** has four other subjects in the indirect statement: **īnsulās** (7), **Rhodum** (8), **Propontida** (9), and **sinum** (9).

    mināx, minācis, *menacing, threatening* (in word or action).

    Hadriāticum, -ī, n., *Adriatic Sea.*

7   **-ve**, enclitic conj., *or.*

    Cȳcladēs, Cȳcladum, f. pl., *Cyclades* (a group of islands in the Aegean Sea). **Cȳcladās**: Greek accusative plural.

8   **Rhodus, -ī**, f., *Rhodes* (an island in the Aegean Sea, east of the Cyclades).

    nōbilis, -is, -e, *well-known, famous.*

    horridus, -a, -um, *bristling* (of hair); *rough, choppy* (of the sea).

    Thracius, -a, -um, *Thracian, on the Thracian side* (referring to Thrace, a territory in northeast Greece).

        Thrāciam: Thomson prints **Thrāciā**, ablative of **Thāciās, -ae**, f. [Greek loan word], *Thracias* (a wind blowing from a direction west of north); **Thrāciā** would be ablative of instrument or cause with **horridam**.

CATULLUS 4

A Ship Retired from Service

The poet commemorates the retirement of a well-traveled ship.

1   Phasēlus ille, quem vidētis, hospitēs,
2   ait fuisse nāvium celerrimus,
3   neque ūllius natantis impetum trabis
4   nequīsse praeterīre, sīve palmulīs
5   opus foret volāre sīve linteō.
6   Et hoc negat minācis Hadriāticī
7   negāre lītus īnsulāsve Cȳcladās
8   Rhodumque nōbilem horridamque Thrāciam

continued

Initial Explorations

1. Who is the speaker? Whom does the speaker address? What is the speaker doing? (1)
2. What claim does the speaker report that the **phasēlus** makes for itself? (2)
3. What denial does the speaker report that the **phasēlus** makes in lines 3–5? What is the tone of the denial? What is the flavor of the words attributed to the **phasēlus** here?
4. In continuing to insist on its swiftness, what tone does the **phasēlus** use in lines 6–9?
5. What words describe the dangers of the waters through which the **phasēlus** claims to have sailed so swiftly? (6–9)
6. Find three words that suggest that the **phasēlus** is being personified. Find one word that suggests it is like a bird. What words suggest the personification of nature? (2–9)

9　**Propontis, Propontidos**, f. [**pro-**, *in front of*, + **Pontus, -ī**, m., *the Black Sea*], *Propontis* (the ancient name for the Sea of Marmora, situated between the Aegean to the west and the Black Sea to the east).

　　Propontida: Greek accusative.

trux, trucis, *harsh, savage, pitiless* (of persons); *cruel, savage* (of the sea).

Ponticus, -a, -um, *Pontic* (referring to the Pontus, the Black Sea).

sinus, -ūs, m., see Catullus 2.2; here, *bay, gulf, sea*.

　　Ponticum sinum: *the Black Sea*.

　　horridamque Thrāciam / Propontida: the three-word phrase is balanced by **trucemve Ponticum sinum**.

10　**iste, ista, istud**, *that, that* (which you see).

　　iste post phasēlus: the adverb **post**, *afterward*, here modifies the noun, **phasēlus**, *that afterward phasēlus, that phasēlus to be*.

11　**comātus, -a, -um**, *long-haired; having much foliage, leafy*.

Cytōrius, -a, -um, *Cytorian, of Mt. Cytorus* (a mountain on the southern shore of the Black Sea, rising up behind the port cities of Amastris and Cytorus).

iugum, -ī, n., *yoke; mountain ridge*.

12　**sībilus, -ī**, m., *whistling sound*.

ēdō, ēdere, ēdidī, ēditus, *to put out; to produce, let out; to utter*.

coma, -ae, f., *hair; foliage, leaves*.

13　**Amastris, Amastris**, f., *Amastris* (a port city on the southern coast of the Black Sea).

　　Amastri: vocative.

Cytōrus, -ī, m., *Cytorus* (both the name of a port city on the southern coast of the Black Sea that was absorbed by Amastris and the name of the mountain behind it, famous as a source of box wood).

buxifer, buxifera, buxiferum [**buxus, -ī**, f., *box tree* + **-fer, -fera, -ferum**, *carrying, bearing*], *producing boxwood trees, boxwood-bearing*.

　　buxifer: compounds of this sort are a common feature of older Latin poetic style.

14　**tibi**: since Cytorus was absorbed by Amastris, the two locations are addressed with a singular pronoun.

haec: either *these things* (just mentioned in lines 10–12) or *the following events*; **haec** is the subject of **fuisse** and **esse** in indirect statement.

cognitus, -a, -um, *recognized, well-known*.

15　**ultimus, -a, -um**, *farthest; earliest*.

orīgō, orīginis, f., *beginning*.

　　ultimā ex orīgine: i.e., from its earliest days.

16　**stetisse dīcit**: the **phasēlus** is the subject of **dīcit** and of the three infinitives **stetisse**, **imbuisse** (17), and **tulisse** (19). Normally Latin would use **sē** as subject of the infinitives in indirect statement, but the ship is again using a Greek construction for indirect statement in which no subject needs to be expressed if it is the same as the subject of the introductory verb, here **dīcit**.

cacūmen, cacūminis, n., *peak, summit*.

 9   Propontida trucemve Ponticum sinum,
10   ubi iste post phasēlus anteā fuit
11   comāta silva; nam Cytōriō in iugō
12   loquente saepe sībilum ēdidit comā.
13   Amastri Pontica et Cytōre buxifer,
14   tibi haec fuisse et esse cognitissima
15   ait phasēlus: ultimā ex orīgine
16   tuō stetisse dīcit in cacūmine,

continued

Initial Explorations

7. Describe a chiastic arrangement of words in lines 8–9.
8. The speaker, quoting the denials of the **phasēlus**, leads us back to its place of origin in lines 6–9. With what words does the poet endow the **phasēlus** with human attributes and abilities when it stood as a forest on Mt. Cytorus? (10–12)
9. Whom did the speaker address in line 1? What does the speaker now address in line 13? What is the technical term for the rhetorical figure involved here?
10. Once more the **phasēlus** is said to refer to an authority for its veracity. (13–15) To what does it refer now and to what did it refer for its veracity before?
11. The word **haec** (14) could refer to what comes before it or to what comes after it. Do you think it refers backward or forward? Present reasons for your answer.

17   **imbuō, imbuere, imbuī, imbūtus,** *to dip, wet* (for the first time, as if in an initiatory rite).

18   **impotēns, impotentis** [**in-,** *not* + **potēns, potentis,** *having power* (over), *able to control*], *powerless* (over oneself); *lacking self-control; wild, violent, raging.*
     fretum, -ī, n., *strait, narrows; sea.*

19   **erus, -ī,** m., *master; owner.*
     laevus, -a, -um, *left, on/from the left.*
       laeva sīve. . . . : the first **sīve** has been omitted here: *whether from the left or. . . .*

20   **vocāret . . . incidisset** (21): for the use of the subjunctive here, see the note to line 5. Note the change in tense from imperfect (*the breeze used to call/invite*) to pluperfect (*had fallen*).
     aura, -ae, f., *breeze.*
     sīve: *or if, or whether.*
     utrumque: modifying **pedem** (21).
     Iuppiter, Iovis, m., *Jupiter;* (by metonymy) *sky; wind.*

21   **secundus, -a, -um** [from **sequor, sequī, secūtus sum,** *to follow*], *following* (in order), *second;* of wind, *following* (producing a tail wind), *favorable.*
     pēs, pedis, m., *foot; sheet* (rope fastening the lower corners of a sail to the ship).

22   **vōtum, -ī,** n., *vow* (promise made to a god to do something in exchange for the god's granting of a request).
     lītorālis, -is, -e, *of/belonging to the shore.*
       lītorālibus deīs: i.e., gods of the sea, who commonly had temples on the shore and to whom sailors in distress would pray begging that the gods bring them safely to shore.

23   **sibi:** *by itself,* dative of agent with the perfect passive infinitive **esse facta,** which here replaces a pluperfect indicative, *had been made,* and requires secondary sequence with the imperfect subjunctive in the **cum** clause.
     venīret: the subject is the **phasēlus.**

24   **novissimus, -a, -um** [superlative of **novus, -a, -um,** *new*], *most recent, latest, last to be reached.*
       ā marī novissimō . . . ad . . . lacum: i.e., *from the last sea* to be crossed, usually identified as the Adriatic, to the inland lake, often identified as the Benacus (Lake Garda), where Catullus' ancestral home was located at Sirmio.
     ad usque + acc., *all the way to.*
     limpidus, -a, -um, *limpid, unclouded, clear.*
     lacus, -ūs, m., *lake.*

Text

24   **novissimō:** a Renaissance conjecture replacing the superlative adverb **novissimē.** The adverb would mean *after all else, lastly* and is probably to be preferred here (Thomson prints it in his text).

17 tuō imbuisse palmulās in aequore,
18 et inde tot per impotentia freta
19 erum tulisse, laeva sīve dextera
20 vocāret aura, sīve utrumque Iuppiter
21 simul secundus incidisset in pedem;
22 neque ūlla vōta lītorālibus deīs
23 sibi esse facta, cum venīret ā marī
24 novissimō hunc ad usque limpidum lacum.

continued

Initial Explorations

12. What rhetorical figure is involved in the repetition of **tuō** (16, 17)?
13. Find words that continue the personification of the **phasēlus** and of nature. (14–24)
14. What word again calls attention to the dangers of the waters through which the **phasēlus** sailed?
15. How had the **phasēlus** emphasized its versatility before? How does it do it now?
16. What is the final boast of the **phasēlus**? (22–24)

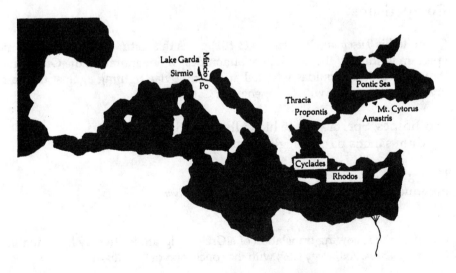

Et hoc negat minācis Hadriāticī
negāre lītus īnsulāsve Cȳcladās
Rhodumque nōbilem horridamque Thrāciam
Propontida trucemve Ponticum sinum. . . .

25   **haec**: *these events.*
      fuēre: = **fuērunt.**
      reconditus, -a, -um, [re-, *back* + **conditus, -a, -um**, *hidden, concealed*], *hidden, secluded.*
26   **seneō, senēre**, *to be old.*
      quiēs, quiētis, f., *relief from labor, rest, repose.*
      tibi: a singular pronoun is here used to refer to the twins, Castor and Pollux, who, as Merrill (12) explains, "were often spoken of . . . under one name,— that of Castor being more frequently used."
27   **gemellus, -a, -um**, *twin-born, twin.*
      Castor, Castoris, m., *Castor* (Castor and his twin brother Pollux were the sons of Zeus and Leda; as the constellation Gemini they were traditionally considered protectors of sailors and ships).
      gemellus, -ī, m., *twin.*
      gemelle Castoris: i.e., Pollux.

Comparisons

Cicero in his *Tusculan Disputations* (1.101) gives this Latin translation of a famous epigram written by the Greek poet Simonides commemorating the Greeks under the command of Leonidas who fell at Thermopylae fighting against the Persian invaders. Compare it with the opening of Catullus 4:

Dīc, hospes, Spartae nōs tē hīc vīdisse iacentēs,
    dum sānctīs patriae lēgibus obsequimur.

lēx, lēgis, f., *law.*
obsequor, obsequī, obsecūtus sum + dat., *to obey.*

Compare the following translation of a Greek epigram written by Macedonius the Consul (*Palatine Anthology* 6.69) with the conclusion of Catullus 4:

Crantas, after many voyages, dedicated his ship to Poseidon,
    anchoring it firmly in the floor of the temple,
now that it is aground it cares no longer for the breeze; on this ground
    Crantas stretching out sleeps without fear.

25   Sed haec prius fuēre: nunc recondītā
26   senet quiēte sēque dēdicat tibi,
27   gemelle Castor et gemelle Castoris.

Initial Explorations

17.   At what point does the speaker again stop letting the **phasēlus** speak for itself?
18.   The words **prius** and **nunc** in line 25 complete the temporal circle of the poem, from the present (**quem vidētis**, 1) to the past (**ait fuisse**, 2) to the present (**nunc . . . senet**, 25–26). What picture does the speaker present of the **phasēlus** in its retirement?
19.   To whom does the **phasēlus** dedicate itself and why?
20.   What rhetorical device used earlier in the poem is used again in the last line?
21.   What is the effect of the meter used in this poem?

Discussion

1.   Examine the structure of the poem as a whole. Define an "introduction," a "conclusion," and a "center." Then locate lines that move toward the center and lines that move away from the center.
2.   In what ways does the **phasēlus** betray its origin as a Greek ship?
3.   In what ways is the **phasēlus** similar to the legendary Argo?
4.   The **phasēlus** is personified. What personality or traits of character does it project as the speaker reports its words?
5.   How do you think the speaker feels about the **phasēlus**? How do you feel about it?

Meter: hendecasyllabic

1   **vīvō, vīvere, vīxī, vīctūrus**, *to live; to live* (in the full sense of the word), *really live, enjoy life.*

      Vīvāmus . . . amēmus . . . aestimēmus (3): explain the mood and construction of these verbs.

   Lesbia, -ae, f., *Lesbia* (the name or pseudonym of the woman to whom the poem is addressed; see Introduction).

   atque, conj., *and, also; and what is more, and in fact, and indeed.*

2   **rūmor, rūmōris**, m., *rumor; gossip.*

   sevērus, -a, -um, *severe in judgment, stern, strict.*

      sevēriōrum: for translation of the comparative, see note to Catullus 3.2.

3   **aestimō, -āre, -āvī, -ātus**, *to estimate the worth of, value.*

   as, assis, m., *copper Roman coin, penny, cent.*

      ūnius assis aestimāre, idiom, *to consider X* (acc.) *as worth just one cent*, genitive of indefinite value. The *i* of **ūnius** is here short for the sake of the meter.

4   **sōlēs**: from **sōl, sōlis**, m., *sun.*

   occidō [ob-, *against* + **cadō, cadere, cecidī, cāsūrus**, *to fall*], **occidere, occidī, occāsūrus**, *to fall; to die; to sink, set* (of celestial bodies).

5   **nōbīs**: emphatic by position, serving as dative of reference, *for us*, with **occidit brevis lūx** and as dative of agent, *by us*, with **est . . . dormienda** (6). Thomson places a comma after **nōbīs**, allowing **nōbīs** to be taken only with **est . . . dormienda** (6).

   semel, adv., *once, once and for all.*

      cum semel occidit: either present or perfect indicative in a present-general temporal clause, *whenever . . . once sets* or *whenever . . . has once set.* Present-general temporal and conditional clauses take the present or perfect indicative in the subordinate clause and the present indicative (here **est . . . dormienda**) in the main clause. The pronoun **nōbīs** will then refer to humankind in general, not to Catullus and Lesbia as individuals.

6   **est . . . dormienda**: gerundive of obligation or passive periphrastic, *must be slept*, with the dative of agent, **nōbīs** (5).

   perpetuus, -a, -um, *everlasting, continuous, uninterrupted.*

7   **Dā mī**: note the reversed and lengthened repetition of vowel sounds from the previous word **dormienda**.

   bāsium, -ī, n., *kiss.*

      bāsia: the word is first attested in Catullus and is rare in later poets; the normal words for *kiss* are **ōsculum** and **suāvium/sāvium**.

8   **dein**: = **deinde**.

9   **usque**, adv., *continuously, without a break, immediately.*

CATULLUS 5

Give me a thousand kisses!

The poet invites Lesbia to a life of love.

1   Vīvāmus, mea Lesbia, atque amēmus,
2   rūmōrēsque senum sevēriōrum
3   omnēs ūnius aestimēmus assis!
4   Sōlēs occidere et redīre possunt;
5   nōbīs cum semel occidit brevis lūx,
6   nox est perpetua ūna dormienda.
7   Dā mī bāsia mīlle, deinde centum,
8   dein mīlle altera, dein secunda centum,
9   deinde usque altera mīlle, deinde centum;

continued

Initial Explorations

1. To whom is this poem addressed? Who is Lesbia? What does the name signify? Of what significance is its position in the line here?
2. With what two exhortations does the poet frame the first line? How does the second exhortation explain the first? How do these exhortations jar with traditional Roman values?
3. How would a well-brought-up young Roman woman react to Catullus' exhortations in line 1?
4. How does Catullus in lines 2–3 anticipate reservations that Lesbia might have?
5. How does Catullus encourage Lesbia to evaluate the **rūmōrēs** of the stern old men? (2–3)
6. What do assonance, alliteration, and word placement contribute to the effect of line 3?
7. What is meant by the phrase **carpe diem**? How do lines 4–6 introduce this theme?
8. Identify, analyze, and comment on the meaning of the imagery and the antitheses in lines 4–6.
9. How does the demand for kisses (7–9) result logically from what the poet has said so far in the poem?
10. How would you characterize Catullus' demand for kisses, and what would the stern old men think of it?

10   **multa mīlia**: supply **basiōrum** as partitive genitive.
      fēcerīmus: future perfect indicative, with long *i* here. In addition to mean-
      ing simply *will have made*, the verb may be understood here in a special
      commercial sense of *making up* or *reaching* a specific sum of money.
11   **conturbō** [con-, *thoroughly* + **turbō, -āre, -āvī, -ātus,** *to stir up, throw into con-
      fusion*], **-āre, -āvī, -ātus,** *to mix up, confound*.
      nē sciāmus: the danger for them is that "to count one's blessings is to invite
      Nemesis and the evil eye" (Fordyce, 108).
12   **quis, qua/quae, quid,** indefinite pronoun after **nē,** *anyone, anybody, somebody,
      anything, something*.
      nē quis malus: *so that no evil person* (lit., *so that somebody evil . . . not . . .*).
      invideō [in-, *in, on* + **videō, vidēre, vīdī, vīsus,** *to see*], **invidēre, invīdī, in-
      vīsus** + dat., *to cast an evil eye* (on), *cast spells* (upon); *to envy*.
      invidēre: use one of the first two translations of the verb given above;
      supply **nōbīs**.
13   **cum**: *when*.
      tantum, -ī, n., *such a quantity, so much; so great a number*.
      tantum: with **bāsiōrum**. According to widely held beliefs of magic, some-
      one knowing the exact number of a person's possessions or actions could
      cast a destructive spell upon them or upon the person.

Text

11   **conturbābimus illa, nē sciāmus**: as a technical commercial term, the verb
      conturbāre may mean *to throw one's accounts* (**ratiōnēs**) *into confusion* (in
      order to give a deceptive appearance of bankruptcy), *to go bankrupt*. The
      technical commercial meaning may be appropriate after lines 7–10; when
      used in this sense, the verb is intransitive and never has an expressed di-
      rect object; one would then place the comma after **conturbābimus** instead
      of after **illa,** and **illa** (*those things = the sum, the total*) would be taken with **nē
      sciāmus**:

11   conturbābimus, illa nē sciāmus
        we will throw our accounts into confusion (i.e., fraudulently go
        bankrupt), *so that we may not know them* (i.e., the numbers of the
        kisses)

      Fordyce remarks, "they will cheat the evil eye [see line 12], as the
      bankrupt cheats his creditors, by faking their books" (108).

10   dein, cum mīlia multa fēcerīmus,

11   conturbābimus illa, nē sciāmus,

12   aut nē quis malus invidēre possit,

13   cum tantum sciat esse bāsiōrum.

Initial Explorations

11.   Analyze the rhetorical effects produced by sound, rhythm, and movement in lines 7–11.
12.   How does line 11 set up a contrast between passion and rationality?
13.   What two threats to the love between himself and Lesbia does Catullus want to protect against? (11–13)

Discussion

1.   How would you divide the poem into sections?
2.   The **malus**, *evil person*, of line 12 is usually thought to represent the stern old men of line 2. To what extent is the following conclusion justified: "The association, or identification, of the *malus* and his envy with the *senes severi* shows them up as hypocrites, and their moral censure stands discredited"? (Fredricksmeyer, 443)
3.   In opposition to the **senēs sevērī** and the **malus**, Catullus stakes out a moral defense of the life of love in this poem. How, in lines 4–6, has he also staked out a rational defense of the life of love?
4.   Assume that the woman addressed as **mea Lesbia** in this poem is the same as the person referred to as **mea puella** in Catullus 2 and 3. To what extent is Catullus 5 an appropriate next step in Catullus' courtship of the **puella**?

Comparisons

Catullus 5 was widely imitated in the Renaissance and later. Compare the following versions, one French and the rest British.

Pierre de Ronsard
(1524–85)

    La Lune est coustumiere
De naistre tous les mois,
Mais quand nostre lumiere
Est esteinte une fois,
Longuement sans veiller
Il nous faut sommeiller.

Tandis que vivons ores,
Un baiser donnez-moy,
Donnez-m'en mille encores.
Amour n'a point de loy,
A sa Divinité,
Convient l'infinité.

Thomas Campion
(1567?–1619)

My sweetest Lesbia let us live and love,
And though the sager sort our deedes reprove,
Let us not way them: heav'ns great lampes doe dive
Into their west, and strait againe revive,
But soone as once set is our little light,
Then must we sleepe one ever-during night.

Ben Jonson
(1571/72–1637)

Come, my Celia, let us prove,
While we can, the sports of love;
Time will not be ours for ever,
He at length our good will sever.
Spend not then his gifts in vain:
Suns that set, may rise again;
But if once we lose this light,
'Tis with us perpetual night.
Why should we defer our joys?
Fame and rumour are but toys.
Cannot we delude the eyes
Of a few poor household spies?
Or his easier ears beguile,
So removed by our wile?
'Tis no sin love's fruit to steal,
But the sweet thefts to reveal,
To be taken, to be seen,
These have crimes accounted been.

Robert Herrick
(1591–1674)

Come, let us goe, while we are in our prime;
And take the harmlesse follie of the time.
    We shall grow old apace, and die
    Before we know our liberty.
    Our life is short; and our dayes run
    As fast away as do's the Sunne:
And as a vapour, or a drop of raine
Once lost, can ne'r be found againe:
    So when or you or I are made
    A fable, song, or fleeting shade;
    All love, all liking, all delight
    Lies drown'd with us in endlesse night.
Then while time serves, and we are but decaying;
Come, my *Corinna*, come, let's goe a Maying.

Richard Crashaw
(1613?–49)

Come and let us live my deare,
Let us love and never feare,
What the sowrest fathers say:
Brightest Sol that dyes to day
Lives againe as blith to morrow;
But if we darke sons of sorrow
Set: O then how long a Night
Shuts the eyes of our short light!
Then let amorous kisses dwell
On our lips, begin and tell
A thousand, and a hundred score,
An hundred and a thousand more,
Till another thousand smother
That, and that wipe off another.
Thus at last when we have numbred
Many a thousand, many a hundred,
Wee'l confound the reckoning quite
And lose our selves in wild delight:
While our joyes so multiply
As shall mocke the envious eye.

Andrew Marvell
(1621–78)

Had we but world enough, and time,
This coyness, lady, were no crime.
We would sit down and think which way
To walk, and pass our long love's day;
Thou by the Indian Ganges' side
Shouldst rubies find; I by the tide
Of Humber would complain. I would
Love you ten years before the Flood;
And you should, if you please, refuse
Till the conversion of the Jews.
My vegetable love should grow
Vaster than empires, and more slow.
An hundred years should go to praise
Thine eyes, and on thy forehead gaze;
Two hundred to adore each breast,
But thirty thousand to the rest;
An age at least to every part,
And the last age should show your heart.
For, lady, you deserve this state,
Nor would I love at lower rate.

But at my back I always hear
Time's winged chariot hurrying near;
And yonder all before us lie
Deserts of vast eternity.
Thy beauty shall no more be found,
Nor in thy marble vault shall sound
My echoing song; then worms shall try
That long preserved virginity,
And your quaint honor turn to dust,
And into ashes all my lust.
The grave's a fine and private place,
But none, I think, do there embrace.

Now, therefore, while the youthful hue
Sits on thy skin like morning glew,
And while thy willing soul transpires
At every pore with instant fires,
Now let us sport us while we may;
And now, like am'rous birds of prey,

Rather at once our time devour,
Than languish in his slow-chapped power.
Let us roll all our strength, and all
Our sweetness, up into one ball;
And tear our pleasures with rough strife
Through the iron gates of life.
Thus, though we cannot make our sun
Stand still, yet we will make him run.

Meter: hendecasyllabic

1   **Flāvius, -ī,** m., *Flavius* (unknown except for mention in this poem).
      dēliciās: see Catullus 2.1.
2   **nī**: = **nisi**, conj., *if . . . not, unless*.
          nī sint: *if she weren't. . . . , unless she were. . . .* ; the present instead of the im-
             perfect subjunctive in the protasis of a contrary-to-fact condition is an ar-
             chaic and perhaps colloquial usage; **vellēs** and **possēs** (3) are the verbs
             of the apodosis.
      illepidus, -a, -um [**in-**, *not* + **lepidus, -a, -um**, see Catullus 1.1], *without*
          grace/refinement; without charm/wit.
      inēlegāns, inēlegantis, *lacking in taste, unrefined.*
3   **dīcere**: + dat. and acc., *to tell* (someone) *about* (something).
      taceō, -ēre, -uī, -itus, intransitive, *to be silent, to keep quiet;* transitive, *to be*
          silent about.
4   **vērum,** conj., *but.*
      nescio quid: see vocabulary note on Catullus 2.6, **nesciō quis**.
          nescio quid: + partitive genitive, *something of a. . . . = some. . . .*
      febrīculōsus, -a, -um [adjective formed from the noun **febris, febris,** f.,
          fever], *fever-ridden, feverish.*
              febrīculōsī: this adjective was used of common whores by Plautus
                 (*Cistellaria* 406); it may suggest over-heated sexuality.
5   **scortum, -ī,** n., *whore.*
      hoc: object of **fatērī**.
      pudet, -ēre, -uit, impersonal, *(it) makes* (someone) *ashamed, causes* (someone)
          shame.
              pudet: supply **tē** as object.
      fateor, fatērī, fassus sum, *to admit.*
              fatērī: subject of **pudet**.
6   **viduus, -a, -um,** *without a husband/wife/mate.*
          viduās . . . noctēs: accusative of duration of time; note the transferred epi-
             thet.
      iacēre: *to lie* (in bed).
          tē nōn viduās iacēre noctēs: indirect statement dependent on **clāmat**;
             nōn may be taken with either **viduās** or **iacēre**.
7   **nēquīquam,** adv., *in vain, to no purpose.*
          nēquīquam: with **tacitum**.
      cubīle, cubīlis, n., *bed.*
      clāmat: find four nouns in lines 7–11 that serve as subjects of this verb.
8   **serta, -ōrum,** n. pl., *wreathes.*
      Syriō . . . olīvō: *perfume* (olive oil from Syria was used as a base for per-
          fumes).
      fragrō, -āre, -āvī, -ātūrus + abl., *to smell strongly* (of).
          fragrāns: neuter nominative singular, modifying **cubīle** (7).
9   **pulvīnus, -ī,** m., *pillow.*
      peraequē, adv. [strengthened form of **aequē**], *equally.*
      ille: = **illīc**, adv., *there.*

CATULLUS 6

Who is your mistress, Flavius?

The poet asks a friend to tell him about his mistress.

1 Flāvī, dēliciās tuās Catullō,
2 nī sint illepidae atque inēlegantēs,
3 vellēs dīcere nec tacēre possēs.
4 Vērum nescio quid febrīculōsī
5 scortī dīligis: hoc pudet fatērī.
6 Nam tē nōn viduās iacēre noctēs
7 nēquīquam tacitum cubīle clāmat
8 sertīs ac Syriō fragrāns olīvō,
9 pulvīnusque peraequē et hīc et ille

continued

Initial Explorations

1. Study the diction of lines 1–5. What important words recall words used in earlier poems? What words import a new tone? What is the effect of the combination of different kinds of diction?
2. What effect is achieved by the use of **Catullō** instead of **mihi** in line 1? Note the line framing.
3. What does Catullus know about Flavius' activities? What does he not know? (1–5)
4. Based on his friend's silence about the identity of the woman he is in love with, what does Catullus assume about her? (2–5)
5. What does Catullus suggest that Flavius is ashamed to admit? (4–5) What incongruity does the juxtaposition of **scortī** and **dīligis** suggest?
6. How is the bed personified? (7)
7. What does the bed shout? (6–7).
8. Why is the bed described as **nēquīquam tacitum** (7)?

10   **attrītus, -a, -um** [**ad-**, *to, toward; thoroughly* + **trītus, -a, -um**, *worn*], *worn down,
      battered, crumpled.*
      tremulus, -a, -um, *trembling.*
      quassus, -a, -um, *shaken.*
          quassa: transferred epithet, in sense describing the bed.
11   **argūtātiō, argūtātiōnis** [a Catullan coinage; **argūtor, -ārī, -ātus sum,** *to chat-
      ter, prattle, babble*], f., *loquacious speaking; a creaking, noise.*
      inambulātiō, inambulātiōnis, f., *a walking up and down, a pacing back and forth*
          (like an orator at a trial); hence, *a restless motion.*
12   **nīl**: = **nihil**; subject of **valet**.
      stuprum, -ī, n., *dishonor, disgrace, debauchery.*
      valet: + infinitive, *is strong enough* (to), *is able* (to).
      nihil: the subject is repeated for emphasis.
      tacēre: cf. **tacēre** (3); here, *to keep* (something) *secret.*
13   **tam**: modifying **ecfutūta**.
      latus, lateris, n., *side, flanks* (of a person).
          latera: a euphemism (one reference of the word is to the seat of male
          strength and vigor), translate, *body.*
      ecfutūtus, -a, -um [**ex-**, *completely* + perfect passive participle of **futuō,
      futuere, futuī, futūtus,** *to have sexual relations with* (a woman)], *worn out
      with sexual intercourse.*
      pandō, pandere, *to spread out.*
          pandās ... faciās (14): present subjunctives in a present contrary-to-fact
          condition. In archaic Latin the present as well as the imperfect subjunc-
          tive was used in present contrary-to-fact conditions, and the present
          subjunctive sometimes continued to be used in poetry.
14   **quis, qua/quae, quid,** indefinite pronoun after **nī,** *anyone, anybody, somebody,
      anything, something.*
      ineptiae, -ārum, f. pl., *instances of foolishness/absurdity/frivolity.*
          quid ... ineptiārum: partitive genitive, *something foolish.*
15   **quisquis, quisquis, quidquid,** indefinite pronoun/adjective, *whoever, what-
      ever.*
          quidquid ... bonī malīque: *whatever of good and bad = whatever good or
          bad thing.*
16   **volo**: = **volō** with iambic shortening.
      amor, amōris, m., *love;* pl., concrete, *the object of one's love, loved one, girlfriend,
      love.*
17   **lepidō**: see Catullus 1.1.
      vocāre: *to summon.*

Text

12   **Nam ... tacēre**: what is printed here is an emendation proposed by Haupt
      for the unintelligible manuscript reading, †**Nam inista prevalet**† **nihil
      tacēre,** which is printed in the Oxford Classical Text with the †s surround-
      ing the words thought to be corrupted. Thomson prints Haupt's emenda-
      tion in his text.

10   attrītus, tremulīque quassa lectī
11   argūtātiō inambulātiōque.
12   Nam nīl stupra valet, nihil, tacēre.
13   Cūr? Nōn tam latera ecfutūta pandās,
14   nī tū quid faciās ineptiārum.
15   Quārē, quidquid habēs bonī malīque,
16   dīc nōbīs. Volo tē ac tuōs amōrēs
17   ad caelum lepidō vocāre versū.

Initial Explorations

9. How does the bed (7–11) reveal the truth of the statement made in line 6?
10. Comment on word placement and sound effects in the description of the bed? (7–11)
11. How does Catullus refer to Flavius' activity in line 12?
12. What imaginary objection from Flavius is the interrogative **Cūr?** (13) meant to address?
13. How does Catullus in line 14 evaluate Flavius' activity?
14. **Quārē** (15) implies that there is a logical connection between the request made in lines 15–16 and the previous part of the poem. Explain the connection.
15. In the last line and a half what does Catullus propose to do?

Discussion

1. Consider the poem as a parody of legal proceedings against Flavius. How does the mock trial develop? What language is borrowed from the courtroom? What charges are brought? Who are the witnesses? How does Flavius defend himself? What is the verdict?
2. How do the last line and a half fit with the rest of the poem?
3. What does the poem celebrate?
4. If Catullus arranged his poems or at least the ones toward the beginning of the corpus in the order in which we now have them, why would he have put poem 6 here?

Meter: hendecasyllabic

1 **bāsiātiō, bāsiātiōnis**, f., *act of kissing, kiss.*
    bāsiātiōnēs: this abstract, polysyllabic noun, formed from **bāsium**, was coined and used only here by Catullus. With **tuae**, in the light of Catullus 5, = *your kissings [of me]*, but editors often translate *[my] kissings of you.*
2 **satis superque**: idiom, *enough and over, enough and more than enough.*
3 **Quam magnus** numerus . . . iacet (4) . . . aut **quam** sīdera **multa** (7) . . . **vident** (8) . . . ; **tam** tē bāsia **multa** bāsiāre (9) . . . est (10): *As great as the number . . . that lies . . . or as many as the stars . . . that see . . . ; for you to kiss so many kisses/to kiss you so many kisses is.* . . . The correlative **quam** in lines 3 and 7 is answered by **tam** in line 9; through two images of infinite numbers Catullus answers Lesbia's question from lines 1–2.
    Libyssa, -ae, f., adjective, *of Libya* (the common term for the whole of North Africa); *of North Africa, African.*
    harēna, -ae, f., *sand;* in collective sense, *sands.*
4 **lāsarpīcifer, -a, -um**, *producing* **lāsarpīcium/lāserpīcium** (a plant thought to have extraordinary curative powers for a wide variety of ailments; see Pliny, *Natural History* 22.100–6).
    lāsarpīciferīs: for the use of a compound adjective, see Catullus 4.13, **buxifer**.
    Cyrēnae, -ārum, f. pl., *Cyrene* (an ancient town in northwest Libya, but here the word is used of a vast region surrounding the town; Cyrene was founded in the 7th century B.C. by the legendary Battus, whose tomb is mentioned in line 6 of this poem. It was also the birthplace of the Greek poet Callimachus, whose style and theories of poetry influenced Catullus; Callimachus actually adopted *Battiades,* "Descendant of Battus," as his pen name).
    Cyrēnīs: locative.
5 **ōrāclum, -ī**, n. [syncope for **ōrāculum**], *oracle.*
    Iuppiter, Iovis, m., *Jupiter.*
    ōrāclum Iovis: the famous North African temple and oracle of Ammon, situated in the oasis of Siwa in the Libyan desert; Ammon was an Egyptian god who was identified by the Romans with Jupiter.
    inter: governing **ōrāclum** (note the anastrophe) and **sepulcrum** (8).
    aestuōsus, -a, -um [**aestus, -ūs**, m., *heat; the fire of love, passion*], *very hot, sweltering;* perhaps, *passionate.*
    aestuōsī: both meanings are possible, the former as a transferred epithet describing the **ōrāclum**, the latter as an apt description of Jupiter.
6 **Battus, -ī**, m., *Battus* (see note to line 4 above).
    sacer, sacra, sacrum, *sacred.*
7 **sīdus, sīderis**, n., *star.*
    nox: an echo of Catullus 5.6.
8 **fūrtīvus, -a, -um**, *stolen; secret, hidden.*
    amor, amōris, m., *love;* pl. here, *love affairs* (cf. Catullus 6.16).

CATULLUS 7

"How many kisses?"

Catullus draws upon two images of infinity to answer Lesbia's question.

1 Quaeris quot mihi bāsiātiōnēs
2 tuae, Lesbia, sint satis superque.
3 Quam magnus numerus Libyssae harēnae
4 lāsarpīciferīs iacet Cyrēnīs
5 ōrāclum Iovis inter aestuōsī
6 et Battī veteris sacrum sepulcrum,
7 aut quam sīdera multa, cum tacet nox,
8 fūrtīvōs hominum vident amōrēs;

continued

Initial Explorations

1. What has Lesbia apparently asked Catullus? Why would she have asked such a question? (1–2)
2. The phrase **bāsiātiōnēs / tuae** (1–2) can be translated two different ways (see note on facing page). Can you argue for translating the phrase one way or the other, or is there deliberate ambiguity here?
3. Catullus inverts his answer by placing two images of infinite number first (3–8) and then giving his statement of how many kisses would suffice (9–10). What is the first image he evokes? (3–6)
4. Generally and specifically where are the sands located? (3–6)
5. The image of infinite sands (3–6) is elaborately developed. What do the connotations and associations of the following words and phrases add to the texture of the image? **lāsarpīciferīs** (4), **aestuōsī** (5), **Battī veteris** (6), and **sacrum sepulcrum** (6)
6. What is the second image? (7–8) How does it differ in tone and mood from the first? How is it similar? What personal reference does it contain?

9   **bāsium, -ī**, n., *kiss*.

     bāsiō, -āre, -āvī, -ātus, *to kiss*.

       tē bāsia multa bāsiāre: **tē** may be taken as the subject of the infinitive, *for you to kiss so many kisses* (compare Catullus 5, where Catullus asks Lesbia for hundreds and thousands of kisses), or the verb **bāsiāre** may govern the two accusatives, *to kiss you so many kisses*. Compare the two different ways of interpreting **tuae** in line 2 above.

10   **vēsānus, -a, -um** [**vē-**, *without, not* + **sānus, -a, -um**, *healthy, sane, sober* (in particular, *free from the passion of love*)], *insane, crazy, frenzied*.

     satis et super: see line 2.

11   **quae**: the antecedent is **bāsia** (9).

     pernumerō [**per-**, *thoroughly* + **numerō, -āre, -āvī, -ātus**, *to count*], **-āre, -āvī, -ātus**, *to make a full accounting of, count completely*.

     cūriōsus, -a, -um, *careful, attentive; inquiring, curious; meddlesome*.

12   **possint**: *could*, potential subjunctive.

     mala . . . lingua: second subject of **possint**.

     fascinō, -āre, -āvī, -ātus, *to bewitch, charm*.

       possint nec mala fascināre lingua: compare Catullus 5.12, **aut nē quid malus invidēre possit**, and with the **cūriōsī** here, compare the **senēs sevēriōrēs** of Catullus 5.2.

lāsarpīciferīs . . . Cyrēnīs

"Weighing and Packing of **Lāsarpīcium**
under the Supervision of King Arkesilas of Cyrene"
Laconian cup, sixth century B.C.
Cabinet des Médailles
Paris, France

9   tam tē bāsia multa bāsiāre
10   vēsānō satis et super Catullō est,
11   quae nec pernumerāre cūriōsī
12   possint nec mala fascināre lingua.

Initial Explorations

7. In line 1, Catullus refers to himself with the first person pronoun, **mihi**; in line 10 the reference shifts to **Catullō**. What is the significance of this shift from first to third person?
8. What view of himself does the speaker take in using the phrase **vēsānō . . . Catullō**?
9. From whom and from what does the speaker wish to protect the kisses? (11–12) What does this echo in Catullus 5?

Discussion

1. How are Catullus 5 and 7 similar and how do they differ in basic matters of form and content?
2. How does Catullus 7 differ from Catullus 5 in style and tone?
3. What is the poet saying through his antithetical images of sand and stars?
4. Why does the poet use the word **bāsiātiōnēs** instead of **bāsia**, which he used in poem 5?
5. How does the third-person reference in the phrase **vēsānō . . . Catullō** (10) suggest that the poet is taking a new, objective perspective on himself and his passion?
6. What role do the **cūriōsī** play in this poem?
7. How would you, if you were Lesbia, respond to Catullus 7?
8. Why might Catullus have placed poem 6 in between poems 5 and 7?

Comparisons

The following poem by Ben Jonson combines themes from Catullus 5 and 7; the lyric of John Oldham is based on Catullus 7 alone.

Ben Jonson
(1571/72–1637)

Kiss me, sweet: the wary lover
Can your fauours keepe, and cover,
When the common courting jay
All your bounties will betray.
Kiss again! no creature comes;
Kiss, and score up wealthy sums
On my lips, thus hardly sundered,
While you breathe. First give a hundred,
Then a thousand, then another
Hundred, then unto the other
Add a thousand, and so more:
Till you equal with the store,
All the grass that Rumney yields,
Or the sands in Chelsea fields,
Or the drops in silver Thames,
Or the stars, that guild his streams,
In the silent Summer-nights,
When youths ply their stolen delights;
That the curious may not know
How to tell 'em as they flow,
And the envious, when they find
What their number is, be pined.

John Oldham
(1653–83)

Nay, *Lesbia*, never ask me this,
How many kisses will suffice?
Faith, 'tis a question hard to tell,
Exceeding hard; for you as well
May ask what sums of Gold suffice
The greedy Miser's boundless Wish:
Think what drops the Ocean store,
With all the Sands, that make its Shore:
Think what Spangles deck the Skies,
When Heaven looks with all its Eyes:
Or think how many Atoms came
To compose this mighty Frame:
Let all these the Counters be,
To tell how oft I'm kiss'd by thee:
Till no malicious Spy can guess
To what vast height the Scores arise;
Till weak Arithmetick grow scant,
And numbers for the reck'ning want:
All these will hardly be enough
For me stark staring mad with Love.

Meter: choliambic

1   **miser, misera, miserum**, *unhappy, miserable, wretched*; as a technical term describing lovers, *obsessed with erotic passion, lovesick*.

     dēsinās . . . dūcās (2): the second person jussive subjunctive is not commonly used with a definite person in mind, as here; it is a milder form of command than an imperative.

     ineptiō [ineptus, -a, -um, *foolish, silly***], ineptīre,** *to be lacking in good judgment; to be a fool, be silly*.

2   **pereō [per-,** *through* **+ eō, īre, iī, itūrus,** *to go***], perīre, periī, peritūrus,** *to die, perish; to come to an end*.

     perdō [per-, *through* **+ dō, dare, dedī, datus,** *to give***], perdere, perdidī, perditus,** *to destroy; to lose*.

        quod . . . dūcās: a pithy, proverbial injunction; supply **id,** *that thing*, as the understood antecedent of **quod**: *consider* (an idiomatic usage of **dūcere**) *that thing* (amplified by **quod vidēs perīsse**) *to have been lost* (supplying **esse** with **perditum**). Compare Plautus, *Trinummus* 1026, **Quīn tū quod periit periisse dūcis?** *Why don't you consider what is gone as gone?*

          perīsse perditum: alliteration and verbal jingle.

3   **fulgeō, fulgēre, fulsī,** *to shine, gleam, glitter*.

     Fulsēre: = **Fulsērunt**.

     quondam, adv., *once, formerly*.

     candidus, -a, -um, *white; bright, dazzling; cheerful, favorable, happy*.

     sōlēs: from **sōl, sōlis,** m., *sun*; Thomson suggests that **sōlēs** here = **diēs**.

4   **ventitō [veniō, venīre, vēnī, ventūrus,** *to come* **+ -itō,** iterative suffix denoting repeated action**], -āre, -āvī, -ātūrus,** *to come often*.

5   **nōbīs**: dative of agent.

     quantum, adv., *as much as*.

     nūlla: supply **puella**.

6   **cum**: *when*, delayed conjunction coming in the middle of its clause.

     iocōsus, -a, -um, *full of jest; funny, playful*.

       iocōsa: *playful things/experiences* (with a suggestion of lovers' play).

7   **nec . . . nōlēbat**: perhaps litotes = **volēbat**, but the double negative may suggest something closer to indifference (*was not refusing*) than enthusiasm; that she was not not wanting these things need not mean that she was really wanting them.

8   **fulsēre . . . sōlēs**: compare with line 3.

CATULLUS 8

Catullus to Himself

*The poet tells himself to harden his heart against his **puella**.*

1 Miser Catulle, dēsinās ineptīre,
2 et quod vidēs perīsse perditum dūcās.
3 Fulsēre quondam candidī tibī sōlēs,
4 cum ventitābās quō puella dūcēbat
5 amāta nōbīs quantum amābitur nūlla.
6 Ibi illa multa cum iocōsa fīēbant,
7 quae tū volēbās nec puella nōlēbat,
8 fulsēre vērē candidī tibī sōlēs.

continued

Initial Explorations

1. What does the speaker's use of the vocative **Miser Catulle** (1) imply about the dramatic situation of this poem? Who is addressing whom? Why?
2. What do the words **miser** (1) and **ineptīre** (1) reveal about Catullus' view of his situation and its cause?
3. Explain the point of the command expressed in line 2.
4. Lines 3 and 8 serve as a frame for a nostalgic memory. What do the words **fulsēre . . . candidī tibī sōlēs** mean?
5. What picture do we get of the relationship between Catullus and the **puella** as presented in lines 4–7?
6. What does each of the following contribute to the meaning and the tone of lines 4–7: the iterative verb, hyperbole, repetition of sounds, and litotes (**nec . . . nōlēbat**)?

9   **nunc iam**, adv., *now at last* (in contrast to what was true in the past).

    illa: i.e., the **puella**.

    volt: archaic form of **vult**.

    inpotēns, inpotentis [**in-**, *not* + **potēns, potentis**, *having power* (over), *able to control*] (see Catullus 4.18, where editors print the alternate spelling, **im-**), *powerless* (over oneself); *lacking self-control, weak in will; wild, violent, raging.*

      inpotēns: vocative and perhaps concessive, *although weak in will* (first sense of the word as given above).

        inpotē<ns nōlī>: the letters in brackets are missing from the manuscripts and have been supplied by editors.

10   **quae fugit**: supply **eam** as the antecedent of **quae** and object of **sectāre**.

    sector [**sequor, sequī, secūtus sum**, *to follow* + **-tō**, iterative suffix], **-ārī, -ātus sum**, *to run after/chase after constantly.*

      sectāre: singular imperative of the deponent verb.

    vīve: colloquial usage of the verb **vīvere**, equivalent in meaning to **es** (imperative), *be!*

      nec miser vīve: see note to line 1: *don't be love-sick, don't be "in love."*

11   **obstinātus, -a, -um** [**ob-**, *in the way of, against* + ***stanō***, a hypothetical form, cf. **stō, stāre**, *to stand*], *stubborn, resolute, determined.*

    perferō [**per-**, *through, completely* + **ferō, ferre, tulī, lātus**, *to carry, bear*], **perferre, pertulī, perlātus**, irreg., *to carry through to the end; to endure, bear through.*

    obdūrō, -āre, -āvī, -ātūrus [**ob-**, *in the way of, against* + **dūrō, dūrāre**, *to become hard*], *to steel oneself, be resolute.*

      perfer, obdūrā: asyndeton.

13   **requīrō** [**re-**, *again* + **quaerō, quaerere, quaesīvī, quaesītus**, *to seek, look for*], **requīrere, requīsīvī, requīsītus**, *to ask, inquire; to seek out, look for; to miss.*

    rogābit: the verb **rogāre** here carries the ideas of invitation, *to request a person be present, to invite*, and of seeking erotic favors, *to woo, court.*

    invītam: modifying **tē**.

14   **nūlla**: colloquial use of the adjective with emphatic adverbial force, *not at all, not ever again.* Compare line 5 where the adjective is used as a substantive.

15   **scelestus, -a, -um**, *accursed; wicked; unlucky, unfortunate.*

    vae, exclamation + dat. or (more rarely) + acc., *woe (to), alas (for).*

    quae: interrogative adjective, modifying **vīta**.

    manet: here + dat., *is in store (for), awaits.*

16   **bellus, -a, -um**, *pretty, cute, smart-looking.*

17   **dīcēris**: what tense and voice (note the long e)? Lesbia will suffer from Catullus' no longer calling her his own **puella**, or so he insists.

18   **bāsiō, -āre, -āvī, -ātus**, *to kiss.*

    Cui: dative of reference expressing personal interest; translate *Whose. . . ?*

    labellum, -ī, n. [**labrum, -ī**, n., *lip* + **-lum**, dim. suffix], *lip.*

    mordeō, mordēre, momordī, morsus, *to bite, nibble.*

19   **dēstinātus, -a, -um** [**dē-**, *down, thoroughly, completely* + ***stanō***, a hypothetical form, cf. **stō, stāre**, *to stand*], *fixed* (in one's mind), *determined, stubborn.*

      dēstinātus: cf. **obstinātā mente** (11); note the force of the different prefixes.

9   Nunc iam illa nōn volt; tū quoque, inpotē<ns, nōlī>,

10   nec quae fugit sectāre, nec miser vīve,

11   sed obstinātā mente perfer, obdūrā.

12   Valē, puella. Iam Catullus obdūrat,

13   nec tē requīret nec rogābit invītam.

14   At tū dolēbis, cum rogāberis nūlla.

15   Scelesta, vae tē! Quae tibī manet vīta?

16   Quis nunc tē adībit? Cui vidēberis bella?

17   Quem nunc amābis? Cuius esse dīcēris?

18   Quem bāsiābis? Cui labella mordēbis?

19   At tū, Catulle, dēstinātus obdūrā.

Initial Explorations

7.   With what temporal adverb earlier in the poem does the phrase **Nunc iam** (9) correlate?

8.   How does Catullus describe the situation as being different now? (9) How does he characterize himself, and what does he order himself to do? (9)

9.   How does the pairing of **inpotēns** and **nōlī** (9) intimate Catullus' dilemma in the poem?

10. How do the words **nec quae fugit sectāre** (10) reverse the memory of the relationship with the **puella** in line 4?

11. How do the iterative verbs **ventitābās** (4) and **sectāre** (10) link and characterize Catullus' behavior before and now?

12. Line 11 concludes Catullus' address to himself, which began in line 1. Comment on his choice of words, use of prefixes, and use of asyndeton in line 11.

13. Beginning with line 12, who is now addressing whom? In what frame of mind is the speaker of this line? With what does he greet his **puella**? What will he not do? (13)

14. What is the purpose of the statement in line 14, the exclamation in line 15, and the rhetorical questions in lines 15–18? For what is the **puella** to be pitied?

15. In warning the **puella** of the consequences of her change of heart toward him by listing the causes of grief that await her (13–18), Catullus is in fact reliving memories of his love affair with her. Do they have a beginning, middle, and end? Do they move toward a climax? What echoes of earlier poems do you find in these memories? What is happening to Catullus' professed resolve?

16. In the last line we again hear the voice of the Catullus of the first eleven lines of the poem. Why does Catullus need to repeat at the end of the poem (19) the command that he had already delivered in line 11? Compare **dēstinātus** (19) with **obstinātā mente** (11). What different meaning does the different

prefix create in line 19?

17.   What effects are produced by the meter of the poem? What tone is produced by absence of enjambement?

Discussion

1.   Reread the poem and note words, phrases, and sounds that are repeated. What is significant about the repeated words, phrases, and sounds? What do the repetitions add to the meaning of the poem?

2.   How does Catullus 8 fit into the story of Catullus' love affair with the **puella**/Lesbia as recorded in Catullus 2, 3, 5, and 7? Does it come as a surprise? Does it seem to fit?

Comparison

Compare the following version of Catullus 8:

Thomas Campion
(1567?–1619)

Harden now thy tyred hart, with more then flinty rage;
Ne'er let her false teares henceforth thy constant griefe asswage.
Once true happy dayes thou saw'st when shee stood firme and kinde,
Both as one then liv'd and held one eare, one tongue, one minde:
But now those bright houres be fled, and never may returne;
What then remaines but her untruths to mourne?

Silly Traytresse, who shall now thy carelesse tresses place?
Who thy pretty talke supply, whose eare thy musicke grace?
Who shall thy bright eyes admire? what lips triumph with thine?
Day by day who'll visit thee and say "th'art onely mine?"
Such a time there was, God wot, but such shall never be:
Too oft, I feare, thou wilt remember me.

Valē, puella. Iam Catullus obdūrat!

"Apollo Citharist"
Red porphyry and white marble
Farnese Collection
National Archaeological Museum
Naples, Italy

Meter: hendecasyllabic

1   **Vērānius, -ī, m.,** *Veranius* (a member of Catullus' inner circle of friends, who has just returned home from provincial service in Spain; he is also mentioned in poems 12, 28, and 47).
     omnibus: take with **meīs amīcīs.**

2   **antistō (antestō)** [**ante-,** *before* + **stō, stāre, stetī, status,** *to stand*], **antistāre, antistitī** + dat., *to surpass, be superior* (to), *be worth more* (than).
     mihi: ethical dative, *in my eyes.*
     trecentī, -ae, -a, *three hundred* (often of an indefinitely large number).
     mīlibus trecentīs: supply **amīcīs,** dative with **antistāns.**

3   **penātēs, penātium,** m. pl. [**penus, -ūs,** f., *food, provisions* (of the household)], *penates* (traditional gods of the household, protectors of the food supply).

4   **ūnanimus, -a, -um,** *of one mind, harmonious, loving.*
     anus, -ūs, f., *old woman;* as an adjective, *old, aged.*

5   **beātus, -a, -um,** *happy; fortunate; supremely happy, blissful, blessed.*
     Ō mihi nūntiī beātī: remember that **nūntius** can mean *messenger* or *message;* exclamatory nominative here (instead of the usual exclamatory accusative), *O messengers (with) fortunate news for me* (implying that Catullus heard the news of Veranius' return from more than one source), or more probably plural for singular, *O happy message for me.*

6   **vīsō, vīsere, vīsī,** *to go and look at/view* (something); *to go and see, visit* (a person).
     Hibērēs, Hibērum, m. pl., *Iberians, Spaniards.*

7   **nārrantem:** a second modifier of **tē** (6).
     loca: this word, masculine in the singular, has both masculine and neuter forms in the plural.
     factum, -ī, n., *deed; exploit.*
     nātiō, nātiōnis, f., *people, race, tribe.*

8   **applicō** [**ad-,** *to, toward* + **plicō, -āre, -āvī, -ātus,** *to fold, bend*], **-āre, -āvī, -ātus** *to bring into contact; to draw* (something) *close.*
     collum, -ī, n., *neck.*
     collum: supply **tuum.**

9   **suāvior (sāvior)** [**suāvis, -is, -e,** *pleasant*], **-ārī, -ātus sum,** *to kiss.*
     suāviābor: Thomson prints **sāviābor.**

10   **Ō quantum est hominum beātiōrum:** *O whatever amount there is of. . . .* = *O however many . . . there are,* cf. Catullus 3.1–2, **ō Venerēs Cupīdinēsque, / et quantum est hominum venustiōrum.** In the present poem, however, the **quantum** clause is not vocative as it is in Catullus 3 but is an exclamatory accusative. It is then to be taken in a partitive sense with **quid** (best translated as if it were **quis**) in the next line: *O of all the rather happy men there are, who is . . . ?*

11   **quid:** neuter, picking up the neuter **quantum** (10), but best translated *who* (see note above).
     laetius . . . bēatius: modifying **quid.** What degree of the adjective are these words? Identify the case of **mē** and explain its use.
     -ve, enclitic conj., *or.*

CATULLUS 9

Joyous news!

Catullus welcomes his close friend Veranius back from Spain.

1   Vērānī, omnibus ē meīs amīcīs
2   antistāns mihi mīlibus trecentīs,
3   vēnistīne domum ad tuōs penātēs
4   frātrēsque ūnanimōs anumque mātrem?
5   Vēnistī. Ō mihi nūntiī beātī!
6   Vīsam tē incolumem audiamque Hibērum
7   nārrantem loca, facta, nātiōnēs,
8   ut mōs est tuus, applicānsque collum
9   iūcundum ōs oculōsque suāviābor.
10   Ō quantum est hominum beātiōrum,
11   quid mē laetius est beātiusve?

Initial Explorations

1. By means again of large numbers (compare Catullus 5 and 7), what point about Veranius does the hyperbole make? (1–2)
2. Behind the simplicity and colloquialism of the Latin in this poem are strong sentiments that celebrate the return of Catullus' close friend. How does Catullus imagine that Veranius' reunion with his home and family unfolded? (3–4)
3. Identify a tricolon in lines 3–4 and a chiasmus in line 4.
4. News of Veranius' arrival home precedes the anticipated reunion of the speaker with his friend. What sequence does the speaker anticipate when the two friends are reunited? How is the intimacy of their friendship revealed through the sequence? (6–9)
5. Lines 6–9 contain three verbs; identify the members of an ascending tricolon in this sentence.
6. As Veranius is singled out by a hyperbole at the start of the poem, who is singled out at the end by an equally strong hyperbole? (10–11)
7. Note that line 10 is almost identical with line 2 of Catullus 3. Does this repetition serve any purpose?
8. Reread the poem and note recurring sound patterns, especially of the letters *m* and *n*. What important words in the poem echo Veranius' name by beginning with the letter *v*? Where is asyndeton used effectively? What do the three elisions in line 6 highlight? Locate strongly placed front and end words in particular lines throughout the poem.

Discussion

1. At what points would you divide the poem into three parts?
2. Printed below are lines from a poem by the third century B.C. Greek poet Theocritus. Catullus may have known this poem, and he may have taken his cue for his repetition of **vēnistī** (3, 5) from the Greek words of Theocritus' poem that are translated "You have come. . . /you have come. . . ." What similarities and what differences between the two poems do you notice? What purpose might Catullus have had in mind in echoing the words from Theocritus?
3. How do the close friendship and bonding between Catullus and Veranius contrast with the relationship between the poet and his **puella** in the preceding poem?

Comparison

The opening lines of Theocritus' *Idyll* 12 are addressed to the poet's boyfriend:

You have come, dear boy; after two nights and days
you have come. But lovers grow old in a day.
As much as spring is sweeter than winter, the apple than the sloe,
as much as the ewe is fleecier than the lamb,
as much as a maiden is more desirable than a thrice-wed woman,
as much as the fawn is swifter than the calf, as much as the
clear voiced nightingale surpasses all other birds in its singing,
so have you cheered me with your appearance, and I run to you
as a traveler runs to a shady oak from the roasting sun.

Ō quantum est hominum beātiōrum,
quid mē laetius est beātiusve?

Fresco from Etruscan Tomb in Paestum
Ca. 470 B.C.

Meter: hendecasyllabic ·

1   **Vārus, -ī**, m., *Varus* (addressed in Catullus 22, he may have been Alfenus
     Varus, a jurist and official in Cisalpine Gaul, or Quintilius Varus, friend of
     Vergil and Horace).

    meus: *my friend*, a colloquialism. The speaker of the poem is Catullus (25).

    amōrēs: *girlfriend, love*, cf. Catullus 6.16.

2   **vīsō, vīsere, vīsī** (see Catullus 9.6), *to go and look at/view* (something); + **ad** +
     acc., *to go and visit* (a person, often a sick person).

        vīsum: this may be a rare supine of **vīsere**, *to go and visit his* (sick?) *girl-
          friend*, or it may be the supine of **vidēre**, *to have a look* (Quinn), or it may
          be the perfect passive participle of **vidēre**, modifying **mē** (1), and be
          taken with **ōtiōsum [esse]**, *me seen to be at leisure*.

    forum, -ī, n., *forum, public square, piazza*.

    ōtiōsus, -a, -um [**ōtium, -ī**, n., *spare time; time free from serious occupations;
     leisure; idleness*], *not occupied by business or politics, having nothing to do, at
     leisure*.

3   **scortillum, -ī**, n. [dim. of **scortum, -ī**, n., *prostitute, whore*], *dear little/young
     prostitute/whore*.

        scortillum: in apposition with **amōrēs** (1); Varus had perhaps romanti-
          cally called her his **amōrēs**, but Catullus with some disparagement
          refers to her with this word.

    repente, adv., *suddenly; at first glance*.

    vīsum est: note that the subject, **scortillum**, is neuter.

4   **sānē**, adv., *certainly, truly*; concessive, *admittedly, to be sure*.

    illepidus, -a, -um [**in-** *not* + **lepidus, -a, -um**, *elegant, charming; smart, witty*]
     (cf. Catullus 6.2), *without charm/wit*.

    invenustus, -a, -um [**in-**, *not* + **venustus, -a, -um**, see Catullus 3.2], *without
     beauty, without charm, unattractive*.

        nōn . . . illepidum . . . invenustum: litotes.

5   **Hūc**: *to this place*, probably to where the woman lived.

    ut: *when*.

    incidō [**in-**, *in, on* + **cadō, cadere, cecidī, cāsūrus**, *to fall*], **incidere, incidī,
     incāsūrus** + dat., *to fall into/onto; to fall to one's lot; to arise, occur*.

        incidēre: = **incidērunt**; topics of conversation came up at random.

6   **quid . . . quō modō** (7) **. . . quōnam** (8): three indirect questions stating
     some of the topics of conversation; the questions, addressed to Catullus,
     pass quickly from a general inquiry about the province of Bithynia (where
     Catullus served for a year) to the profitability of his year abroad.

7   **sē habēret**: *[it] held itself, [it] was faring*.

8   **quīnam, quaenam, quodnam** [**quī, quae, quod**, *what, which?* + **nam**, parti-
     cle, *now*], interrogative adjective, *what kind of?*

    prōsum, prōdesse, prōfuī, *to be of use*; + dat., *to benefit, profit* (someone).

    prōfuisset: the subject is Bithynia.

    aes, aeris, n., *copper, bronze; money*.

        quōnam . . . aere: ablative of means, *by what kind of money*. Thomson
          prints **ecquōnam**, *whether from any*.

CATULLUS 10

Visiting a Scortillum

The poet, caught in a shameless lie, defends himself by vilifying the **scortillum**.

1 Vārus mē meus ad suōs amōrēs
2 vīsum dūxerat ē forō ōtiōsum,
3 scortillum, ut mihi tum repente vīsum est,
4 nōn sānē illepidum neque invenustum.
5 Hūc ut vēnimus, incidēre nōbīs
6 sermōnēs variī: in quibus, quid esset
7 iam Bīthȳnia; quō modō sē habēret;
8 et quōnam mihi prōfuisset aere.

continued

Initial Explorations

1. Unlike the earlier poems, Catullus 10 does not set up the situation of a dramatic dialogue in which Catullus addresses someone. There is no addressee. What form does this poem take? (1–4)
2. What are Catullus' first impressions of the woman that Varus takes him to visit? (3–4)
3. What direction does their conversation take? (5–8)
4. Locate the members of a tricolon in lines 6–8.

9   **id quod erat**: *that, which was*, i.e., *the truth*.
     nihil: with **esse**, *there was nothing* = *there was no money*.
     ipsīs: usually interpreted as meaning *for the natives*; some editors take it as
       modifying **praetōribus** (10) and regard **neque . . . / nec** as a colloquial
       pleonasm, thus **neque ipsīs / nec praetōribus** (possibly plural for singu-
       lar; see next note) . . . **nec cohortī** = *neither for the governor himself nor his
       staff*.
10   **praetor, praetōris**, m., *magistrate; governor*.
     praetōribus: possibly plural for singular; the praetor, or, more properly,
       the propraetor was appointed by the Senate to govern a province for a
       year. Catullus served under Gaius Memmius in 57 B.C.
     cohors, cohortis, f., *cohort; bodyguard; staff, retinue*.
     cohortī: the **cohors praetōria** had evolved by Catullus' time into a fash-
       ionable assembly of young men, called **comitēs**, *companions*, who ac-
       companied a provincial governor on his tour of duty. In some cases, as
       probably with Memmius, poets and artists were enlisted to provide cul-
       tural relief amid provincial backwaters.
11   **cūr**: *[as to] why*.
     quisquam, quisquam, quicquam, indefinite pronoun, *anyone, anything*.
     ūnctus, -a, -um, *oiled, anointed*; metaphorical, *enriched*.
     caput ūnctius: *a more richly combed head of hair*; literally, *a more oiled head*;
       the use of expensive hair lotions at banquets and celebrations was a
       mark of class and prosperity in Rome.
         caput ūnctius referret: = *should return enriched*. Catullus is implying
           that with Memmius as governor, no one in his entourage was able to
           make any profit.
12   **praesertim**, adv., *especially*.
     quibus . . . esset: short for **eīs quibus esset**, *for those* (continuing the datives
       from lines 9 and 10) *to/for whom* (dative of the possessor) *there was*. . . .
     irrumātor, irrumātōris, m., *a man who forces others to engage in unnatural sex
       with him; a pervert, s.o.b.*
13   **praetor**: C. Memmius, governor of Bithynia in 57/56 B.C., was at that time
       married to Sulla's daughter, Fausta, and was hostile to Caesar; he was a
       man of reputed literary taste, favoring, as did Catullus, Greek Alexan-
       drian poetry; a patron of the Latin poet Lucretius, he took both Catullus
       and the poet C. Helvius Cinna with him to Bithynia.
         quibus esset irrumātor / praetor: the governor may literally have
           abused his staff sexually, but the words may be taken figuratively to
           suggest the disdain with which the governor treated his staff by not
           sharing his profits with them. Catullus again bitterly excoriates
           Memmius for sexual abuse of his staff in poem 28.
     nec faceret: *and [who] was not considering/regarding*.
       esset (12) . . . **faceret** (13): relative clauses in indirect statement require the
         subjunctive.
     pilus, -ī, m., *a hair*.
       pilī: genitive of value, *worth a hair, of any value*.

9   Respondī, id quod erat, nihil neque ipsīs

10 nec praetōribus esse nec cohortī,

11 cūr quisquam caput ūnctius referret,

12 praesertim quibus esset irrumātor

13 praetor, nec faceret pilī cohortem.

continued

Initial Explorations

5. How does Catullus characterize his reply to these questions? (9)
6. Locate three words or phrases with the colloquial flavor of everyday or street language in lines 11–13.
7. How does Catullus characterize his service on the governor's staff in Bithynia? What complaints does he make? (9–13)

14 **quod . . . esse** (15): *[that] which is said to have been born there = that which is said to be native to that place;* the **lectīca octōphoros** (note the Greek adjectival ending), *litter carried by eight men*, was proverbially associated with the kings of Bithynia.

15 **comparāstī**: syncope for **comparāvistī**.

16 **ad lectīcam**: *for [the purpose of carrying] a litter.*
puellae: *in the eyes of the girl*, ethical dative (cf. Catullus 9.2 **mihi**).

17 **mē facerem**: *I might make myself [out to be].* . . .
beātus, -a, -um, *happy; fortunate; wealthy.*
    beātiōrem: not *more.* . . . but *rather.* . . .
        ūnum . . . beātiōrem: when **ūnus** is used with a superlative adjective it intensifies it, *one [above all]*, *most*; here it intensifies the comparative, *the one [fellow] in particular [who was] rather fortunate.*

18 **malignē**, adv., *stingily, scantily, insufficiently.*
    nōn . . . mihi tam fuit malignē: *I didn't make out so badly.*

19 **quod**: *just because.*
incidisset: supply **mihi**.

20 **parō, -āre, -āvī, -ātus**, *to prepare*; here and in lines 30 and 32, *to purchase, buy.*
rēctus, -a, -um, *right, proper; straight; tall.*

21 **mī**: dative of the possessor.
illīc: i.e., in Bithynia.

22 **grabātus, -ī**, m. [Greek loan word], *(a simple, poor man's) bed, cot.*

23 **collum, -ī**, n., *neck.*
collocō [**con-**, *together* + **locō, -āre, -āvī, -ātus**, *to place*], **-āre, -āvī, -ātus**, *to place.*

24 **Hīc**: *At this point.*
illa: i.e., Varus' girlfriend.
decet, decēre, decuit, impersonal + acc., *(it) is fitting for, befits.*
cinaedus, -a, -um [adjective made from the Greek loan word **cinaedus, -ī**, m., *catamite* (a male whore, usually regarded as exceedingly mercenary and opportunistic)], *resembling/typical of a* **cinaedus**.
    cinaediōrem: perhaps translate *the rather shamelessly opportunistic [girl].*

25 **quaesō, quaesere**, *to seek; to ask, beg.*
    Quaesō: *I beg, Please.*
inquit, "mihi, mī: Thomson gives this line as:
    "Quaesō," inquit mihi, "mī Catulle, paulum
        mī: vocative of **meus**.

26 **iste, ista, istud**, *that (of yours).*
    istōs: *those [litter-bearers] of yours.*
commodō [**commodus, -a, -um**, *convenient, beneficial* + **-ō**, verbal suffix], **-āre, -āvī, -ātus**, *to lend.*
    commoda: imperative with short *a* for the sake of the meter or possibly in imitation of colloquial speech.
ad Serāpim: *to the temple of Serapis.* Serapis was an Egyptian goddess, who was popular in Rome, especially among women who went to her temple in the city for treatment of various illnesses.

27 **Mane**: iambic shortening = **Manē**, *Wait!*
inquiī: perfect of **inquam**; the form is found only here in classical Latin.

14	"At certē tamen," inquiunt, "quod illīc
15	nātum dīcitur esse, comparāstī
16	ad lectīcam hominēs." Ego, ut puellae
17	ūnum mē facerem beātiōrem,
18	"Nōn," inquam, "mihi tam fuit malignē,
19	ut, prōvincia quod mala incidisset,
20	nōn possem octō hominēs parāre rēctōs."
21	At mī nūllus erat nec hīc neque illīc,
22	frāctum quī veteris pedem grabātī
23	in collō sibi collocāre posset.
24	Hīc illa, ut decuit cinaediōrem,
25	"Quaesō," inquit, "mihi, mī Catulle, paulum
26	istōs commoda; nam volō ad Serāpim
27	dēferrī." "Mane," inquiī puellae,

continued

Initial Explorations

8. What do Varus and the **scortillum** suppose that Catullus must have acquired in Bithynia and why? (14–16)
9. Why do you suppose that Varus and the **scortillum** remark that Catullus surely acquired these? (14–16)
10. What motivates Catullus' reply? To whom does he explain his motivation? (16–17)
11. What does Catullus say he was able to purchase? (20)
12. Is he telling the truth? How do we know? (21–23)
13. What does the **puella** request? (25–27) How does Catullus characterize her for making this request? (24) What reason does the **puella** give for her request? (26–27) Might she have some other reason for making it? If so, what is it?

28   **istud**: object of **parāvit** (30).
      modo, adv., *only; just now.*
29   **ratiō, ratiōnis**, f., *reason, common sense, good judgment.*
         fūgit mē ratiō: a colloquial expression for one's wits going astray, causing
         one to make a mistake.
      sodālis, sodālis, m., *companion, friend.*
30   **Cinna . . . Gāius**: Gaius Helvius Cinna, poet and friend of Catullus and au-
         thor of a poem titled *Zmyrna*, much admired by Catullus (see poem 95).
         Gāius: scan as three syllables.
31   **vērum**, conj., *but.*
      utrum . . . an . . . : *whether [the litter-bearers are] . . . or. . . .*
      illius . . . meī: *his . . . mine*, possessive genitives; **illius** = **illīus**; **meī** is proba-
         bly the genitive of **ego**, although the genitive of **ego** is not usually used to
         show possession, the adjective **meus, -a, -um** being used instead (the form
         would be the same here, **meī**).
      quid ad mē: supply **attinet**, *is [that] of concern.*
32   **tam bene quam . . . parārim** (= **parāverim**): supply **sī**, *as well as if I have/
         had. . . .* , perfect subjunctive in a conditional clause of comparison.
33   **īnsulsus, -a, -um** [**in-**, *not* + **salsus, -a, -um**, *salted; salty; witty*], *unsalted; dull,
         tasteless, without wit.*
      male: *especially, quite, very*, a colloquial use.
      vīvis: colloquial for **es** (see Catullus 8.10).
34   **esse neglegentem**: supply **quemquam**, *anyone*, or **mē**, *me*; the phrase
         [**quemquam/mē**] **esse neglegentem** is the subject of **nōn licet**, *[for any-
         one/for me] to be careless is not permitted.*

28   "istud quod modo dīxeram mē habēre,

29   fūgit mē ratiō: meus sodālis—

30   Cinna est Gāius—is sibī parāvit.

31   Vērum, utrum illius an meī, quid ad mē?

32   Ūtor tam bene quam mihī parārim.

33   Sed tū īnsulsa male et molesta vīvis,

34   per quam nōn licet esse neglegentem."

Initial Explorations

14.   What does the faltering speech of lines 27–30 imply about the speaker?
15.   What is unusual about the order of words in the first half of line 30? Why do you suppose the speaker does what he does here?
16.   Is Catullus' explanation in lines 29–30 credible?
17.   How does Catullus' assessment of the woman differ at the end of the poem (33–34) from what it was at the beginning (4)?
18.   What does Catullus imply about his behavior in referring to himself as **neglegentem** (34)?

Discussion

1.   This poem does not have an addressee, but Catullus tells a story about himself. What are the consequences of this difference in form? How does this poem differ in tone from those preceding it?
2.   What device does the poet use to guide the reader's response to his portrayal of himself in this poem?

Meter: Sapphic Strophe

1 **Fūrī ... Aurēlī**: vocative. Furius and Aurelius are two friends of Catullus, who are dealt with abusively in other poems but are presented as loyal comrades here.

    comitēs: vocative, in apposition with **Fūrī et Aurēlī**.

2 **sīve ... sīve** (5): *whether ... or. ...*

    sīve ... penetrābit ... sīve ... gradiētur (9): Catullus is the subject of these verbs in an extended travelogue that runs from line 2 through line 12. The correlative **sīve** in lines 2, 5, 6 (where the alternate form **seu** appears), 7, and 9 separates the various places in the world that Furius and Aurelius are invited to visit with Catullus.

    in extrēmōs ... Indōs: *among the. ...*

    extrēmus, -a, -um, *last; lying at the end; far distant;* (situated) *at the end of the world.*

    penetrō, -āre, -āvī, -ātus, *to penetrate;* + **in** + acc., *to enter among.*

    Indī, -ōrum, m. pl., *inhabitants of India, Indians* (India marked the furthest extent of the conquests of Alexander the Great).

3 **lītus**: the shore of the ocean that was thought to surround the circle of the world's lands.

    ut, relative adv., *where.*

    ut: delayed relative adverb, coming as the second rather than the first word in its clause.

    longē, adv., *far, far and wide.*

    resonō [**re-**, *back* + **sonō, sonāre, sonuī, sonitus**, *to sound*], **-āre, -āvī**, *to resound.*

    resonante: what form, tense, and voice? What does it modify?

    Eōus, -a, -um, *Eastern.*

4 **tundō, tundere, tutudī, tūsus**, *to strike, beat, pound.*

    tunditur: the subject is **lītus**.

        tunditur unda: note the play on sounds.

CATULLUS 11

A Parting of the Ways

*Catullus sends a final message to his **puella**.*

1   Fūrī et Aurēlī, comitēs Catullī,
2   sīve in extrēmōs penetrābit Indōs,
3   lītus ut longē resonante Eōā
4   tunditur undā,

continued

Initial Explorations

1. Analyze the grammar of lines 2–12.
   a. What two verbs are introduced by the repeated conjunction **sīve**?
   b. What two verbs are parts of subordinate clauses within clauses introduced by **sīve**?
   c. What two prepositional phrases are parallel to one another?
   d. Where has the preposition **in** been omitted where it could have been expressed?
   e. What relative adverb has been delayed?
   f. What antecedent has been placed within the relative clause dependent on it?

5   **Hyrcānī, -ōrum**, m. pl., *the Hyrcani* (a people who lived on the south shore of the Caspian Sea and were associated in the popular mind with the conquests of Alexander the Great).

       Arabēs, Arabum, m. pl., *the Arabians*.

         Arabas: Greek accusative plural.

       -ve, enclitic conj., *or*.

       mollis, -is, -e, *soft; luxurious*.

         in Hyrcānōs Arabasve mollēs: supply **penetrābit** from line 2.

6   **seu**: = **sīve**.

       Sagae, -ārum, m. pl., *the Sacae* (a nomadic Scythian people who lived east of the Caspian Sea and were dangerous enemies of Rome).

       sagittiferus, -a, -um [**sagitta, -ae**, f., *arrow* + **-fer, -fera, -ferum**, *carrying*], *arrow-carrying*.

       Parthī, -ōrum, m. pl., *the Parthians* (an eastern people whose kingdom reached from the Euphrates to the Indus and who were hostile to Rome; they were notorious for the skilled tactics of their mounted archers; in November, 55 B.C., Marcus Licinius Crassus set out with a Roman army to defeat the Parthians but was trapped and killed near Carrhae).

         Sagās sagittiferōsve Parthōs: supply **penetrābit in**.

7   **quae . . . Nīlus** (8): the antecedent of **quae** is **aequora** (8), placed inside the relative clause.

       septemgeminus, -a, -um [**septem**, *seven* + **geminus, -a, -um**, *twin*], *sevenfold* (referring to the delta of the Nile).

       colōrō, -āre, -āvī, -ātus, *to color, stain, darken*.

8   **aequor, aequoris**, n., *a smooth, level surface; a level stretch of ground, plain*; often, in sing. or pl., *the sea*.

         aequora: supply **penetrābit in**; **aequora** is the final element in the list of imagined localities dependent on **penetrābit** (2).

            colōrat / aequora Nīlus: probably referring to silt carried into the Mediterranean (**aequora** = *the sea*), but possibly referring to the Nile staining the plains (**aequora**) with alluvial deposits during its annual flooding.

5   sīve in Hyrcānōs Arabasve mollēs,

6   seu Sagās sagittiferōsve Parthōs,

7   sīve quae septemgeminus colōrat

8   aequora Nīlus,

continued

Initial Explorations

2. Examine the elements of elevated style in lines 2–12.
   a. Identify examples of anaphora and of asyndeton.
   b. Comment on the effectiveness of word placement in line 2. Consider in particular the placement of the verb **penetrābit**.
   c. Identify and explain the sound effects of the words in lines 3–4.
   d. Diagram the arrangement of nouns and adjectives in lines 5–6. Identify a chiastic noun-adjective, adjective-noun arrangement.
   e. Describe the effect of the use of polysyllabic adjectives.
   f. Describe the effect of adverbial and adjectival words that convey ideas of distance, size, or stature.
3. Trace on the map the succession of places mentioned from line 2 to the end of line 12. What is the overall pattern? What word at the end rounds out the passage by echoing a word at the beginning? What do these words contribute to the tone of the passage?
4. The words **sagittiferōsve Parthōs** (6) allude to Crassus' expedition to Parthia, to which he set out in 55 B.C. and where he was defeated near Carrhae in 53 B.C.; lines 9–12 refer to Caesar's bridging of the Rhine in 55 B.C. and his crossing into Britain in 55 and 54 B.C. Why do you suppose Catullus included this allusion in line 6 and these references in lines 9–12?

9   **gradior, gradī, gressus sum**, *to walk, go.*

10   **Caesar, Caesaris**, m., *Julius Caesar* (whose campaigns in Gaul are alluded to here; early in 54 B.C., Catullus, who had viciously lampooned Caesar and his henchmen in a number of poems, was reconciled with him).

     vīsō, vīsere, vīsī, *to go and look at/view* (something).

     monimentum, -ī, n. [**moneō, -ēre, -uī, -itus**, *to remind; to warn*], *reminder; memorial; testimonial; monument.*

     magnī: which word does this adjective modify?

11   **Gallicus, -a, -um**, *of Gaul, Gallic.*

     Rhēnus, -ī, m., *the Rhine River* (the Rhine formed the natural boundary between Gaul and Germany; Caesar crossed the Rhine with his army in the summer of 55 B.C.).

     horribilis, -is, -e, *inspiring fear/horror; rough.*

       horribile aequor: i.e., the British Channel, which Caesar first crossed in August of 55 B.C. and again in the late summer of 54.

         Gallicum Rhēnum horribile aequor: asyndeton.

     ultimus, -a, -um, *far, distant.*

12   **Britannī, -ōrum**, m. pl., *inhabitants of Britain.*

13   **omnia haec**: i.e., the places and peoples in the previous list.

     quīcumque, quaecumque, quodcumque, indefinite relative pronoun, *whoever, whatever.*

       quaecumque: neuter accusative plural, *whatever.*

     feret: what mood and tense?

     voluntās, voluntātis, f., *will.*

14   **caeles, caelitis** [archaic and poetic], *dwelling in heaven*; as substantive, usually plural, **caelitēs, caelitum**, m. pl., *gods.*

     simul, adv., *in company, together; at the same time, simultaneously.*

     parātī: modifying the vocatives in line 1.

15   **pauca**: which word does this adjective modify?

     nūntiō, -āre, -āvī, -ātus, *to announce.*

     meae puellae: what case? What is your clue?

16   **nōn bona**: litotes; the "words" or message are the final two stanzas.

Text

11   **horribile aequor ulti- / mōsque Britannōs**: the manuscripts have **horribilēsque ulti- / mōsque Britannōs**, with both adjectives modifying **Britannōs**:

     11   Gallicum Rhēnum horribilēsque ulti-

     12   mōsque Britannōs,

With this reading, however, the meter is preserved only if elision does not occur between **horribilēsque** and **ulti-**. In order to avoid this hiatus, editors usually print the emendation **horribile aequor**, as in this text. Another reading, **horribilem gelū** [**gelū, -ūs**, n., *cold, frost, ice*], has also been proposed, with the adjective modifying **Rhēnum**:

     11   Gallicum Rhēnum horribilem gelū ulti-

     12   mōsque Britannōs,

9   sīve trāns altās gradiētur Alpēs,

10   Caesaris vīsēns monimenta magnī,

11   Gallicum Rhēnum horribile aequor ulti-

12   mōsque Britannōs,

13   omnia haec, quaecumque feret voluntās

14   caelitum, temptāre simul parātī,

15   pauca nūntiāte meae puellae

16   nōn bona dicta.

continued

Initial Explorations

5. How is the elevated style of lines 1–12 continued in lines 13–14? Include discussion of hyperbole and poetic vocabulary.
6. What appears to be the purpose of the imagined or projected travels? Who will decide what travels will be undertaken? What is the relationship of Furius and Aurelius to Catullus?
7. Lines 1–16 constitute one main clause of a single sentence. What is the main verb in this clause?
8. How do lines 15–16 depart from the elevated style of lines 1–4?
9. What word in lines 15–16 echoes what word in lines 13–14?

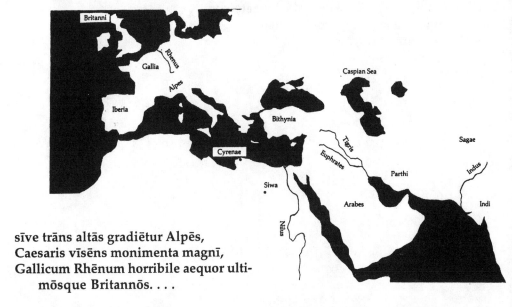

sīve trāns altās gradiētur Alpēs,
Caesaris vīsēns monimenta magnī,
Gallicum Rhēnum horribile aequor ulti-
    mōsque Britannōs. . . .

Locate on this map all the places and peoples mentioned in Catullus 11.

17   **Cum:** *With.*
     valeō, valēre, valuī, *to grow stronger; to thrive, prosper, fare well.*
        cum suīs vīvat valeatque: jussive subjunctives (the subject is **puella**) in a
           formula for leave-taking = *good-by to her with her.* . . . , but expressing
           more literal meanings as well: *may she live and may she fare well with
           her.* . . .
     moechus, -ī, m., *adulterer.*
18   **quōs:** with **trecentōs,** *300 of whom.*
     complector, complectī, complexus sum, *to embrace.*
        complexa: the perfect participle of a deponent verb is often best translated
           with a present participle in English.
     trecentī, -ae, -a, *three hundred* (often of an indefinitely large number).
        trecentōs: hyperbole; cf. Catullus 9.2, **mīlibus trecentīs.**
19   **omnium:** what case and number? Pronounce **omnium** as two syllables by
        synaeresis or elide with the next line (synapheia).
20   **īlia, īlium,** n. pl., *groin, male organs.*
21   **respectō [respiciō, respicere,** *to look back at* + **-tō,** verbal suffix], **-āre,** *to look
        around for; to await.*
        respectet: what mood, tense, and construction? The subject is **puella.**
22   **quī:** the antecedent is **amōrem.**
     illius: = **illīus,** referring to the **puella.** What case and number is the pronoun?
     culpa, -ae, f., *fault, blame; wrongdoing;* (of sexual misconduct) *infidelity.*
        culpā: ablative of cause.
     prātum, -ī, n., *meadow.*
        prātī: the line is hypermetric, and the final syllable is elided (synapheia).
           prātī / ultimī: *of the furthest [part of the] meadow.*
23   **praetereunte . . . arātrō** (24): ablative absolute, not instrumental ablative,
        which would have required **praetereuntī.**
     postquam: delayed conjunction.
24   **arātrum, -ī,** n., *plow.*

17   Cum suīs vīvat valeatque moechīs,
18   quōs simul complexa tenet trecentōs,
19   nūllum amāns vērē, sed identidem omnium
20   īlia rumpēns;

21   nec meum respectet, ut ante, amōrem,
22   quī illius culpā cecidit velut prātī
23   ultimī flōs, praetereunte postquam
24   tāctus arātrō est.

Initial Explorations

10. Does the message in lines 17–20 come as a shock after the buildup of lines 1–16? What is shocking about it?
11. How are the style, tone, and perspective of lines 17–20 different from those of lines 1–16? Is hyperbole present in lines 17–20?
12. In what ways is the scene described in lines 17–20 the opposite of the travels described in lines 1–12?
13. Notice that two words are repeated in lines 17–20 from the previous stanza: **simul** (18) = **simul** (14) and **omnium** (19) = **omnia** (13). What contrast do these repetitions invite between the two groups of people and their activities, i.e., between Catullus and his male companions (**comitēs**) on the one hand and the **puella** embracing three hundred adulterers at a time on the other?
14. What words in lines 17–20 express leave-taking? What words in lines 21–24 reiterate this message?
15. Examine the simile of the flower and the plow. What does the flower represent? What does the plow represent? What is the significance of the fact that the flower is at the edge of the meadow? Is there any suggestion as to whether the plowman cuts the flower accidentally or on purpose?
16. Look at the last line in each stanza. How does each last line bring its stanza to an effective closure?

Discussion

1. Consider this poem as part of the cycle of poems dealing with Catullus' love affair with his **puella**/Lesbia. What position does this poem occupy in the cycle? What is different from the situation in Catullus 8?
2. Gloria S. Duclos has compared the fifth stanza of Catullus 11 with Catullus 5 as follows. To what extent do you agree with her observations?

> C.11 . . . is in some ways a response to . . . earlier enthusiasm. Just as Catullus now truly sees Lesbia for what she is, . . . so he also weaves into this last poem themes and verbal reminiscences from other poems to and about Lesbia. The most rapturous poem of the Catullus-Lesbia affair is c.5, which opens

with the startling equation of living and loving: *vivamus atque amemus* (1). The two lovers are exhorted to live a life of loving and kissing, excluding all others. The isolation and uniqueness of Catullus and Lesbia in their love for each other are stressed in c.5. In the fifth stanza of c.11, there are ironic and bitter echoes of c.5. *Vivamus atque amemus* becomes *vivat valeatque* of 11.17. The union of the two lovers, expressed in the verbs, has been broken irrevocably and one partner now fornicates indiscriminately, to the disgust of the other. The percussive *centum, centum, centum* of 5.7,8,9 is ironically reflected in the *trecentos* of 11.18; Catullus now counts Lesbia's other lovers, not her kisses given to him. 5.1 and 11.17 show in the very word order how far apart the lovers have grown: *vivamus* and *amemus* encircle, as it were, the beloved *mea Lesbia*; living and loving should be the alpha and omega of the lovers' existence. In c.11, however, Lesbia is encircled, in the line as well as in life, by her adulterers, *cum suis . . . moechis*; she lives her life with them and thrives on her sexual excesses. The *amemus* of 5.1 is answered by the flat statement of 11.19: *nullum amans vere*, and the ecstatic exhortation of 5.1 degenerates into a true assessment of what Lesbia's "love" really is: *ilia rumpens* (11.20). It is not only Lesbia who has withdrawn from the *amemus*; Catullus' love, too, has gone, destroyed by Lesbia herself (11.21–22). Catullus had declared in c.5 that living and loving were the same thing and thus in c.11 he pictures his love dying as a flower dies; when love is gone, so is life extinguished.

(Gloria S. Duclos, "Catullus 11: Atque in perpetuum, Lesbia, ave atque vale," *Arethusa* 9, 1976, 79–80)

3. The comparison of Catullus' love to a flower cut down as a plow passes by (22–24) is indebted to an image of a hyacinth in lines preserved from a wedding hymn written by the Greek poetess Sappho (seventh to sixth centuries B.C.):

    like the hyacinth that shepherds trample under foot in the mountains, and the purple flower <lies crushed> on the ground. . . .

Gloria S. Duclos has written as follows on this fragment of Sappho and the image of the flower in the last stanza of Catullus' poem. Again, to what extent do you agree with her observations?

The image which dominates this stanza, the lonely flower at the meadow's edge cut down by the plough, has its origin in a fragment attributed to Sappho. Catullus had used a variant of it in another, presumably earlier, poem (62.39–47), but what is interesting about its use in c.11 is the inversion to which Catullus has subjected it. In the Sapphic fragment, the hyacinth trampled by the shepherds is presumably likened to a maiden's virginity. The passage in c.62 explicitly compares the plucked flower to a girl's maidenhood. The image, then, is traditionally used to express the finality of a girl's loss of her virginity. In c.11, the finality is still there (*cecidit*, 22) but the subject of the image has been changed, the flower has become Catullus' love for Lesbia. As he inverted the first part of the Sapphic image from feminine to masculine, so also he transforms the second element from masculine to feminine, for the passing plough of the simile must correspond to Lesbia. Not only is ploughing ordinarily a masculine activity, but the metaphoric use of ploughing to denote male sexual activity is commonplace in ancient literature.

Catullus has clearly reversed the usual terms of the image: the girl's virginity becomes Catullus' love, and the shepherds' trampling feet become Lesbia's plough. In this final renunciation of his love, the poet's tendency to think of himself in feminine rather than masculine terms is . . . apparent.

(Duclos, 86–87)

4. Divide the poem into three parts according to the tenses of the indicative verbs. In what temporal direction do the poet's thoughts move? On what note does the poem end?

CATULLUS 1–11

Review Catullus 1–11

1. Outline the course taken by Catullus' love affair with Lesbia in poems 2, 3, 5, 7, 8, and 11, as they are arranged here (which need not be the order in which they were composed).

2. Note the theme of travel in poems 4, 9, 10, and 11.

3. Observe the theme of the whore in poems 6, 10, and 11.

4. Show how Catullus 11 recapitulates the main themes of the collection as a whole and provides an appropriate conclusion.

Make a diagram showing the pattern of relationships among the poems in the collection, noting how the themes of Lesbia, travel, and the whore are interwoven.

Charles Segal has argued that poems 1–11 "form a unified block held together by some coherent pattern of arrangement" (67), noting that "six of these poems concern Lesbia" and "are so arranged that they form a progression: from light to serious and from optimistic to bitter" (70). He sees a progression in "the terms of address used for Lesbia," noting that in the final poem Catullus "refuses to address Lesbia at all or even to mention her name" (73–74). Throughout the Lesbia poems, Segal notes "a complex of related themes and images, namely love, death, light, and darkness" (75). He also calls attention to the placement of the poems dealing with travel and the whore, noting that Catullus 4 and 9 "are both happy poems" and that in Catullus 11 "Lesbia is herself little better than a **scortum**" (79). (Charles Segal, "The Order of Catullus, Poems 2–11," *Latomus* 27 [1968], 305–21)

What other interrelations can you find among these poems? Consider the placement of Catullus 6 at the center of poems 1–11. Does Catullus 10 foreshadow the poem that follows it in any important ways? Do you think Catullus gathered these poems into a collection and arranged them in this order? What does the collection as a whole say that the poems read individually do not? How is the collection greater than the sum of its parts?

Meter: hendecasyllabic

1   **Marrūcīnus, -a, -um**, *of/belonging to the Marrucini* (a people living on the
    Adriatic coast of central Italy).
        Marrūcīne Asinī: Asinius Marrucinus, an acquaintance of Catullus. The
        order of the **nōmen (Asinius)** and **cognōmen (Marrūcīnus)** is re-
        versed. The family of the Asinii came from Teate, the chief town of the
        Marrucini.
    manū sinistrā: why are these two words in the ablative? The left hand was
        proverbially associated with thievery.
2   **bellē**: for the adjective **bellus, -a, -um**, see on Catullus 3.14; the adverb has a
        colloquial tone, *nicely, well.*
    ūteris: present or future? What is the clue?
    in iocō atque vīnō: i.e., at dinner parties full of joking and drinking.
3   **linteum, -ī**, n., *linen; towel, napkin.*
        lintea: see Catullus 4.5 for use of the word **linteum** in a different sense. The
        Romans brought their own napkins to dinner parties, and napkins were
        important because the Romans ate with their fingers.
    neglegentiōrum: what degree, case, and number is the adjective? What
        noun could you supply for this adjective to modify? Cf. Catullus 10.34.
4   **salsus, -a, -um** (cf. Catullus 10.33, **īnsulsa**), *salty; humorous, witty.*
    Fugit tē: *[It] escapes you. That's where you're wrong.* Cf. Catullus 10.29, **fūgit
        mē ratiō**.
    ineptus, -a, -um [in-, *not* + **aptus, -a, -um**, *tied, bound; appropriate, fitting]*, *un-
        aware of what is appropriate; silly, foolish.*
        inepte: cf. Catullus 6.14, **ineptiārum**, and 8.1, **ineptīre**.
5   **quamvīs [quam**, *as much as* + **vīs**, *you want/wish]*, adv., *as much as you please;
        ever so, extremely.*
    sordidus, -a, -um, *sordid, filthy, disgraceful.*
    invenustus, -a, -um [in-, *not* + **venustus, -a, -um**, see Catullus 3.2 and 10.4],
        without beauty, without charm, unattractive.
6   **mihi? . . . Polliōnī**: in what case are these two words and why?
    Polliō, Polliōnis, m., *Pollio* (brother of Asinius and most likely the Roman
        orator, historian, and poet, Gaius Asinius Pollio, 76 B.C.–A.D. 4., who was
        later a friend of Horace and Vergil and who founded the first public library
        in Rome).
7   **fūrtum, -ī**, n., *theft.*
    vel, particle, *even.*
    talentum, -ī, n. [Greek loan word], *talent* (a Greek unit of weight and an ex-
        pression for a very large sum of money equaling the weight of a talent of
        gold or silver).
        vel talentō: *with even a talent*, ablative of means or instrument.
8   **mūtō, -āre, -āvī, -ātus**, *to change; to exchange; to undo.*
        mūtārī: what form, tense, and voice?
    velit: from what verb? Identify the mood, tense, and construction.
        quī (7) . . . velit (8): i.e., he would give a talent to undo his brother's thefts.
    lepos, lepōris, m., *charm, grace; wit, humor*; pl., *witticism.*

CATULLUS 12

A Thief at Large

What has Asinius Marrucinus stolen? How does Catullus threaten to get it back? Why is it valuable?

1   Marrūcīne Asinī, manū sinistrā
2   nōn bellē ūteris: in iocō atque vīnō
3   tollis lintea neglegentiōrum.
4   Hoc salsum esse putās? Fugit tē, inepte;
5   quamvīs sordida rēs et invenusta est.
6   Nōn crēdis mihi? Crēde Polliōnī
7   frātrī, quī tua fūrta vel talentō
8   mūtārī velit: est enim lepōrum

continued

Initial Explorations

1. What words characterize Asinius and his crime in lines 1–5?
2. Why does Catullus mention Pollio, Asinius' brother? (6–9)

"A Reading from Homer"
Sir Lawrence Alma-Tadema, British, 1836–1912
Philadelphia Museum of Fine Arts
Philadelphia, Pennsylvania
Can you imagine this as Catullus reading poem 12 to his friends from his **libellus**?

9   **differtus, -a, -um** + gen., *stuffed* (with), *chockfull* (of).
     facētiae, -ārum, f. pl., *cleverness; facetiousness, wit.*

10   **hendecasyllabī, -ōrum**, m. pl. [Greek loan word], *hendecasyllables* (eleven-
     syllable verses, the meter of this poem and a meter often used by Catullus
     for satire and abuse as well as for love poems).
     trecentī, -ae, -a, *three hundred* (often of an indefinitely large number).
     trecentōs: hyperbole.

12   **quod**: relative pronoun and subject of **movet**. Identify the antecedent, gen-
     der, and number.
     aestimātiō, aestimātiōnis, f., *valuation; monetary worth, value.*

13   **vērum**, conj., *but.*
     mnēmosynum, -ī, n. [Greek loan word], *souvenir, memento, keepsake.*
     sodālis, sodālis, m., *companion, friend.*

14   **sūdārium, -ī**, n., *sweat cloth, handkerchief, napkin.*
     Saetabus, -a, -um, *Saetaban, from Saetabis* (a town in Spain known for its linen
     goods).
     Hibērī, Hibērōrum, m. pl., *Iberians, Spaniards.*
     ex Hibērīs: *from the [land of the] Iberians*, i.e., *from Spain.*

15   **mihi mūnerī**: double dative, *to me for [the purpose of] a gift, to me as a gift.*
     Fabullus: he and **Vērānius** (16) were friends of Catullus, on provincial ser-
     vice in Spain; for Veranius, see Catullus 9.1.

16   **haec**: i.e., the **sudāria** (14).
     haec amem: supply **ut** (which is often left out with impersonal verbs and
     the impersonal phrase **necesse est**); the clause **ut haec amem** is the
     subject of **necesse est**.

17   **ut**: *just as*, supply **amō**.
     Vērāniolus, -ī, m. [dim. of **Vērānius**], *Veraniolus.*
     Vērāniolum: what does the diminutive express here? How can you best
     translate it into English?

Text

9   **differtus**: the manuscripts have **dissertus** or **disertus**, *skilled in speaking*,
     which does not produce good sense; Thomson notes that the conjecture
     printed in our text, **differtus**, should take an ablative and not a genitive as
     here; Thomson proposes reading **disertē pater**, *clearly the father*, with the
     genitives in lines 8 and 9 depending on **pater** = *he is clearly the father [= the
     very essence] of. . . .* Thus:
           8   est enim lepōrum
           9   disertē pater ac facētiārum.

9   differtus puer ac facētiārum.

10   Quārē aut hendecasyllabōs trecentōs

11   exspectā, aut mihi linteum remitte,

12   quod mē nōn movet aestimātiōne,

13   vērum est mnēmosynum meī sodālis.

14   Nam sūdāria Saetaba ex Hibērīs

15   mīsērunt mihi mūnerī Fabullus

16   et Vērānius; haec amem necesse est

17   ut Vērāniolum meum et Fabullum.

Initial Explorations

3.   What reading in line 9 makes more sense?
4.   What threat does Catullus make in lines 10–11? What rhetorical device does he use to highlight the threat?
5.   The poem ends on a sentimental note. Why does Catullus really want the napkin back?
6.   In line 1, look closely at the two pairs of words. How do they echo each other?
7.   Locate other pairs of words or phrases in the poem.

Discussion

1.   What key words are used in the comparison of the two brothers in lines 4–9? How do they define a conception of **urbanitās**, i.e., the sophistication and manners appropriate to a refined city-dweller?
2.   The literary genre of satire is often aimed at people who act in self-interested, thoughtless, greedy, and ultimately self-destructive ways. To what extent is this poem satirical, and what strategies does the poet use in lines 1–11 to bring Asinius to his senses and to correct his ways?
3.   How does the poet's valuation of the napkin as expressed in the last section of the poem differ from that of Asinius?
4.   Divide the poem into three sections. How do the themes of the poem develop from beginning to end?

Meter: hendecasyllabic

1   **mī**: vocative singular of **meus**, often used with close friends (compare Catullus 10.25).

    Fabullus, -ī, m., *Fabullus* (a dear friend of Catullus; see Catullus 12.17).

2   **paucīs ... diēbus**: how do you translate the ablative of time here? Note how Catullus has framed the line with these two words. Find another example of line framing in this poem.

    sī ... favent: equivalent to our expression, *God willing*; the use of the present tense in the if-clause (protasis) of the future-more-vivid condition is colloquial.

        dī: = **deī**, nom. pl.

3   **attuleris**: the future perfect, used in the protasis of a future-more-vivid conditional sentence. Where is the second half or conclusion (apodosis)? What is the tense of the verb in the apodosis?

4   **nōn sine**: litotes, equivalent to **cum**.

    candidus, -a, -um (see Catullus 8.3, 8), *white, fair-skinned, pretty*.

5   **sal, salis**, m. (see Catullus 10.33, **īnsulsa**, and 12.4, **salsum**), *salt*; by metonymy, *wit*.

    cachinnus, -ī, m. [onomatopoetic], *loud laughter*.

6   **venustus, -a, -um** (see Catullus 3.2, 10.4, 12.5), *endowed/involved with Venus; attractive, charming*.

    venuste: in what case is the adjective here? What noun is understood?

    noster: Catullus often uses the plural possessive adjective instead of the singular; translate, *my*.

7   **tuī Catullī**: genitive of possession with **sacculus** (8).

8   **sacculus, -ī**, m. [dim.], *small sack, bag, purse, pouch*.

    arānea, -ae, f., *spider's web, cobweb*.

9   **contrā**, adv., *in return*.

    merus, -a, -um, *undiluted, pure*.

    amor, amōris, m., *love*; pl., *love affairs* (cf. Catullus 7.8), or concrete, *the object of one's love, loved one, girlfriend* (cf. Catullus 6.16 and 10.1).

        amōrēs: not *girlfriend* here; the phrase **merōs amōrēs** points forward to **unguentum** (11), a perfume that is anticipated in the phrase **merōs amōrēs**, "pure, unadulterated love" (Fordyce), "something you'll absolutely fall in love with" (Quinn), or "love's pure essence" (Ker in translating Martial 14.206.1, where Martial borrows Catullus' phrase **merōs amōrēs**).

10   **seu**: = **sīve**, *or if*.

    quis, qua/quae, quid, indefinite pronoun after **seu**, *anyone, anybody, somebody, anything, something*.

        seu quid ... est: i.e., you could describe the perfume with some word or phrase other than **merōs amōrēs** if there is anything more delightful or more elegant than that.

    -ve, enclitic conj., *or*.

CATULLUS 13

A Fantasy of an Unusual Dinner

What prediction does Catullus make in the first half of the following poem? What does he promise in the second half?

1   Cēnābis bene, mī Fabulle, apud mē
2   paucīs, sī tibi dī favent, diēbus,
3   sī tēcum attuleris bonam atque magnam
4   cēnam, nōn sine candidā puellā
5   et vīnō et sale et omnibus cachinnīs.
6   Haec sī, inquam, attuleris, venuste noster,
7   cēnābis bene—nam tuī Catullī
8   plēnus sacculus est arāneārum.
9   Sed contrā accipiēs merōs amōrēs
10   seu quid suāvius ēlegantiusve est:

continued

Initial Explorations

1. What will Fabullus do? Where? When? On what condition? (1–2)
2. What does Catullus imagine that Fabullus will bring? (3–5)
3. Why can't Catullus provide the usual essentials of a good dinner? (7–8)
4. What will Fabullus receive in return? (9–10)

... unguentum dabo. ....

11   **unguentum, -ī**, n., *perfume.*
      dabo: iambic shortening.
         unguentum dabo: Catullus as host of the dinner party will provide the
            perfume that was usual on such occasions; in Horace, *Odes* 4.12.16–17,
            Horace invites Vergil to bring perfume while he, Horace, will provide
            the wine.
      quod: what are the antecedent, gender, number, and case of this relative
         pronoun and of the one in line 13?
      meae puellae: the **puella** is usually identified with Lesbia.
      dōnārunt: syncope for **dōnāvērunt**.
      Venerēs Cupīdinēsque: *[all] Venuses and Cupids;* cf. Catullus 3.1.
13   **olfaciō, olfacere, olfēcī, olfactus** *to catch the scent of, smell, sniff.*
      tū cum olfaciēs: temporal **cum** clause.
14   **tōtum**: this may be taken with either **tē** or **nāsum**.
      ut tē faciant: on what word does this indirect command depend?

Comparison

Thomas McAfee, a modern poet, has created a dialogue across centuries in the following poem. From the poems you have read, which *personae* of Catullus does
McAfee appear to admire and envy? What is meant in the last line?

If I had your gall, Catullus,
I wouldn't worry about the phone bill
Or the end of the month
Or how much you owe for last year's
Income tax. You could live
On ink and my sweat. I saw
The dinner invitation you sent:
Bring your own food (and make sure
I'll like it), a beautiful woman,
And a good wine. Don't forget
Witty talk, and you have to do
The laughing.
                    I know. You don't
Have to tell me. He might even show
And you could get drunk and flirt
With the woman. If he doesn't,
You'd be depressed anyway.

11   nam unguentum dabo, quod meae puellae

12   dōnārunt Venerēs Cupīdinēsque,

13   quod tū cum olfaciēs, deōs rogābis

14   tōtum ut tē faciant, Fabulle, nāsum.

Initial Explorations

5. What specifically will Catullus give Fabullus? (11–12)
6. What will this make Fabullus do? (13–14)
7. Structure:
    a. Analyze the chiastic arrangement of phrases and words in lines 1–7 by finding in lines 6 and 7 words and phrases that correspond in reverse order to the following phrases and words in lines 1–4: **Cēnābis bene** (1), **mī Fabulle** (1), **sī . . . attuleris** (3), **cēnam** (4).
    b. What three words positioned at the beginning of three of lines 1–7 echo one another?
    c. The arrangement of words that you have analyzed in lines 1–7 reinforces the tight logic of the statement being made in these lines, namely, that Fabullus will dine well if he brings the dinner, etc., with him. What Catullus will contribute is described in lines 9–14. Discuss the significance of the following correspondences between phrases and words in these lines and in lines 1–7: **accipiēs merōs amōrēs** (9) = **Haec . . . attuleris** (6); **unguentum dabo** (11) = **attuleris . . . / cēnam** (3–4); **puellae** (11) = **puellā** (4); **deōs** (13) = **dī** (2); and **Fabulle** (14) = **Fabulle** (1).

Discussion

1. This poem is often described as an invitation to dinner. Is it? What would a normal dinner invitation be like, and how does this poem invert and parody what one would expect in a dinner invitation? How does this inversion and parody produce a humorous and comical effect?
2. How does Catullus set up an opposition between the dinner that Fabullus will provide and the perfume that Catullus will offer? Note the verbal correspondences that you analyzed above.
3. What is the point of the inverted situation of guest and host in which the guest brings all the food, etc., and the host supplies only the perfume?
4. What precisely is the perfume that Catullus will give? Is it more or less important than what Fabullus is imagined as contributing to the imagined dinner?
5. Is the poem a serious description of a possible dinner with Fabullus, or does it have some quite different purpose? If so, what is it?

Meter: choliambic

1   **Suffēnus, -ī**, m., *Suffenus* (the poet about whom Catullus is writing this poem; he is mentioned in Catullus 14.19; nothing of his work has survived).

       iste, ista, istud (usually pejorative or disparaging), *that (of yours).*

       Vārus, -ī, m., *Varus* (see on Catullus 10.1).

       probē, adv., *correctly; thoroughly, well.*

       nōscō, nōscere, nōvī, nōtus, inceptive, *to become acquainted with;* pf., *to know.*

          nōstī: syncope for **nōvistī**.

2   **venustus**: see Catullus 3.2, 10.4, 12.5, and 13.6.

       dicāx, dicācis, *sharp-tongued, witty.*

       urbānus, -a, -um, *of the city; urbane, sophisticated* (in speech and manners).

3   **īdem**: pronoun, *the same* (person as previously mentioned); often, as here, introducing an inconsistency, translate, *at the same time* or *on the other hand.*

       longē, adv., *far, far and wide, by far.*

4   **esse**: take with **perscrīpta** in line 5 to form a perfect passive infinitive.

       illī: dative of agent.

       mīlia: supply **versuum**.

       aut decem aut plūra: modifying **mīlia**, as a kind of afterthought, the main point being that Suffenus writes verses by the thousands.

5   **perscrībō [per-**, *fully* + **scrībō, scrībere, scrīpsī, scrīptus**, *to write*], **perscrībere, perscrīpsī, perscrīptus**, *to write out fully; to write down.*

       ut fit: *as it happens, as is usual/common.*

       palimpsestum, -ī, n. [from a Greek word meaning *scraped again*], *palimpsest* (parchment or papyrus from which the old writing has been scraped off, mentioned here as an example of ordinary, everyday writing material).

6   **relāta**: supply **esse**; the subject of the infinitive is **mīlia (versuum)** (4).

       carta, -ae, f. (see Catullus 1.6), *sheet of papyrus.*

       cartae . . . membrānae (7): supply **sed** to introduce this list.

       rēgius, -a, -um, *royal, fit for kings; high-quality, expensive.*

       liber, librī, m., *papyrus roll* (the ancient form of what we think of as a book).

7   **umbilīcus, -ī**, m., *navel; stick/cylinder* (on which papyrus was rolled); pl., *knobs* (at either end of the stick or cylinder of a papyrus roll).

       lōrum, -ī, n., *strap, leather tie.*

       ruber, rubra, rubrum, *red.*

       membrāna, -ae, f., *skin of a sheep or goat prepared for use as writing material, parchment; cover/wrapper made of parchment.*

          membrānae: genitive or dative, *of/for the wrapper.*

CATULLUS 22

On a Local Poetaster

Suffenus is a charming person, but as a poet—. Still, there is a Suffenus in us all.

1 Suffēnus iste, Vāre, quem probē nōstī,
2 homō est venustus et dicāx et urbānus,
3 īdemque longē plūrimōs facit versūs.
4 Putō esse ego illī mīlia aut decem aut plūra
5 perscrīpta, nec sīc ut fit in palimpsestō
6 relāta: cartae rēgiae, novī librī,
7 novī umbilīcī, lōra rubra membrānae,

continued

Text

5 **palimpsestō**: Thomson prints this reading rather than the accusative **palimpseston**, found in older editions.
6 **cartae rēgiae, novī librī**: Thomson prints **cartae rēgiae novae librī**, making the whole phrase refer to the sheets of the papyrus roll.
7 **lōra rubra membrānae**: Thomson punctuates **lōra rubra, membrānae**, with **membrānae**, *parchment wrappers*, nominative plural, thus:
    6 relāta: cartae rēgiae novae librī,
    7 novī umbilīcī, lōra rubra, membrānae,

Initial Explorations

1. In lines 1–2, how does Catullus characterize Suffenus as a person?
2. What picture of Suffenus as a poet does Catullus build up in lines 3–8?
3. Does Catullus seem to approve or disapprove of Suffenus as a poet?

8   **dērigō** [**dē-**, *thoroughly* + **regō**, *to keep* (things) *in line, direct, rule*], **dērigere,**
       dērēxī, dērēctus, *to arrange along a fixed line; to line, rule* (a sheet of pa-
       pyrus).
     plumbum, -ī, n., *lead* (used for making lines on papyrus).
     pūmex, pūmicis, m. (see Catullus 1.2), *pumice-stone* (used like sandpaper to
       smooth the ends of a papyrus roll).
     omnia: modified by **dērēcta** and **aequāta.**
     aequō, -āre, -āvī, -ātus, *to make level/smooth.*
9   **bellus, -a, -um** (see Catullus 3.14, 15; colloquial, cf. the more formal **pulcher,**
       pulchra, pulchrum, *beautiful, handsome, lovely*), *handsome, pretty; charming;*
       "*smart.*"
10   **ūnus, -a, -um,** *one* (of a class), *an ordinary.*
     caprimulgus, -ī, m. [**caper, caprī,** m., *billy goat* + **mulgeō, mulgēre, mulsī,**
       mulsus, *to milk* (an animal)], *goat-milker, goatherd.*
     fōssor, fōssōris, m., *ditch-digger.*
11   **rūrsus,** adv., *again; on the contrary, on the other hand; at another moment.*
     vidētur: supply **esse** or **fierī.**
     abhorreō, abhorrēre, abhorruī, *to shrink back from; to be out of accordance, be at*
       variance; to be different from.
         abhorret: i.e., *is different from the appearance he gave earlier.*
     mūtō, -āre, -āvī, -ātus, *to change.*
12   **putēmus:** deliberative subjunctive.
     Quī: the antecedent is **īdem** in line 14; for a smoother translation, bring the
       idea expressed in **īdem** to the front, *The same man who. . . .*
     modo, adv., *only; just now.*
     scurra, -ae, m., *an urbane and witty man, a wit.*
13   **quis, qua/quae, quid,** indefinite pronoun after **sī,** *anyone, anybody, somebody,*
       anything, something.
     scītus, -a, -um [**scīscō, scīscere, scīvī, scītus,** inceptive, *to get to know*],
       knowing, shrewd, sharp.
         hāc rē: i.e., *than a* **scurra.**
14   **īdem:** see notes on lines 3 and 12.
     īnficētus, -a, -um [**in-,** *not* + **facētus, -a, -um,** *clever*], *witless, dull-witted,*
       crude.
         īnficētō . . . īnficētior: some editions have **īnfacētō . . . īnfacētior.**
15   **simul:** = **simul ac,** conj., *as soon as.*
     poēma, poēmatis, n. [Greek loan word], *poem.*
     attingō [**ad-,** *to, toward* + **tango, tangere, tetigī, tāctus,** *to touch*], **attingere, at-**
       tigī, attāctus, *to touch; to undertake, put one's hand to.*
16   **aequē . . . ac . . . cum:** *equally . . . as when.*
     beātus, -a, -um, *happy.*

8   dērēcta plumbō et pūmice omnia aequāta.

9   Haec cum legās tū, bellus ille et urbānus

10   Suffēnus ūnus caprimulgus aut fōssor

11   rūrsus vidētur: tantum abhorret ac mūtat.

12   Hoc quid putēmus esse? Quī modo scurra

13   aut sī quid hāc rē scītius vidēbātur,

14   īdem īnficētō est īnficētior rūre,

15   simul poēmata attigit, neque īdem umquam

16   aequē est beātus ac poēma cum scrībit:

17   tam gaudet in sē tamque sē ipse mīrātur.

continued

Initial Explorations

4.   According to lines 9–11, what contradiction is noticed when one reads Suffenus' poetry?

5.   How does Catullus further describe the contradictions in Suffenus? (12–15)

6.   How does Suffenus feel about his activity as a poet? Are his feelings justified? (15–17)

18   **nīmīrum** [**nī-**, negative adverb + **mīrum**, *it would be a wonder if . . . not*], parti-
     cle, *without doubt, clearly.*
     idem: with a short *i*, neuter, internal accusative with **fallimur.**
     fallō, fallere, fefellī, falsus, *to mislead, deceive;* passive, *to be deceived, be mis-
     taken.*
          idem . . . fallimur: *we make the same mistake.*
     quisquam, quisquam, quicquam, indefinite pronoun, *anyone, anything.*
19   **in aliquā rē**: *in some situation.* The second foot of this line consists of three
     short syllables.
     Suffēnum: *[as] a Suffenus.*
20   **possīs**: what mood is this and why?
     Suus . . . error: *one's own defect, one's imperfection.*
     quisque, quaeque, quidque, pronoun, *each, every one, every thing.*
          cuique: what case and number?
     attribuō, attribuere, attribuī, attribūtus, *to allot, assign.*
     error, errōris, m., *wandering; mistake; mental aberration, delusion.*
21   **mantica, -ae**, f., *wallet, knapsack.*
          manticae quod . . . est: *[the part] of the knapsack that is. . . .*

18   Nīmīrum idem omnēs fallimur, neque est quisquam
19   quem nōn in aliquā rē vidēre Suffēnum
20   possīs. Suus cuique attribūtus est error;
21   sed nōn vidēmus manticae quod in tergō est.

Initial Explorations

7.   What observation on human nature does Catullus make in lines 18–21?
8.   How many elisions can you find in line 4? What effect do they produce?
9.   Find an example of asyndeton and describe its effect on the reader.

Discussion

1.   Repetition is an effective device in poetry; the same word or phrase used two or three times can emphasize a point or feeling. How does the repetition of **īdem** (3, 14, 15) reinforce the theme of this poem?
2.   Why are the terms **caprimulgus** and **fossor** (10) appropriate descriptions of Suffenus when he publishes his poetry?
3.   What point of literary criticism does Catullus make in this poem?
4.   Compare the external appearance and the inner contents of Suffenus' **librī** with those of Catullus' **libellus** as he describes it in his first poem.
5.   What larger moral does Catullus draw from his observations on Suffenus?

Comparison

Compare the ending of Catullus' poem with this fable of Phaedrus (Latin poet of the first half of the first century A.D.):

De vitiīs hominum

Pērās imposuit Iuppiter nōbīs duās:
propriīs replētam vitiīs post tergum dedit,
aliēnīs ante pectus suspendit gravem.
    Hāc rē vidēre nostra mala nōn possumus;
aliī simul dēlinquunt, cēnsōrēs sumus.

Jupiter has put upon us two bags:
the one that is filled with our own faults he put on our back,
the other sagging with the faults of others he hung on our chest.
    For this reason we cannot see our own faults;
but as soon as others do something wrong, we become fault-finders.

—Phaedrus, *Fables* 4.10

Meter: hendecasyllabic

1   **minister, ministrī**, m., *servant, attendant*, here + gen.
     Minister: vocative, in apposition with **puer** (here referring to a slave boy).
     vetulus, -a, -um [dim.], *fairly old;* here expressing endearment, *good old.*
     Falernus, -a, -um, *Falernian* (referring to a district in northern Campania, famous for its wine).
       Falernī: supply **vīnī**.
2   **ingerō, ingerere, ingessī, ingestus**, *to heap on; to pour on/in.*
     inger: form found only here = **ingere**, imperative singular.
     calix, calicis, m. [cf. Greek *kylix*, "drinking-cup"], *drinking cup;* here by metonymy, *the contents of drinking cups, wine.*
     amārus, -a, -um, *bitter;* of wine, *dry, tart.*
       amāriōrēs: comparative adjective, *drier;* the following lines indicate that it is intended here to mean *mixed with less water.*
3   **lēx, lēgis**, f., *law, dictate, decree.*
     Postumia, -ae, f., *Postumia* (name of the Roman matron who is presiding over this drinking party as **magistra bibendī**, *mistress of drinking*, replacing the usual **magister bibendī**, the individual who decided on the wine and the proportion of water, **lympha**, cf. 5, to pure wine, **merum**, cf. 7, that was to be drunk. This may be the same Postumia who was the wife of Servius Sulpicius Rufus and mistress of Julius Caesar; there may also be an allusion here to the Lex Postumia from the time of the reign of King Numa that regulated the use of wine in certain rituals, see Pliny, *Natural History* 14.88).
4   **ēbriōsus, -a, -um**, *addicted to drink.*
     acinus, -ī, m., *berry; grape.*
5   **vōs**: i.e., the **lymphae**, which Catullus here addresses.
     quō lubet: archaic for **libet**, *wherever [to go] pleases [you], wherever it pleases [you] [to go].*
     hinc, adv., *from here.*
     lympha, -ae, f. [from Greek *nymphē*, "bride, nymph, water,"], *water-nymph; water.*
6   **perniciēs, -ēī**, f., *ruin, destruction.*
     vīnī perniciēs: in apposition with **lymphae**.
     sevērus, -a, -um (see Catullus 5.2), *severe in judgment, stern, strict.*
7   **merus, -a, -um** (see Catullus 13.9), *undiluted, pure.*
     Thyōniānus, -ī, m. [noun coined by Catullus; cf. **Thyōnē, Thyōnēs**, f., *Thyone* (another name for Semele, the mother of Bacchus); **Thyōneus, -ī**, m., *Thyoneus* (a name of Bacchus); cf. formations such as **Caesariānus**, *a supporter of Caesar*, and **Pompeiānus**, *a supporter of Pompey*], *a follower/adherent of Bacchus.*
       Thyōniānus: Catullus and his fellow neoteric poets coined many new words.
         Hīc merus est Thyōniānus: perhaps, *Here is an undiluted Thyonian* = *Here is a follower of Bacchus who drinks his wine undiluted*, perhaps = *I am. . . .*

CATULLUS 27

Stronger drink, please!

Catullus sets the serving boy straight at a drinking party.

1 Minister vetulī puer Falernī,
2 inger mī calicēs amāriōrēs,
3 ut lēx Postumiae iubet magistrae
4 ēbriōsō acinō ēbriōsiōris.
5 At vōs quō lubet hinc abīte, lymphae,
6 vīnī perniciēs, et ad sevērōs
7 migrāte. Hīc merus est Thyōniānus.

Initial Explorations

1. Consider possible ambiguity in line 1. After the words **Minister vetulī**, do you expect the line to end with the name of a person or of a wine? Is the wine being personified here?
2. How is the juxtaposition of the words **vetulī** and **puer** particularly effective?
3. Explain the figure of speech in the phrase **inger . . . calicēs amāriōrēs**.
4. What is unusual about the person in charge of the drinking on this occasion?
5. What is striking about the choice, sound, and arrangement of the words in line 4? Locate an example of personification and an example of a transferred epithet.
6. What rule for the drinking was laid down by Postumia? (2–4)
7. How does the speaker go beyond Postumia's provisions for drinking? (5–7)

Discussion

1. Where does the poem divide into segments, and how does line 4 fit in?
2. Compare this poem with the lines of Diphilus quoted below. What are the similarities? How does Catullus' poem move to a climax?
3. What role do the **sevērī** play in this poem? How does their role here compare with their role in Catullus 5?

Comparison

Now pour us something to drink. Give stronger stuff, by Zeus, boy! For everything watery is an evil for the soul!

—Diphilus (Greek comic poet, fourth century B.C., fragment 58K)

Meter: choliambic

1   **paene īnsulārum**: = **paenīnsulārum**. The genitives in line 1 depend on the word **ocelle** (2).

     Sirmiō, Sirmiōnis, f., *Sirmio* (a small peninsula or promontory overlooking Lake Garda, Lago di Garda in Italian, the ancient **lacus Bēnācus**, where Catullus' family had a villa).

2   **ocellus, -ī**, m. [dim. of **oculus, -ī**, m., *eye*], *little eye, dear eye*; figurative, *jewel*.

     ocelle: vocative (affectionate diminutive), in apposition with **Sirmiō** (1).

       Sirmiō (1) . . . / **ocelle**: personification.

     quīcumque, quaecumque, quodcumque, indefinite relative pronoun, *whoever, whatever*.

     liquēns, liquentis, *clear*.

     stagnum, -ī, n., *pool; lake*.

3   **vastus, -a, -um**, *desolate*; of the sea, *dreary, endless, immense, huge*.

     uterque Neptūnus: i.e., each of the two Neptunes, referring to the tradition that there was a Neptune of saltwater seas and one of fresh-water lakes.

4   **quam . . . quamque**: *how . . . and how. . . .*

     invīsō, invīsere, invīsī, invīsus, *to come to see, to visit; to look upon*.

5   **mī**: dative with **crēdēns**.

     crēdēns: introducing indirect statement; supply **mē** as subject of **līquisse** (6) and **vidēre** (6).

     Thȳnia (Thūnia), -ae, f., *Thynia* (the country on the south shore of the Black Sea inhabited by the Thyni).

     Bīthȳnus (Bīthūnus), -a, -um, *Bithynian, of/belonging to Bithynia* (the Roman province in Asia Minor inhabited by the Thyni and the Bithyni).

       Thȳniam atque Bīthȳnōs . . . campōs (6): objects of **līquisse** (6).

6   **līquisse**: = **relīquisse**.

     līquisse . . . vidēre: what tense is each infinitive?

     tūtus, -a, -um, *safe, secure*.

     in tūtō: *in one piece, safely*.

     solūtīs . . . cūrīs: ablative of comparison; instead of translating *than anxieties that have been relieved*, turn the idea expressed in the participle into a noun; compare **ab urbe conditā** = *from the foundation of the city*.

     beātius: for the word, see note on 9.5.

8   **repōnō** [**re-**, *back* + **pōnō, pōnere, posuī, positus**, *to put, place*], **repōnere, reposuī, repositus**, *to put aside*.

     peregrīnus, -a, -um, *foreign*.

     peregrīnō / labōre (9): the phrase refers to the hardships of travel and public service in foreign lands.

9   **fessī**: = **dēfessī**.

     lar, laris, m., *household god, household altar*; by synecdoche, *home*.

10   **acquiēscō** [**ad-**, intensive + **quiēscō, quiēscere, quiēvī, quiētūrus**, *to fall asleep; to rest*], **acquiēscere, acquiēvī**, inceptive, *to rest, relax*.

     lectō: = **in lectō**.

CATULLUS 31

Coming Home after Work

Catullus arrives home to his villa at Sirmio in the spring of 56 B.C. for a welcome rest after spending a trying year in Bithynia on the staff of Gaius Memmius.

1 Paene īnsulārum, Sirmiō, īnsulārumque
2 ocelle, quāscumque in liquentibus stagnīs
3 marīque vastō fert uterque Neptūnus,
4 quam tē libenter quamque laetus invīsō,
5 vix mī ipse crēdēns Thӯniam atque Bīthӯnōs
6 līquisse campōs et vidēre tē in tūtō.
7 Ō quid solūtīs est beātius cūrīs,
8 cum mēns onus repōnit, ac peregrīnō
9 labōre fessī vēnimus larem ad nostrum,
10 dēsīderātōque acquiēscimus lectō?

continued

Initial Explorations

1. What is the tone of the poet's opening address to Sirmio? (1–3)
2. What words and phrases are paired in these lines? Which words are arranged in a chiasmus? Find an example of homoioteleuton.
3. What does the poet reveal in lines 4–6 about what he is doing now and what he has done in the recent past?
4. Locate an example of anaphora in lines 4–6. Locate three pairs of words in these lines. What effect do such figures of speech and pairing of words have on the reader?
5. What further factual information does the poet reveal about himself in lines 7–10?
6. What emotions or feelings does the poet express in lines 7–10?
7. Locate the members of an ascending tricolon in lines 7–10. Which of the three clauses in the tricolon is the longest? Which is climactic?
8. What words or phrases in lines 7–10 are set in contrast or concordance with each other?

11   **ūnus, -a, -um**, here, *alone, by itself.*
      prō, prep. + abl., *for; in return for, in compensation for.*
         Hoc est quod ūnum est prō: *This is [that] which alone is in compensation*
         for. . . . = *This is what alone makes up for.* . . .
12   **venustus, -a, -um**: see Catullus 3.2, 10.4, 12.5, 13.6. Use of the adjective here
      personifies Sirmio.
      erus, -ī, m.: see Catullus 4.19.
         erō: with **gaudente** (13). What case and construction?
13   **Lȳdius, -a, -um**, *Lydian, Etruscan* (the area around Sirmio had once been
      ruled by the Etruscans, who were thought to have come from Lydia in Asia
      Minor).
      lacus, -ūs, m., *lake.*
      Lȳdiae lacūs undae: transferred epithet.
14   **quisquis, quisquis, quidquid**, indefinite pronoun/adjective, *whoever, what-*
      ever.
      domī: locative, here not literally *at home*, but idiomatically, *at your disposal, in*
      your stock, in store.
      cachinnus, -ī, m. [onomatopoetic] (see Catullus 13.5), *loud laughter.*
         quidquid . . . cachinnōrum: **quidquid** with its dependent partitive geni-
         tive functions as internal or cognate accusative with the intransitive verb
         rīdēte, *laugh whatever (of) laughter*; we would say *with whatever laughter.*

Text

13   **vōsque, ō Lȳdiae lacūs undae**: Thomson argues for reading **vōsque lūci-**
      dae lacūs undae:
         13   gaudente, vōsque lūcidae lacūs undae
      [**lūdicus, -a, -um**, *clear, bright, translucent*] This eliminates the learned ref-
      erence to Lydia. Goold prints **limpidae**, *clear, transparent*, in his text.

11   Hoc est quod ūnum est prō labōribus tantīs.

12   Salvē, ō venusta Sirmiō, atque erō gaudē

13   gaudente, vōsque, ō Lȳdiae lacūs undae,

14   rīdēte quidquid est domī cachinnōrum.

Initial Explorations

9.   With what word in line 7 does **labōribus** (11) correspond?
10. Locate the members of an ascending tricolon in lines 12–14. Which clause is longest? Is it also climactic?
11. Identify the transferred epithet in the phrase **Lȳdiae lacūs undae**. Some editors eliminate the learned allusion in the description of the lake as Lydian and substitute descriptive adjectives instead (see **Text** on the opposite page). What arguments could you make for and against the substitution of descriptive adjectives?
12. How do lines 12–14 echo lines 1–3? How do these sets of lines provide an effective frame for the poem? How is the tone of lines 12–14 different from that of lines 1–3? Why is it different?

Discussion

1.   This poem is an example of a literary genre that the ancients described with the Greek word *epibaterion*, which refers to a speech or poem recited by someone who steps onto the shore of his homeland upon returning from travels abroad. The Greek poem translated below is an example, representing the words of Ulysses upon his return home after the Trojan War and his subsequent wanderings. What similarities do you find with Catullus' poem? What differences?
2.   What role does personification play in Catullus' poem? How is it important?
3.   Compare Catullus 31 with Catullus 9 on Veranius' return home. What similarities and what differences do you find?

Comparison

Ithaca, hail! After my labors, after the bitter woes
of the sea, with joy I come to your soil, hoping to see
Laertes and my wife and my glorious only son.
Love of you enticed my heart; I have learnt for myself that
"Nothing is sweeter than a man's country and his parents."

—Anonymous, *Palatine Anthology* 9.458

Meter: The first three lines of each stanza are glyconics, the fourth line a pherecratean.

1   **Diāna, -ae**, f., *Diana* (Roman goddess identified with the Greek goddess Artemis).

    in fidē: *in the custody, under the protection* (as a patron would protect a client in Roman society).

2   **puellae et puerī**: subjects of **sumus** (1), both modified by **integrī**.

    integer, integra, integrum [**in-**, *not* + **tangō, tangere, tetigī, tāctus**, *to touch*], *untouched; whole, complete; youthful; morally unblemished, chaste; unmarried.*

3   **<Diānam puerī integrī>**: this line, missing in the manuscripts, has been supplied by modern editors; note the anaphora with line 1.

4   **canō, canere, cecinī, cantus**, *to sing about, glorify in song.*

5   **Lātōnia, -ae** [matronymic], f., *Latonia, daughter of Latona* (= Diana, daughter of Leto, who was called Latona by the Romans).

6   **prōgeniēs, -ēī**, f., *offspring.*

    Iuppiter, Iovis, m., *Jupiter* (king of the gods).

        maximī / magna prōgeniēs Iovis: embedded phrasing.

7   **Dēlius, -a, -um**, *Delian, of/belonging to Delos* (island in the Aegean where Latona gave birth to Diana and Apollo under an olive tree).

8   **dēpōnō** [**dē-**, *down* + **pōnō, pōnere, posuī** (archaic **posīvī**), **positus**, *to put, place*], **dēpōnere, dēposuī** (archaic **dēposīvī**), **dēpositus**, *to lay down; to bring forth, deliver.*

    olīvam: other accounts of the birth of Apollo and Artemis/Diana mention the tree as a palm or laurel.

9   **montium domina ut**: the subordinating conjunction introducing the purpose clause is delayed to third position.

        montium . . . silvārumque (10) **. . . saltuumque** (11) **. . . amniumque** (12)**. . . .** : the genitives depend on **domina** (9) and list the places over which Diana presides as the goddess of wild beasts and of hunting.

    forēs: = **essēs**; the subject, *you*, refers to **Lātōnia** = Diana.

10   **vireō, virēre, viruī**, *to be green; to flourish.*

11   **saltus, -ūs**, m., *wooded pasture land.*

    reconditus, -a, -um, [**re-**, *back* + **conditus, -a, -um**, *hidden, concealed*], *hidden, secluded.*

        saltuumque reconditōrum / amniumque: line 11 is hypermetric and **reconditōrum** elides with the first word of the next line (synapheia).

12   **amnis, amnis**, m., *river.*

    sonō, sonāre, sonuī, sonitus, *to resound, echo.*

    sonantum: = **sonantium**.

CATULLUS 34

A Hymn to Diana

A chorus of unmarried boys and girls supplicates Diana as a goddess of nature and fertility in a traditionally styled hymn and makes a patriotic prayer.

1 Diānae sumus in fidē
2 puellae et puerī integrī:
3 <Diānam puerī integrī>
4   puellaeque canāmus.

5 Ō Lātōnia, maximī
6 magna prōgeniēs Iovis,
7 quam māter prope Dēliam
8   dēposīvit olīvam,

9 montium domina ut forēs
10 silvārumque virentium
11 saltuumque reconditōrum
12   amniumque sonantum:

continued

Initial Explorations

1. How does the first stanza introduce the hymn?
2. How do anaphora, conduplicatio, and chiasmus contribute to the tone of the first stanza?
3. How is Diana invoked in the second stanza? What is implied or stated about her parentage and her birth?
4. What deities do the adjectives **maximī** (5) and **magna** (6) describe? Why is it tactful for the adjective **maximī** to come before the adjective **magna**?
5. What activities of Diana are celebrated in the third stanza?
6. What is the effect of the positioning of words in the third stanza?

13   tū ... dicta (14): with dicta, supply es (cf. 15–16).

      tū ... tū (15) ... tū (17): anaphora and ascending tricolon.

      Lūcīna ... Iūnō (14): Diana is here identified with Iūnō Lūcīna, Juno in her
         role as goddess of childbirth, a role Juno took over from the Greek goddess
         of childbirth Eileithyia.

14   dīcō, dīcere, dīxī, dictus, *to say; to tell; to name, call.*

      puerpera, -ae, f. [puer, puerī, m., *child* + pariō, parere, peperī, partus, *to give
         birth*], *woman in labor.*

         dolentibus (13) ... puerperīs: dative of agent.

15   potēns, potentis [often describing sorcerers and witches], *powerful.*

      Trivia, -ae, f., *Trivia* (another name for Diana, as identified with the Greek
         goddess Hecate, goddess of the underworld and goddess of witchcraft and
         sorcery, worshiped at places where three roads meet, called a trivium
         [trēs, tria, *three* + via, -ae, f., *road*]).

      nothus, -a, -um, *bastard; not genuine, spurious; derivative;* here, *reflected.*

16   lūmen, lūminis, n., *light.*

      nothō (15) ... lūmine: ablative of cause with es (15) ... dicta.

      Lūna: once Diana was identified with the Greek goddesses Artemis and
         Hecate, she became a moon-goddess too. Artemis had already been identi-
         fied with the Greek moon goddess, Selene.

17   cursus, -ūs, m., *course* (here, of the moon).

      mēnstruus, -a, -um [mēnsis, mēnsis, m., *month*], *monthly.*

18   mētior, mētīrī, mēnsus sum, *to measure.*

      mēnstruō / mētiēns: there is an etymological play on words here, since
         mēnstruus, mēnsis, and mētior are all derived from the same root; the
         Indo-European root also produced the English words *month* and *moon.*

      annuus, -a, -um, *annual, yearly.*

19   rūsticus, -a, -um, *rustic, rural.*

      rūstica: what does this modify?

      agricolae: genitive with tēcta (20) or dative of reference (advantage).

20   tēctum, -ī, n., *roof; home; shed.*

      frūgēs, frūgum, f. pl., *grain, produce.*

      expleō, explēre, explēvī, explētus, *to fill.*

21   Sīs: with sāncta (22). What mood, tense, and construction is Sīs?

      quīcumque, quaecumque, quodcumque, indefinite adjective, *whatever.*

         quōcumque ... nōmine (22): ablative with sāncta (22), *hallowed with
         whatever name.* In hymns and prayers, it was common to appeal to the
         divinity with as many names as possible to be sure to incorporate the
         right one for the occasion and to include an open-ended appeal as here.

22   Rōmulus, -ī, m., *Romulus* (legendary first king of Rome).

      Rōmulī: with gentem (24).

         sāncta nōmine, Rōmulīque: hypermetric line with synapheia again.

23   antīquē, adv., *in olden times, long ago, of old.*

      antīquē: translate with solita es.

      solita es: from the semi-deponent verb solēre.

24   sōspitō [sospes, sospitis, *safe and sound*], -āre, *to preserve.*

      ops, opis, f., *help, aid.*

13   tū Lūcīna dolentibus
14   Iūnō dicta puerperīs,
15   tū potēns Trivia et nothō es
16   dicta lūmine Lūna;

17   tū cursū, dea, mēnstruō
18   mētiēns iter annuum,
19   rūstica agricolae bonīs
20   tēcta frūgibus explēs.

21   Sīs quōcumque tibi placet
22   sāncta nōmine, Rōmulīque,
23   antīquē ut solita es, bonā
24   sōspitēs ope gentem.

Initial Explorations

7.   Locate the members of an ascending tricolon articulated by anaphora in lines 13–20.
8.   Now look at the fourth stanza (13–16), and locate the members of a tricolon in this stanza. Is it an ascending tricolon?
9.   What three aspects or manifestations of Diana are celebrated in the fourth stanza (13–16)? To what three Greek goddesses is she equivalent in these roles? What three realms are involved here?
10.   Which manifestation of Diana mentioned in the fourth stanza is elaborated in the fifth (17–20)? How does Diana in this manifestation benefit mankind?
11.   What two prayers are expressed in the sixth stanza (21–24)? What is the relationship between them?
12.   How is the last word, **gentem** (24), a fitting conclusion for the hymn?

Discussion

1.   What conception of the goddess Diana is presented in the three stanzas (9–20) that celebrate her powers, and how does the poet organize his presentation of that conception of the deity?
2.   To what extent does Catullus present, celebrate, and appeal to Diana as a particularly Roman goddess?

Meter: hendecasyllabic

1   **Poētae tenerō, meō sodālī ... Caeciliō**: datives with **dīcās** (2).
    tener, tenera, tenerum, *soft, tender, delicate; sensitive.*
       tenerō: probably simply *tender* here; later often used to describe love poets.
    sodālis, sodālis, m. (see Catullus 10.29 and 12.13), *companion, friend.*
2   **velim ... dīcās**: *I would like you to. ...* , potential subjunctive (**velim**) intro-
    ducing an indirect command; supply **ut** to introduce **dīcās**.
    Caecilius, -ī, m., *Caecilius* (known only from this poem).
    papȳrus, -ī, m., *papyrus* (paper made from papyrus reeds).
       papȳre: by metonymy the sheet of papyrus refers to the poem that Catul-
       lus is writing.
3   **Vērōna, -ae**, f., *Verona* (city in northern Italy, birthplace and family home of
    Catullus).
       Vērōnam: what case and construction?
    veniat: supply **ut** to introduce a second indirect command.
    Novī ... Comī (4): *Novum Comum* (a town north of Milan and about 130
    miles west of Verona; the name **Novum Comum** dates from 59 B.C., when
    Julius Caesar repopulated the town with 5000 colonists); genitive with
    moenia (4).
    relinquēns: the subject is Caecilius.
4   **Lārius, -a, -um**, *Larian, of/belonging to Lake Larius* (now the Lago di Como,
    Lake Como, on the southern shore of which was situated **Novum Comum**,
    the modern Como).
5   **volo**: iambic shortening.
    cōgitātiō, cōgitātiōnis, f., *thought; opinion, view.*
6   **accipiat**: supply **ut** to introduce the indirect command.
7   **sapiō, sapere, sapīvī**, *to be wise; to have sense.*
       sapiet: what mood and tense? What kind of conditional sentence is this?
    vorō, -āre, -āvī, -ātus, *to devour, eat up.*
       viam vorābit: an unusual metaphor.
8   **quamvīs**, relative adv. + subjunctive, *even if, although.*
    candidus, -a, -um (see Catullus 8.3, 8 and 13.4), *white, fair-skinned, pretty.*
    mīliēs, adv. = **mīliēns**, *a thousand times.*
       mīliēs: although this adverb should be translated with **revocet** (9), its
       placement suggests that the **puella** is a thousand times dazzling too.
9   **euntem**: present participle from **eō, īre**; supply **eum**.
    manūs: what case, gender, and number? By synecdoche the word here
    refers to arms.
    collum, -ī, n. (see Catullus 9.8), *neck.*
10 **iniciēns**: scanned with a long first syllable.
    roget morārī: poetic equivalent of **roget ut [Caecilius] morētur**.
       morārī: from **moror** or **morior**? What is the difference in meaning?

CATULLUS 35

Go, papyrus, bring my friend!

The poet wants to see his friend, but he understands his delay.

1   Poētae tenerō, meō sodālī,
2   velim Caeciliō, papȳre, dīcās
3   Vērōnam veniat, Novī relinquēns
4   Cōmī moenia Lāriumque lītus:
5   nam quāsdam volo cōgitātiōnēs
6   amīcī accipiat suī meīque.
7   Quārē, sī sapiet, viam vorābit,
8   quamvīs candida mīliēs puella
9   euntem revocet, manūsque collō
10 ambās iniciēns roget morārī.

continued

Initial Explorations

1. How is Caecilius described in the first line? Identify the elements of a chiasmus.
2. Note that Catullus addresses the papyrus (2) on which he is writing and not Caecilius. How is this unusual? Why do you suppose he does this?
3. What does Catullus want the papyrus to tell Caecilius? (3–4)
4. Why does Catullus want Caecilius to come to Verona? (5–6)
5. Is there any suggestion as to what the **cōgitātiōnēs** (5) might be and who the mutual **amīcus** (6) might be?
6. What will Caecilius do if he is wise? (7)
7. How is the person of the verbs **veniat** (3), **accipiat** (6), **sapiet** (7), and **vorābit** (7) dependent on Catullus' choice of addressing the sheet of papyrus instead of addressing Caecilius directly? How does the person of the verbs affect the tone of what is said here?
8. Who may hold Caecilius back in Novum Comum? (8–10) Why do you suppose she would do this?
9. What physical means of gaining her end does the **puella** employ? (9–10) How does the arrangement of words reflect her action?

11   **Quae**: the antecedent is **puella** (8); a relative pronoun at the beginning of a
      sentence is common in Latin as a link to the previous sentence; translate
      And she. . . .
      vēra: nom. pl., *true [reports].*
      nūntiō, -āre, -āvī, -ātus, *to announce.*
12   **illum**: what case, gender, and number? To whom does this pronoun refer?
      dēpereō [dē-, *thoroughly* **+ pereō, perīre, periī, peritūrus,** *to perish*],
          dēperīre, dēperiī, *to perish;* + acc., *to be madly in love with.*
      impotēns, impotentis [in-, *not* **+ potēns, potentis,** *having power* (over), *able to
          control*] (see Catullus 4.18 and 8.9), *powerless* (over oneself); *lacking self-
          control; wild, violent, raging.*
          impotente: ablative.
13   **quō tempore . . . ex eō** (14): = **ex eō tempore quō,** *from that time at which;*
          then do not translate **ex eō** in line 14.
      lēgit: the **puella** is the subject.
      incohō, -āre, -āvī, -ātus, *to begin; to make a sketch/first draft of* (a literary work).
          incohātus, -a, -um, *only begun, just sketched out, unfinished, in progress.*
14   **Dindymon, -ī,** n., *Dindymon* (a mountain in Phrygia in northern Asia Minor,
          sacred to Cybele, the **Magna Māter,** Great Mother).
          Dindymī dominam: perhaps the opening words of Caecilius' poem,
              which was about Cybele.
      misellus, -a, -um [dim. of **miser, misera, miserum,** *wretched*] (see Catullus
          3.16), *poor little, wretched.*
          misellae: supply **puellae,** genitive dependent on **medullam** (15) or da-
              tive of reference (disadvantage).
15   **ignēs**: i.e., of love or desire.
      interior, interior, interius, gen., **interiōris,** *inner.*
      edunt: note the present tense; with **ex eō** translate, *(they) have been eating.*
      medulla, -ae, f., *marrow of bones; one's innermost parts, vitals, heart* (as the seat
          of emotions).
16   **ignōscō, ignōscere, ignōvī, ignōtus** + dat., inceptive, *to forgive.*
      Sapphicus, -a, -um, *Sapphic, of Sappho* (Greek poetess of Lesbos, seventh to
          sixth centuries B.C.).
      puella: vocative.
17   **mūsa, -ae,** f., capitalized, *Muse* (goddess who inspires poetry); lower case, *po-
          etry.*
          Sapphicā (16) **. . . mūsā:** *than Sappho's poetry* or *than Sappho as a poet* or
              than Sappho's muse.
      doctus, -a, -um (see Catullus 1.7), *learned, full of learning; well versed* (in po-
          etry), *tasteful, discriminating.*
      venustus, -a, -um (see Catullus 3.2, 10.4, 12.5, 13.6, 31.12), *endowed/involved
          with Venus; attractive, charming.*
          venustē: *charmingly,* with **est . . . incohāta** (18); the context also suggests
              a secondary meaning for **venustē**—*in a manner that inspires erotic pas-
              sion.*
18   **Magna . . . Māter**: perhaps the title of Caecilius' poem.
      Caeciliō: dative of agent.

11 Quae nunc, sī mihi vēra nūntiantur,

12 illum dēperit impotente amōre:

13 nam quō tempore lēgit incohātam

14 Dindymī dominam, ex eō misellae

15 ignēs interiōrem edunt medullam.

16 Ignōscō tibi, Sapphicā puella

17 mūsā doctior: est enim venustē

18 Magna Caeciliō incohāta Māter.

Initial Explorations

10. Is your answer to the second part of question 8 confirmed by lines 11–12?

11. Why is it tactful for Catullus to include the words **sī mihi vēra nūntiantur** (11)?

12. How does the description of the love of the **puella** for Caecilius harmonize with her imagined actions described in lines 8–10?

13. When did the **puella** fall in love with Caecilius? (13–15)

14. How does Catullus describe the intensity of the love felt by the **puella**? (14–15) Was the **puella** wretched (**misellae**, 14) before or after she fell in love? Why is the word **misellae** placed so early in its clause?

15. For what does Catullus pardon the **puella**? (16)

16. Up to this point the **puella** and her actions have been described in the third person. What reasons can you think of as to why Catullus now refers to the **puella** in the second person (**tibi**, 16) and addresses her directly in the vocative (**puella / . . . doctior**, 16–17)?

17. Why does Catullus pardon the **puella**? (16–18)

18. What word is repeated in the last line from the first section of the poem? What is the effect of this repetition?

Sapphicā puella mūsā doctior

"Young Woman with
Writing Tablet and Stylus"
Fresco from Pompeii
Museo Archeologico Nazionale
Naples, Italy

Discussion

1. Outline the poem's structural symmetry.

2. What message is conveyed in the last six lines of the poem?

Meter: hendecasyllabic

1   **annālis, annālis**, m. [**annus, -ī**, m., *year*], *a book of annals or chronicles;* pl., *annals, chronicles* (in several volumes).

> **Annālēs**: vocative: *Annals* of Volusius, referring to a verse chronicle written by the poet Volusius, who is lambasted here and in Catullus 95 for being a verbose writer.

cacō, -āre, -āvī, -ātus, *to defecate; to expel as excrement.*

carta, -ae, f., *sheet of papyrus;* by extension, *papyrus roll* (i.e., sheets of papyrus glued together).

> **cacāta carta**: *papyrus expelled as excrement*, in apposition with **Annālēs** and a bold metaphor; Volusius suffers from verbal diarrhea.

2   **vōtum, -ī**, n., *vow* (a promise to dedicate or sacrifice something to a deity if the deity should grant a favor or answer a prayer); *offering or sacrifice made in repayment of a vow, votive offering.*

solvō, solvere, solvī, solūtus, *to loosen, untie; to relax, relieve;* here, *to pay off, discharge, fulfill.*

> **vōtum solvite**: translate **vōtum** in the first of the two senses given in the vocabulary entry above.

prō, prep. + abl., *on behalf of, for.*

4   **voveō, vovēre, vōvī, vōtus**, *to promise* (something to a god in return for a favor), *vow.*

sī . . . restitūtus essem dēsīssemque (5) **. . . (sē) datūram (esse)** (7): *if I would be . . . and would . . . (she) would. . . . ,* an example of a conditional sentence in an indirect statement, here, introduced by **vōvit**. The verb in the if-clause (protasis) is in the subjunctive since subordinate clauses in indirect statements use subjunctives; the verb in the conclusion (apodosis) is an infinitive in indirect statement. The type of the conditional sentence will determine the tense of the subjunctive and infinitive. In this case, Lesbia's vow was in the form of a future-more-vivid condition: **sī Catullus mihi restitūtus erit dēsieritque trucēs vibrāre iambōs, dabō. . . .** In indirect statement the future perfect indicatives become pluperfect subjunctives, and the future indicative becomes a future infinitive.

sibi: i.e., Lesbia.

restituō [**re-**, *back, again* + **statuō, statuere, statuī, statūtus**, *to set; to stand up; to place*], **restituere, restituī, restitūtus**, *to set up again; to restore; to bring back;* + dat., *to reinstate in favor* (with).

5   **dēsīssem**: syncope for **dēsiissem**.

trux, trucis, *fierce, vicious.*

vibrō, -āre, -āvī, -ātus, *to fling, hurl* (as a spear or a bolt of lightning).

iambus, -ī, m., *iamb; poem written in iambic meter* (including the choliambic or "limping iambic" meter); pl., *invective written in iambic meter.*

> **trucēs . . . iambōs**: possibly referring to Catullus 37, a scabrous indictment of Lesbia's promiscuity, which is written in choliambics.

CATULLUS 36

Good riddance to the *Annals* of Volusius!

Catullus at a time of estrangement from his **puella** *eagerly sacrifices the* Annals *of Volusius to Vulcan, the fire-god, in fulfillment of a playful vow that his* **puella** *made.*

1   Annālēs Volusī, cacāta carta,
2   vōtum solvite prō meā puellā.
3   Nam sānctae Venerī Cupīdinīque
4   vōvit, sī sibi restitūtus essem
5   dēsīssemque trucēs vibrāre iambōs,

continued

Initial Explorations

1. What is Catullus addressing in the opening lines and what command does he give? (1–2) On whose behalf is his command to be carried out? Who is the **puella**?
2. Analyze the first line as a chiasmus. What role do alliteration and assonance play in the effectiveness of the line?
4. What can we infer about recent events in the relationship of Catullus and his **puella** from lines 4 and 5?

6   ēlēctus, -a, -um [ēligō, ēligere, ēlēgī, ēlectus, *to pick out, choose*], *select, choice.*
    ēlēctissima pessimī poētae: i.e., *the very worst.* . . . (Thomson).

7   scrīptum, -ī, n., *writing, written work.*
    tardipēs, tardipedis [tardus, -a, -um, *slow* + pēs, pedis, m., *foot*], *slow-footed.*
    tardipedī deō: what case? The slow-footed god is the limping Vulcan.
    datūram: = sē datūram esse.

8   īnfēlīx, īnfēlīcis [in-, *not* + fēlīx, fēlīcis, *fruitful, productive; auspicious; lucky*],
    unproductive, sterile; inauspicious; unlucky.
    ūstulō, -āre, -āvī, -ātus, *to burn partially, char, scorch.*
    ūstulanda: modifying scrīpta (7).
    lignum, -ī, n., *wood, firewood.*
    īnfēlīcibus . . . lignīs: firewood from a tree thought of as īnfēlīx because it
      does not grow from seed or bear fruit; such trees were consecrated to the
      gods of the underworld, condemned criminals were hung from them in
      primitive times, and their wood was used to burn deformed creatures
      thought of as prodigies or monsters (Fordyce, 180).

9   hoc: supply vōtum.

10 iocōsē, adv., *in jest, humorously, playfully.*
    lepidē, adv., *charmingly, pleasantly, wittily.*
    iocōsē lepidē: asyndeton; the words describe how the **puella** saw herself
      making her vow to the gods, *playfully and wittily.*
    dīvus, -ī, m., *god.*

11 ō . . . creāta: *O [goddess] created/born.* . . . , i.e., Venus.
    caeruleus, -a, -um, *blue.*
    pontus, -ī, m., *sea.*
    caeruleō . . . pontō: ablative of origin; Aphrodite, Venus' Greek counter-
      part, was thought to have been born from the foam (Greek, *aphros*) of the
      sea.

12 quae . . . colis (14): *you who.* . . . ; the first of several relative clauses naming
      the various locations at which Venus was worshiped throughout the
      Mediterranean world. In a hymn or appeal to a god or goddess, it was
      common practice to list the names and places of worship associated with
      the particular divinity. The verb colis (14) is understood in each clause.
    Īdalium, -ī, n., *Idalium* (a cult site of Aphrodite on the island of Cyprus).
    Ūriī, -ōrum, m. pl., *Urii* (possibly an alternate spelling for Urion [Greek] or
      Urium [Latin], a town in Apulia on the east coast of Italy). Nothing is
      known about worship of Venus there.
    apertus -a, -um, *open; exposed* (i.e., to the elements).
    apertōs: this describes Urii as an "open roadstead, in the nautical sense, in
      contrast to a safe, well-sheltered harbour" (Thomson, 298).

13 Ancōn, Ancōnis, acc. Ancōna, f., *Ancon* or *Ancona* (a seaport on the central
      east coast of Italy; a temple of Venus was located there, and representations
      of Venus appeared on its coins).
    Cnidus, -ī, m., *Cnidus* (a city on the southwest coast of Asia Minor; Praxiteles'
      famous statue of Aphrodite stood in a temple in this city).
    harundinōsus, -a, -um [harundō, harundinis, f., *reed*], *full of reeds* (reeds
      were exported from Cnidus and used for the production of paper).

6   ēlēctissima pessimī poētae
7   scrīpta tardipedī deō datūram
8   īnfēlīcibus ūstulanda lignīs,
9   et hoc pessima sē puella vīdit
10 iocōsē lepidē vovēre dīvīs.
11 Nunc, ō caeruleō creāta pontō,
12 quae sānctum Īdalium Ūriōsque apertōs
13 quaeque Ancōna Cnidumque harundinōsam

continued

Initial Explorations

5. What exactly did the **puella** promise, and on what conditions? (3–8)
6. What might the **puella** have had in mind when she spoke of **ēlēctissima pessimī poētae / scrīpta**? (6–7)
7. Locate elements of humor and wit in the vow as it is quoted in lines 3–8.
8. How does a phrase in line 9 answer a phrase in the vow of the **puella**?
9. What do lines 9–10 tell us about the attitude of the **puella** toward the vow she made?
10. What is bizarre about the vow made by the **puella**? How can it be said truly to have been made **iocōsē lepidē**?
11. What does the word **Nunc** (11) signal with regard to the structure of the poem?

14   **colō, colere, coluī, cultus,** *to cultivate; to live in, inhabit.*
     colis: deities were thought to dwell in the places where they were wor-
        shiped.
     Amathus, Amathuntis, acc. **Amathunta,** f., *Amathus* (a seaport town in
        Cyprus and cult site of Aphrodite).
     Golgī, -ōrum, m. pl., *Golgi* (a town in Cyprus, famous for its very ancient cult
        of Aphrodite).
15   **Dyrrachium (Durrachium), -ī,** n., *Dyrrachium* (a seaport in southern Illyria,
        across the Adriatic from Brundisium and a prosperous trading center).
     Hadria, -ae, f., *the Adriatic Sea.*
     taberna, -ae, f., *shop; inn.*
     Hadriae tabernam: in apposition with **Durrachium.** The town of
        Dyrrachium is described metaphorically as the *inn of the Adriatic* because
        sailors would frequently put in there. The town had a bad reputation,
        and the word **taberna** can be used of a house of ill repute. In Plautus,
        Menaechmi 258–62, the inhabitants of Dyrrachium are described as "the
        greatest pleasure-lovers and drinkers . . . lots of swindlers, cajolers . . .
        prostitutes nowhere in the world more blandishing." The word **taberna**
        has disreputable connotations in Catullus 37, the only other poem in
        which Catullus uses this word and possibly the poem referred to in the
        phrase **trucēs . . . iambōs** (above, line 5).
16   **face:** archaic for **fac.**
     reddō [re-, *back* + **dō, dare, dedī, datus,** *to give*]**, reddere, reddidī, redditus,**
        to give back; to pay (a debt); *to render* (ritual offerings); *to discharge, fulfill* (a
        vow).
     acceptum face redditumque vōtum: the words **acceptum face . . . vō-**
        tum, literally, *make the votive offering received* = **accipe vōtum,** *receive*
        the votive offering (note that **vōtum** is used here in the second of the two
        senses given in the vocabulary entry for line 2). The words **face reddi-**
        tum . . . vōtum mean *regard the vow as discharged/fulfilled* (**vōtum** is
        used here in the first of the two senses given in the vocabulary entry
        for line 2).
17   **nōn illepidum neque invenustum:** litotes; see Catullus 10.4.
18   **vōs:** addressed again to the *Annals* of Volusius.
     intereā: here not in its temporal sense, *meanwhile,* but in its adversative sense,
        no matter how that is, regardless.
19   **īnficētiae, -ārum [in-,** *not* + **facētiae, -ārum,** f. pl., *skillfulness, cleverness, face-*
        tiousness] (compare Catullus 22.14), *unrefinement, coarseness.*
     īnficētiārum: some editors print **īnfacētiārum.**

14   colis quaeque Amathunta quaeque Golgōs
15   quaeque Dyrrachium Hadriae tabernam,
16   acceptum face redditumque vōtum,
17   sī nōn illepidum neque invenustum est.
18   At vōs intereā venīte in ignem,
19   plēnī rūris et īnficētiārum
20   annālēs Volusī, cacāta carta.

Initial Explorations

12.   What is the tone of the poet's invocation of Venus? (11–15) How does it display the poet's learning? Is it entirely serious, or does it contain some humor? Is it a respectful eulogy of Venus' power?
13.   What does the poet request of Venus (16) after his invocation of her?
14.   Explain how the descriptive phrases in line 17 apply to the two different things that are referred to with the word **vōtum** in line 16.
15.   What does the use of the qualifying word **intereā** (18) imply?
16.   How does line 18 echo line 2?
17.   How does line 20 echo line 1?
18.   What is accomplished by Catullus' violating the symmetry of the opening and closing lines of the poem by adding line 19?

Discussion

1.   What does the poem imply about the present and future relationship between Catullus and the **puella**?
2.   Compare Catullus 36 with Catullus 35. What are some of the similarities and differences?

Meter: hendecasyllabic

1   **minimō . . . nāsō**: ablative of description, as are the other ablative phrases in
     lines 2–4.
2   **bellus, -a, -um** [colloquial, cf. the more formal **pulcher, pulchra, pulchrum**,
     beautiful, handsome, lovely], *handsome, pretty, charming.*
     ocellus, -ī, m. [dim. of **oculus, -ī**, m., *eye*], *little eye.*
3   **siccus, -a, -um**, *dry.*
4   **sānē**, adv. (see Catullus 10.4), *certainly, truly, really.*
     nimis, adv., *too much, especially, very.*
     ēlegante: = **ēlegantī**.
       ēlegante linguā: here of elegant speech or wit more than of physical ap-
       pearance.
5   **dēcoctor, dēcoctōris**, m. [**dēcoquō, dēcoquere, dēcoxī, dēcoctus**, *to boil
     down; to melt down; to squander money; to go bankrupt*], *insolvent debtor;
     bankrupt.*
     amīca: *paid mistress*, = the **puella** of line 1.
     Fōrmiānus, -a, -um, *from Formiae* (a resort town south of Rome).
       Dēcoctōris . . . Fōrmiānī: usually identified as the bankrupt Mamurra,
       one of Caesar's generals, who had served in Gaul and whom Catullus at-
       tacks along with Caesar in poem 47 (not in this book); the girl would then
       be Ameana, his mistress, lampooned by Catullus in poem 41 (not in this
       book).
6   **tēn**: = **tēne**. What does the **-ne** signify?
     prōvincia: the Roman province of Cisalpine Gaul, where the woman re-
     ferred to in line 5 lived.
7   **comparō** [**compar, comparis**, *similar, alike*], **-āre, -āvī, -ātus**, *to place together;
     to treat as equal; to compare.*
       comparātur: distinguish this verb from its homonym, **comparō** [**con-** *to-
       gether* + **parō, -āre, -āvī, -ātus**, *to prepare, get ready*], *to buy, obtain; to get
       ready.*
8   **saeclum, -ī**, n. [syncope for **saeculum**] (see Catullus 1.10), *age, lifetime, genera-
     tion, century; era.*
     īnsipiēns, īnsipientis [**in-**, *not* + **sapiēns, sapientis**, *wise*], *unwise, foolish.*
       īnsipiēns: some editors print **īnsapiēns**.
     īnficētus, -a, -um [**in-**, *not* + **facētus, -a, -um**, *clever, humorous*] (cf. Catullus
     12.9 **facētiārum**, 22.14 **īnficētō est īnficētior rūre**, and 36.19 **īnficētiārum**),
     boorish, humorless, insensitive, tasteless.
       īnficētum: some editors print **īnfacētum**.

CATULLUS 43

Hello, girl, with neither. . . .

Catullus describes a girl whom many consider attractive and even compare to Lesbia.

1   Salvē, nec minimō puella nāsō
2   nec bellō pede nec nigrīs ocellīs
3   nec longīs digitīs nec ōre siccō
4   nec sānē nimis ēlegante linguā.
5   Dēcoctōris amīca Fōrmiānī,
6   tēn prōvincia nārrat esse bellam?
7   Tēcum Lesbia nostra comparātur?
8   Ō saeclum īnsipiēns et īnficētum!

Initial Explorations

1. Specifically, what does Catullus find distasteful about the girl? (1–4)
2. Identify examples of litotes in lines 1–4, and explain why the device is effective.
3. What other rhetorical device heightens the impact of lines 1–4? How is line 3 related to line 2 in positioning of words? What word in line 4 corresponds to **minimō** in line 1? How is line 4 an appropriate climax in the series?
4. What does line 5 add to the disparaging attack on the girl?
5. What is the tone of the last three lines? What two rhetorical devices add to the effect?
6. What generalization does Catullus make in the last line? What has led him to this conclusion?
7. How might this poem give us a glimpse of what the poet found most attractive about Lesbia?

Discussion

1. Summarize how Catullus in such a brief span draws a devastating portrait of the **puella** and her lover.
2. Why does the poet mention Lesbia in such an unpleasant context?

Comparisons

With **īnficētum** (43.8), compare Catullus' use of other words to describe and evaluate the qualities of people and life around him in poems earlier in the collection:

facētus 12.9	**īnficētus** 22.14; 36.19
salsus 12.4	**īnsulsus** 10.33
venustus 3.2; 13.6; 22.2; 31.12; 35.17	**invenustus** 10.4; 12.5; 36.17
ēlegāns 13.10	**inēlegāns** 6.2
urbānus 22.2	**rūsticus** 34.19

*   *   *

For Catullus' adaptation of the following poem of Sappho, see page 153.

Sappho 31

1   Φαίνεταί μοι κῆνος ἴσος θέοισιν
2   ἔμμεν' ὤνηρ, ὄττις ἐνάντιός τοι
3   ἰσδάνει καὶ πλάσιον ἆδυ φωνεί-
4   σας ὐπακούει

5   καὶ γελαίσας ἰμέροεν, τό μ' ἦ μὰν
6   καρδίαν ἐν στήθεσιν ἐπτόαισεν·
7   ὠς γὰρ ἔς σ' ἴδω βρόχε', ὤς με φώναι-
8   σ' οὐδ' ἒν ἔτ' εἴκει,

9   ἀλλὰ κὰμ μὲν γλῶσσά ⟨μ'⟩ ἔαγε, λέπτον
10   δ' αὔτικα χρῷ πῦρ ὐπαδεδρόμηκεν,
11   ὀππάτεσσι δ' οὐδ' ἒν ὄρημμ', ἐπιρρόμ-
12   βεισι δ' ἄκουαι,

13   κὰδ δέ μ' ἴδρως κακχέεται, τρόμος δὲ
14   παῖσαν ἄγρει, χλωροτέρα δὲ ποίας
15   ἔμμι, τεθνάκην δ' ὀλίγω 'πιδεύης
16   φαίνομ' ἔμ' αὔτᾳ.

17   ἀλλὰ πὰν τόλματον, ἐπεὶ †καὶ πένητα†

Ezra Pound (1885-1972), a modern poet who also found himself at odds with the tastes and values of his time, translated Catullus 43 as follows. How well does the translation convey the tone of the original? Where has Pound taken liberties?

To Formianus' Young Lady Friend
After Valerius Catullus

All Hail; young lady with a nose by no means too small,
With a foot unbeautiful, and with eyes that are not black,
With fingers that are not long, and with a mouth undry,
And with a tongue by no means too elegant,
You are the friend of Formianus, the vendor of cosmetics,
And they call you beautiful in the province,
And you are even compared to Lesbia.

O most unfortunate age!

*   *   *

The following is a translation of the Greek poem on the opposite page.

Sappho 31

1   That man appears to me to be equal
2   to the gods, who sits opposite
3   you and listens to your sweet voice
4   close at hand

5   and your lovely laughter, which truly sets
6   the heart in my breast aflutter,
7   for when I look at you for a moment, I can
8   no longer speak,

9   but my tongue is tied, a thin
10 flame has at once run beneath my skin,
12 I cannot see even one thing with my eyes,
13   my ears are buzzing,

14 sweat pours down me, a trembling
15 takes hold of all of me, I am paler
16 than grass, and I seem to myself little
17   short of being dead.

18 But all must be endured. . . .

Meter: choliambic

1   **noster**: i.e., *my*.

       Ō funde noster: personification, as in Catullus' address to Sirmio in poem 31.

       seu . . . seu, conj., *whether . . . or*.

       Sabīnus, -a, -um, *Sabine* (i.e., in the territory of the Sabines, a rustic, agricultural people living to the northeast of Rome, just beyond Tibur).

       Tīburs, Tīburtis, *of/belonging to Tibur* (the modern Tivoli, a fashionable resort town on the Anio River, eighteen miles northeast of Rome).

          seu Sabīne seu Tīburs: Tibur was an expensive resort area; the Sabine hills and farming lands, north of Tibur, were less prosperous and pretentious. The argument in lines 1–5 is one of prestige: is the estate in the high- or low-rent district?

2   **autumō, -āre, -āvī, -ātus** [archaic], *to assert, insist*.

       autumant: the subject is the understood antecedent of **quibus**; translate: *they, for whom . . . , insist that you* (**tē**). . . .

       quibus nōn est / cordī: idiom with double dative, *for whom . . . is not to/for the heart, is not dear/pleasing to*. The subject is the infinitive **laedere**.

3   **laedō, laedere, laesī, laesus**, *to hurt*.

       at quibus cordī est: supply **Catullum laedere** as subject.

4   **quīvīs, quaevīs, quodvīs** [**quī, quae, quod** + **vīs**, *you wish*], *any that you please, no matter what*.

       Sabīnum . . . esse: supply **tē**; parallel to **tē esse Tīburtem** (2); note the chiastic arrangement of infinitives and adjectives.

       pignus, pignoris, n., *stake* (offered in a wager).

       quōvīs . . . pignore: *on any stake, for any amount*.

       contendō [**con-**, intensive + **tendō, tendere, tetendī, tentus**, *to stretch*], **contendere, contendī, contentus**, *to stretch; to hasten; to assert, maintain; to contend*.

5   **sīve**: = **seu**.

6   **fuī libenter**: *I was glad to be*.

       suburbānus, -a, -um, *located close to a city*.

7   **pectore**: ablative of separation.

       tussis, tussis, acc. **tussim**, f., *cough*.

8   **inmerēns, inmerentis** [**in-**, *not* + **merēns, merentis**, *deserving*], *undeserving, blameless*.

          nōn inmerentī: litotes.

       quam: delayed relative pronoun; in normal word order it would occur at the beginning of this line. The verb for this relative clause is **dedit** in line 9, which peculiarly interrupts the **dum** clause in that line (an example of hyperbaton).

       mihī: the second *i* is sometimes long in poetry.

       venter, ventrī, m., *stomach*.

CATULLUS 44

Ō funde noster. . . .

As if praying to a deity, Catullus addresses his country estate in a poem of thanks that ends with a prayer.

1   Ō funde noster seu Sabīne seu Tīburs
2   (nam tē esse Tīburtem autumant, quibus nōn est
3   cordī Catullum laedere; at quibus cordī est,
4   quōvīs Sabīnum pignore esse contendunt),
5   sed seu Sabīne sīve vērius Tīburs,
6   fuī libenter in tuā suburbānā
7   vīllā, malamque pectore expulī tussim,
8   nōn inmerentī quam mihī meus venter,

continued

Initial Explorations

1. In what two ways do people refer to Catullus' country estate? (1–5)
2. Why do some people refer to it in one way and some the other way? (2–4)
3. What word in line 5 indicates how Catullus would like people to refer to his country estate?
4. How does line 5 echo line 1?
5. Why was Catullus glad to be at his country estate? (6–7)
6. How does Catullus describe himself in line 8? What figure of speech does he use?

9   **dum . . . appetō**: *while . . .* , translate the present tense in a **dum** clause as an
     imperfect when the verb of the main clause is in the perfect tense.
     sūmptuōsus, -a, -um, *expensive, costly; sumptuous.*
     appetō [**ad-**, *to, toward* + **petō, petere, petīvī, petītus**, *to look for, seek*], **ap-**
     petere, appetīvī, appetītus (see Catullus 2.3), *to seek; to hunger after.*
     dedit: hyperbaton, the verb is separated from the rest of its clause in line 8
     and interrupts the subordinate clause in line 9.

10   **Sestiānus, -a, -um**, *of/belonging to Sestius* (Publius Sestius was a senator
     known for supporting conservative causes and for a dull, frigid speaking
     and writing style; he was quaestor in 63 B.C. and a friend of Cicero's).
          Sestiānus: take with **convīva**, *a Sestian guest*, an inflated way of saying *a*
          guest of Sestius.
     dum: delayed conjunction; for translation of the verb in the clause, see the
     note on **dum** in line 9 above; **dum**, *while*, may also express cause, *as, since.*

11   **ōrātiōnem**: a speech written by Sestius.
     in: *against.*
     Antius, -ī, m., *Antius* (possibly the C. Antius who was responsible for legisla-
     tion against electoral fraud).
     petītor, petītōris, m. [**petō, petere, petīvī, petītus**, *to look for, seek*], *one who*
     seeks political office, a candidate.

12   **venēnum, -ī**, n., *poison.*
     pestilentia, -ae, f., *plague.*

13   **hīc**, adv., *here; thereupon, then.*
     gravēdō, gravēdinis, f. [**gravis, -is, -e**, *heavy*], *cold, sickness.*
     frequēns, frequentis, *repeated, frequent; constant.*
          gravēdō frīgida et frequēns tussis: chiasmus.

14   **quassō, -āre, -āvī, -ātus**, *to shake.*
          quassāvit: the two subjects here take a singular verb.
     usque, adv., *continuously, constantly.*
     dum: *until.*
     tuum: i.e., the estate's.
     sinus, -ūs, m. (see Catullus 2.2), *fold of a toga; bosom.*

15   **recūrō** [**re-**, *back, again* + **cūrō, -āre, -āvī, -ātus**, *to look after, take care of*], **-āre,**
     -āvī, -ātus, *to restore* (by medical treatment), *cure.*
     ōtium, -ī, n., *leisure.*
     urtīca, -ae, f., *stinging nettle.*
          ōtiōque et urtīcā: the use of **-que et** is archaic; nettle leaves are sharp, bitter
          greens that would have made a potent medicine for a variety of ills.
               mē recūrāvī ōtiōque et urtīcā: an example of zeugma; the verb is
               used in its literal, medical sense with **urtīcā** but in a figurative sense
               with **ōtiō**.

16   **grātēs, grātium**, f. pl. [archaic, used especially in religious contexts and
     eventually replaced by **grātiae**], *thanks.*

17   **ulcīscor, ulcīscī, ultus sum**, *to take vengeance on; to punish.*
          es ulta: from **ulcīscor**; the subject is the **vīlla**.
     peccātum, -ī, n., *fault, error.*

9   dum sūmptuōsās appetō, dedit, cēnās:

10   nam, Sestiānus dum volō esse convīva,

11   ōrātiōnem in Antium petītōrem

12   plēnam venēnī et pestilentiae lēgī.

13   Hīc mē gravēdō frīgida et frequēns tussis

14   quassāvit usque, dum in tuum sinum fūgī,

15   et mē recūrāvī ōtiōque et urtīcā.

16   Quārē refectus maximās tibī grātēs

17   agō, meum quod nōn es ulta peccātum.

continued

Initial Explorations

7.   Judging from line 9, why does Catullus describe himself as **nōn inmerentī** in line 8?

8.   What does the phrase **Sestiānus . . . convīva** (10) imply about the status of being invited to dinner by Sestius?

9.   When did Catullus read Sestius' oration against Antius? Why do you suppose he would have read it? (10–12)

10. How does Catullus describe the oration? (12)

11. What happened to Catullus when he read the oration? (13–14)

12. How does the description of the oration in line 12 prepare for or explain what happened to Catullus as described in lines 13–14?

13. How did Catullus treat his illness? (14–15)

14. For what two things is Catullus grateful? (16–17)

15. What was Catullus' **peccātum** (17)? What word earlier in the poem is recalled by Catullus' blaming himself for a **peccātum** here?

18   **dēprecor** [**dē-**, indicating a reversal + **precor, -ārī, -ātus sum,** *to pray*], **-ārī,**
     -ātus sum, *to try to avert by prayer;* + **quīn** + subjunctive, *to offer a prayer to*
     prevent X *from doing* Y.
         Nec dēprecor . . . quīn (19) **. . . ferat frīgus** (20): *And I offer no prayer . . .*
         to prevent . . . the frigidity (of Sestius' **nefāria scrīpta**) *from bringing. . . .*
     nefārius, -a, -um, *abominable, awful.*
     scrīpta, -ōrum, n. pl., *writings.*
19   **recepsō:** an archaic future formation from the verb **recipere**, here used as the
     equivalent of **recēperō**, the future perfect; the meaning of the verb here, *to*
     take up again, is different from its usual meaning, *to receive, take back.*
20   **frīgus, frīgoris,** n., *cold, chill; frigidity* (of rhetorical style), *flatness* (in the style
     of a speech).
21   **tunc . . . , cum. . . . :** *then . . . , when = only . . . , when.*
     vocat . . . , cum . . . lēgī: present general, with present indicative in the
     first clause and perfect indicative in the temporal clause; translate the per-
     fect as a present, *when(ever) I read.*
     liber, librī, m., *papyrus roll* (book in the form of a papyrus roll).
     malum librum: i.e., his lousy speech written out on a papyrus roll.

18   Nec dēprecor iam, sī nefāria scrīpta
19   Sestī recepsō, quīn gravēdinem et tussim
20   nōn mī, sed ipsī Sestiō ferat frīgus,
21   quī tunc vocat mē, cum malum librum lēgī.

Initial Explorations

16.   The prayer as stated in lines 18–20 begins with a double negative, literally, *And I offer no prayer to prevent*. . . .   Rephrase and translate it as a positive prayer, introduced by *I pray that*. . . .
17.   Explain how the poet puns on the two different meanings of the word **frīgus** (20).
18.   What words earlier in the poem are recalled by the following words: **nefāria** (18), **gravēdinem et tussim** (19), **frīgus** (20).
19.   Why does Catullus think that Sestius deserves to catch a cold? (21)

Discussion

1.   Consider the poem as a kind of address to a deity.   Locate the following:
    a.   Invocation
    b.   Narrative of service rendered by the deity
    c.   Expression of thanks by the speaker
    d.   Prayer
2.   In calling upon their deities, the Romans tried to be as inclusive as possible in listing the deity's names, epithets, or places of worship (see, for example, Catullus 34.9–22 and 36.12–15). How does Catullus work this inclusiveness of epithet into his invocation of his country estate? (1–5)
3.   The Romans tended to preserve archaic words and forms in their religious language. Locate the archaic words and forms in this poem.
4.   What phrase and words in lines 17–18 add to the religious tone of the poem?
5.   In one common form of ancient prayer, the suppliant prays that a god may turn some evil back upon its perpetrator, e.g., "If someone wrongs me, turn the wrong back upon him." How does Catullus' prayer in lines 18–21 fit this pattern?
6.   How is Sestius described and evaluated as a social figure in this poem?
7.   How comfortably does Catullus fit into the social world evoked by this poem?

Meter: hendecasyllabic

1   **Acmē, Acmēs**, acc. **Acmēn**, f., *Acme* (name of a young woman, probably a Greek freedwoman; her Greek name means *summit, prime, flowering*).
    Septimius, -ī, m., *Septimius* (name of a young Roman man; it is not known whether Acme and Septimius were real people or not).
    suōs amōrēs: see Catullus 6.16 and 10.1; the phrase is in apposition with **Acmēn**.

2   **gremium, -ī**, n. (see Catullus 3.8), *lap* (of a person).

3   **nī**: = nisi.
    perditē, adv., *recklessly, desperately, madly.*
    amāre: dependent on **parātus** (4).
    porrō, adv., *onward, hereafter, into the future, on and on.*

4   **omnēs**: which word does **omnēs** modify? What case and usage?
    assiduē, adv., *continually, unceasingly.*

5   **quantum quī**: *as much as [he loves] who, as much as [anyone] who.*
    potis or **pote**, indeclinable adjective + infinitive, *having the power (to), able (to).*
    pote: supply **est** = **potest**.
    pereō [**per-**, *through* + **eō, īre, iī, itūrus**, *to go*], **perīre, periī, peritūrus**, *to die, perish; to come to an end; to perish* (with love), *be madly in love.*
        perīre: = **perditē amāre.**

6   **Libya, -ae**, f., *Libya* (name used generally for all of North Africa).
    India, -ae, f., *India* (name used for much of Asia, including modern day India and China).
    tostus, -a, -um, *burned, sun-baked, parched.*

7   **caesius, -a, -um**, *having gray, gray-blue, or gray-green eyes.*
    veniam obvius: + dat., optative subjunctive expressing a wish or prayer, *may l come face-to-face* (with).

8   **dīxit**: Septimius is the subject.
    Amor, Amōris, m., *Love, Cupid.*
    sinistrā . . . / dextrā: supply **manū**; ablative of place where without a preposition.
        sinistrā ut ante / dextrā: the meaning of this refrain, repeated in lines 17–18, has prompted much discussion; most agree, however, that the god is giving his approval of the lovers' vows by sneezing twice. The words **ut ante**, *as before*, may be taken alternately with both **sinistrā** and **dextrā**.

9   **sternō, sternere, sternuī**, *to sneeze.*
    approbātiō, approbātiōnis, f., *approval.*

CATULLUS 45

A Love Duet

"The most charming picture in any language of a light and happy love" —Munro

1 Acmēn Septimius suōs amōrēs
2 tenēns in gremiō, "Mea," inquit, "Acmē,
3 nī tē perditē amō atque amāre porrō
4 omnēs sum assiduē parātus annōs,
5 quantum quī pote plūrimum perīre,
6 sōlus in Libyā Indiāque tostā
7 caesiō veniam obvius leōnī."
8 Hoc ut dīxit, Amor sinistrā ut ante
9 dextrā sternuit approbātiōnem.

continued

Initial Explorations

1. Describe the scene as presented in lines 1–2.
2. How do the first two words and the people to whom they refer contrast with one another?
3. How does the arrangement of subject and object in the first line visually undercut the sense of the line?
4. What letter do the words **Acmēn Septimius . . . amōrēs** have in common?
5. Septimius describes his love for Acme in a conditional sentence with its protasis introduced by **nisi**, *unless* (3). What does Septimius say about himself in the protasis? (3–5)
6. What does Septimius wish or pray for in the apodosis (6–7) of his conditional sentence?
7. How do Septimius' words characterize his declaration of his love? (2–7)
8. Study the alliteration of *ps*, *ss*, and *qs* in lines 3–5. How does sound reinforce sense?
9. For the Greeks "right" was regarded as lucky and "left" as unlucky; the reverse was true in early times for the Romans, but later they tended to adopt the Greek way of thinking. Remember that Acme is Greek and Septimius Roman and that Acme is sitting in Septimius' lap and facing him. How would you interpret Amor's intentions here? (8–9)

10   **leviter**, adv., *lightly, gently, a little.*
        caput: i.e., her own.
        reflectō [re-, *back* + **flectō, flectere, flexī, flexus**, *to bend*], **reflectere, reflexī, reflexus**, *to bend back.*
11   **dulcis, -is, -e**, *sweet; charming; dear.*
        dulcis puerī: what case?
        ocellus, -ī, m. [dim. of **oculus, -ī**, m., *eye*], *little eye, dear eye.*
12   **purpureus, -a, -um**, *deep red, wine-colored; radiant, glowing.*
        suāvior (sāvior) [**suāvis, -is, -e**, *pleasant*], **-ārī, -ātus sum**, *to kiss.*
        suāviāta: Thomson prints **sāviāta**.
13   **Sīc**: take with **serviāmus** (14), optative subjunctive expressing a wish or prayer.
        Septimillus, -ī, m. [dim.], *dear little Septimius.*
14   **dominō**: i.e., Amor.
        usque, adv., *continuously, constantly.*
15   **ut**: *as surely as,* but need not be translated here. Acme's main thought, namely that her love is greater than Septimius', is expressed in the subordinate clause introduced by **ut** (15–16); proof of this is offered in her wish or prayer expressed in lines 13–14. The sentence structure of **sīc** + optative subjunctive in the main clause and **ut** + indicative in the subordinate clause is fairly common in Latin but has no direct equivalent in English. As Fordyce remarks (207), we reverse the construction and would say "as I hope we may serve to the end the one master (i.e. Amor) whom we now own (*huic*), the passion that burns in me is far fiercer than yours."
        ācer, ācris, ācre, *keen; sharp; violent; strong.*
16   **medulla, -ae**, f. (see Catullus 35.15), *marrow of bones; one's innermost part, vitals, heart* (as the seat of emotions).

10   At Acmē leviter caput reflectēns
11   et dulcis puerī ēbriōs ocellōs
12   illō purpureō ōre suāviāta,
13   "Sīc," inquit, "mea vīta Septimille,
14   huic ūnī dominō usque serviāmus,
15   ut multō mihi maior ācriorque
16   ignis mollibus ārdet in medullīs."
17   Hoc ut dīxit, Amor sinistrā ut ante
18   dextrā sternuit approbātiōnem.

continued

Initial Explorations

10.   What is Acme's physical response to Septimius' declaration of his love? (10–12)
11.   How does Acme's declaration of her love for Septimius (13–16) differ from his for her (2–7)? Include in your answer a description of how Acme's wish or prayer expressed with the optative subjunctive differs from that of Septimius.
12.   Study the alliteration of *ms*, *ls*, and *ss* in lines 13–16. How does sound reinforce sense? How many *ps* did Septimius use in his speech? How many *ms* does Acme use? How are these letters related to the names Septimius and Acme?
13.   What words in Acme's speech repeat or recall words in Septimius'?

19   **auspicium, -ī**, n., *sign, omen.*
      profectī: modifying the subjects, Acme and Septimius. From what deponent
      verb? What form and tense?
20   **animus, -ī**, m., *mind* (as the seat of consciousness and thought); *soul, heart* (as
      the seat of feelings and emotions).
      amant amantur: asyndeton, anaphora, and antithesis.
21   **misellus, -a, -um** [dim. of **miser, misera, miserum**, *wretched*] (see Catullus
      3.16), *poor little, wretched* (here from longing or desire).
            Ūnam Septimius misellus Acmēn: note the embedding of the phrase
            Septimius misellus within the phrase **Ūnam . . . Acmēn**.
22   **māvult**: from **mālō, mālle**.
      māvult quam: *prefers . . . to.*
      Syriās Britanniāsque: i.e., all the Syrias and Britains in the world; Septimius
      is thinking of military service on the borders of the Roman empire. Men-
      tion of Syria and Britain may help provide a date for the poem; in 55 B.C.
      Crassus set out for Syria and Parthia, and Caesar led his first invasion of
      Britain (see Catullus 11.6 and 12 for references to Parthia and Britain).
23   **in**: here perhaps translate as *with.*
24   **dēliciae, -ārum**, f. pl. [usually pl. in form, sing. in meaning] (see Catullus 2.1),
      pleasure, delight; pet; darling, sweetheart.
            dēliciās facere, idiom, *to find pleasure, enjoy oneself.*
      libīdō, libīdinis, f., *sexual appetite/desire;* pl., *lovemaking.*
            facit dēliciās libīdinēsque: translate as hendiadys.
25   **beātus, -a, -um**, *happy, fortunate.*
26   **Venus, Veneris**, f., *Venus* (the goddess of love); *lovemaking.*
      auspicātus, -a, -um, *auspicious, fortunate, lucky.*

19   Nunc ab auspiciō bonō profectī
20   mūtuīs animīs amant amantur.
21   Ūnam Septimius misellus Acmēn
22   māvult quam Syriās Britanniāsque:
23   ūnō in Septimiō fidēlis Acmē
24   facit dēliciās libīdinēsque.
25   Quis ūllōs hominēs beātiōrēs
26   vīdit, quis Venerem auspicātiōrem?

Initial Explorations

14. In what ways does the language of line 19 suggest an army marching out to battle?
15. In what two ways does line 20 emphasize the reciprocity of Acme and Septimius' love?
16. Compare the arrangement of words in line 21 with that in line 1.
17. What is said about Septimius in lines 21–22?
18. What is said about Acme in lines 23–24?
19. Identify the corresponding words in lines 21 and 23 and in lines 22 and 24.
20. Identify the corresponding words in lines 25 and 26.
21. What is the expected answer to the rhetorical questions in lines 25 and 26?

Discussion

1. Divide the poem into its three major sections, and divide the third section into subsections.
2. Septimius and Acme have been described as "spokesmen, as it were, of their sexes." Discuss the way they are portrayed in the poem and evaluate the applicability of this statement.
3. Some readers have thought that the picture of an ideal love affair presented in the poem is too good to be true and have seen ironic double meanings undercutting its idyllic surface. What elements of irony, if any, do you detect in the poem?
4. What lines show Septimius' adherence to the saying "Make love, not war"? To what extent did Catullus share this preference?

Meter: hendecasyllabic

1   vēr, vēris, n., *spring*.
     ēgelidus, -a, -um [ex-, *thoroughly; without* + gelū, -ūs, n., *frost; cold*], *extremely
         cold; having the chill removed, no longer chill, mild.*
     tepor, tepōris, m., *warmth*; pl., *warm weather.*
2   furor, furōris, m., *fury, rage; storminess.*
     aequinoctiālis, -is, -e [aequus, -a, -um, *equal* + nox, noctis, f., *night*],
         equinoctial (i.e., at the spring equinox).
         aequinoctiālis: take with caelī.
3   Zephyrus, -ī, m., *Zephyr* (the west wind of spring).
     silēscō, silēscere, inceptive, *to become silent, quiet down.*
         silēscit: why is an inceptive verb appropriate for this poem?
     aura, -ae f., *wind, breeze.*
         aureīs: an archaic spelling of the ablative (of instrument with silēscit),
             scanned as two syllables. Thomson prints aurīs.
4   Linquantur: = Relinquantur.
         Linquantur: what mood and why? Catullus left Bithynia, where he had
             served on the governor's staff, in spring of 56 B.C. (see Catullus 10).
     Phrygius, -a, -um, *Phrygian* (referring to an area in central and north west-
         ern Asia Minor, including the western part of Bithynia).
5   Nicaeus, -a, -um, *Nicaean, of Nicaea* (one of the two major cities in Bithynia,
         its rival being Nicomedia, the seat of Roman provincial government).
     ūber, ūberis, *rich, fertile.*
     aestuōsus, -a, -um (see Catullus 7.5), *very hot, sweltering.*
6   clārus, -a, -um, *bright; brilliant; famous.*
     Asia, -ae f., *Asia* (a Roman province on the western coast of what is now
         Turkey, famous for its cities such as Pergamum and Ephesus).
     volō, -āre, -āvī, -ātūrus, *to fly, speed, go quickly.*
         volēmus: what mood and construction?
7   praetrepidāns, praetrepidantis [prae-, *ahead; very* + trepidō, -āre, -āvī,
         -ātūrus, *to tremble*], *trembling/excited in anticipation.*
     aveō, avēre, *to wish, want, long* (to do something).
     vagor, -ārī, -ātus sum, *to wander, roam.*
8   vigēscō, vigēscere, inceptive, *to grow strong, come alive.*
9   dulcis, -is, -e, *sweet.*
     comes, comitis, m., *companion.*
     coetus, -ūs, m., *group, company.*
         coetūs: vocative plural; comitum . . . coetūs: the members of the gover-
             nor's staff, his cohors, cf. Catullus 10.10.
10   longē: take with quōs . . . ā domō profectōs, *whom, having journeyed far
         from home*, with the participle profectōs here referring to the entire jour-
         ney and not just to its beginning.
11   variē, adv., *variously, by different routes.*

CATULLUS 46

Spring has arrived.

The poet is eager to journey home.

1   Iam vēr ēgelidōs refert tepōrēs,
2   iam caelī furor aequinoctiālis
3   iūcundīs Zephyrī silēscit aureīs.
4   Linquantur Phrygiī, Catulle, campī
5   Nicaeaeque ager ūber aestuōsae:
6   ad clārās Asiae volēmus urbēs.
7   Iam mēns praetrepidāns avet vagārī,
8   iam laetī studiō pedēs vigēscunt.
9   Ō dulcēs comitum, valēte, coetūs,
10   longē quōs simul ā domō profectōs
11   dīversae variē viae reportant.

Initial Explorations

1. What do the first three lines of the poem celebrate and what feelings do they evoke? What does Catullus urge in lines 4–6? What does he state in lines 7–8? Whom does he address and with what feelings in the last three lines?
2. Repetition of words, letters, and sounds is significant in this poem. Why is the word **iam** repeated four times?
3. Words that have the letter *v* in them are central to the poem. Locate these words and describe the pattern that you see in their use. What sounds link words in lines 4, 5, and 9?
4. Compare and contrast line 1 with line 7 and lines 2 and 3 with line 8. How does the arrival of spring influence and mirror the poet's state of mind?
5. Find a chiasmus in lines 7–8. What is its effect?
6. Does the tone of the last three lines differ from that of the rest of the poem? If so, how?

Discussion

1. Divide the poem into groups of lines as follows:
   a. 1–3
   b. 4–6
   c. 7–8
   d. 9–11

continued

How do lines 7–8 relate to lines 1–3?
How do lines 9–11 relate to lines 4–6?

2. Study the poet's use of the following words in the poem: **ēgelidōs** (1), **volē-mus** (6), **praetrepidāns** (7), and **vigēscunt** (8). How is each word especially appropriate and expressive in its context?

Comparisons

The arrival of spring has served as a metaphor for many poets. Read the following excerpts from Chaucer's *The Canterbury Tales* and T. S. Eliot's *The Waste Land*. What aspects of spring and springtime activity do these two passages share with Catullus 46? How are the attitudes of the three poets toward spring similar and how are they different?

As soon as April pierces to the root
The drought of March, and bathes each bud and shoot
Through every vein of sap with gentle showers
From whose engendering liquor spring the flowers;
When zephyrs have breathed softly all about
Inspiring every wood and field to sprout. . . .
Then off as pilgrims people long to go,
And palmers to set out for distant strands
And foreign shrines renowned in many lands.

—Geoffrey Chaucer, ca. 1340–1400

April is the cruellest month, breeding
Lilacs out of the dead land, mixing
Memory and desire, stirring
Dull roots with spring rain.

—T. S. Eliot, 1888–1965

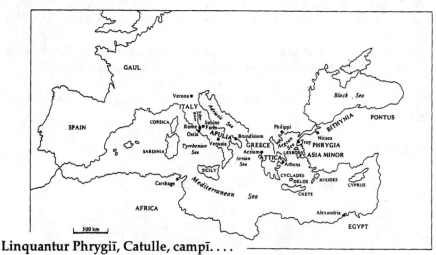

Linquantur Phrygiī, Catulle, campī. . . .

The Mediterranean area as it was in Catullus' time

Iam vēr ēgelidōs refert tepōrēs. . . .

"Spring"
Fresco from the Villa of Ariadne at Stabiae
National Archaelogical Museum
Naples, Italy

Meter: hendecasyllabic

1   **disertus, -a, -um**, *articulate, eloquent.*
     Disertissime: what form and case?
    Rōmulus, -ī, m., *Romulus* (first king of Rome).
    nepōs, nepōtis, m., *grandson; descendant.*
2   **quot**, indeclinable adjective, *as many as, however many.*
    fuēre: = **fuērunt**.
    Mārcus Tullius, -ī, m., *Marcus Tullius Cicero* (106–43 B.C., Rome's greatest
       orator and a contemporary of Catullus; here addressed formally with
       praenōmen and **nōmen**).
6   **tantō . . . quantō** (7), *as much . . . as.*
7   **patrōnus**: supply **es**.

Comparison

Christopher Smart (1722–71)

(Imitated after Dining with Mr. Murray)

O Thou, of British orators the chief
That were, or are in being, or belief;
All eminence and goodness as thou art,
Accept the gratitude of Poet Smart,—
The meanest of the tuneful train as far,
As thou transcend'st the brightest at the bar.

Disertissime Rōmulī nepōtum. . . .

"Bust of Cicero"
Uffizi
Florence, Italy

CATULLUS 49

A Thank You Note to Cicero

For what is the poet thanking Cicero? Is he sincere or ironic?

1 Disertissime Rōmulī nepōtum,
2 quot sunt quotque fuēre, Mārce Tullī,
3 quotque post aliīs erunt in annīs,
4 grātiās tibi maximās Catullus
5 agit pessimus omnium poēta,
6 tantō pessimus omnium poēta
7 quantō tū optimus omnium patrōnus.

Initial Explorations

1. What is the effect of the anaphora in lines 2–3?
2. What is the effect of the particular way Cicero is addressed in line 2?
3. Locate five superlative adjectives in the poem.
4. Locate examples of parallel word order.
5. Locate examples of alliteration.
6. Locate examples of homoioteleuton.
7. What is the structure of the poem?

Discussion

1. What indication, if any, does Catullus give for why he is thanking Cicero with this poem?
2. On the surface, this is a very flattering poem of thanks to Cicero. Some readers have felt that it is ironic. What is there in the poem that could lead one to suspect irony on the part of Catullus?

Meter: hendecasyllabic

1   **hesternus, -a, -um**, *of/belonging to yesterday*.
     Hesternō . . . diē: *Yesterday*.
     Licinius, -ī, m., *C. Licinius Calvus Macer* (a close friend of Catullus, an orator
     and one of the **poētae novī**; see Catullus 53 and 96).
     ōtiōsus, -a, -um [**ōtium, -ī**, n., *spare time; time free from serious occupations;*
     leisure; idleness] (see Catullus 10.2), *not occupied by business or politics, hav-*
     ing nothing to do, at leisure.
          ōtiōsī: modifying the subject of **lūsimus** (2). Catullus describes himself
          and Calvus spending an afternoon together, when other people were
          engaged in business (**negōtium**).
2   **lūsimus**: *we played/had fun*, the verb is often used of writing poetry and in
     particular of composing playful light verse, as opposed to doing serious
     business in the real world.
     tabella, -ae, f., *board*; pl., *waxed tablets* (for writing).
3   **conveniō, convenīre, convēnī, conventūrus**, *to come together, meet, assem-*
     ble; to make an agreement; impersonal, *(it) is agreed*.
          convēnerat (nōs) esse dēlicātōs: the infinitive phrase is the subject of
          the impersonal verb.
     dēlicātus, -a, -um, *at ease, frivolous, self-indulgent*.
4   **versiculus, -ī**, m. [dim. of **versus, -ūs**, m., *verse*], *a brief line of verse*; pl., *light*
     verse; scraps of verse.
     nostrum: genitive (partitive here) of **nōs**.
5   **numerus, -ī**, m., *number; meter*.
          numerō: = **in numerō**.
     modo . . . modo, adv., *now . . . now*.
     illōc: = **illō**, with retention of a demonstrative suffix, **-c(e)**, seen in **hic, haec**
     hoc.
6   **reddēns mūtua**: i.e., exchanging verses in turn, perhaps capping one anoth-
     er's verses.
     per iocum atque vīnum: cf. Catullus 12.2, **in iocō atque vīnō**.
7   **Atque**: here introducing a following event, *And then*.
     illinc, adv., *from there*.
     lepos, lepōris, m. (see Catullus 12.8), *charm, grace; wit, humor*.
     lepōre: what case and why?
8   **facētiae, -ārum**, f. pl. (see Catullus 12.9, 36.19, and 43.8), *cleverness; facetious-*
     ness, wit.
          lepōre (7) **. . . facētiīsque**: cf. Catullus 12.8–9 **lepōrum / . . . facētiārum**.
9   **ut**: purpose or result clause? What is your clue?
     miserum: an adjective appropriate to lovesickness; compare the opening
     word of Catullus 8.
     iuvō, iuvāre, iūvī, iūtus, *to help, benefit, relieve*.
10   **ocellus, -ī**, m. [dim. of **oculus, -ī**, m., *eye*], *little eye, dear eye, tender eye*.

CATULLUS 50

Inflamed by Poetry

The poet details how moved he was by a literary evening at his friend's.

1 Hesternō, Licinī, diē ōtiōsī
2 multum lūsimus in meīs tabellīs,
3 ut convēnerat esse dēlicātōs:
4 scrībēns versiculōs uterque nostrum
5 lūdēbat numerō modo hōc modo illōc,
6 reddēns mūtua per iocum atque vīnum.
7 Atque illinc abiī tuō lepōre
8 incēnsus, Licinī, facētiīsque,
9 ut nec mē miserum cibus iuvāret
10 nec somnus tegeret quiēte ocellōs,

continued

Initial Explorations

1. When were Catullus and Calvus together? What were they doing? Where were they? Was anyone else there? (1–7)
2. How are the two men and their activity characterized? (1–6)

11   **tōtō**: with **lectō**.

indomitus, -a, -um [**in-**, *not* + **domitus, -a, -um**, *subdued by taming, broken in, tamed*], *unable to be controlled, unbridled; wild*.

furor, furōris, m., *fury, rage; delirium; ecstasy; inspiration*.

indomitus furōre: = **indomitō furōre**, *with uncontrollable delirium*, ablative of manner with **versārer**. **Indomitus** is a transferred epithet.

12   **versō** [**vertō, vertere, vertī, versus**, *to turn* + iterative suffix **-sō**], **-āre, -āvī, -ātus**, *to keep turning around, to turn over and over*.

versārer: passive used in middle/reflexive sense, *I was turning myself, I was tossing and turning*.

13   **ut**: purpose or result? What is your clue?

loquerer: what mood, tense, and person?

ut essem: supply **tēcum** from the first half of the line.

ut tēcum loquerer simulque ut essem: hysteron proteron.

14   **At . . . postquam**: **At** introduces the main clause in line 16; **postquam** is in delayed position.

labōre: *from suffering/pain*.

membrum, -ī, n., *limb* (of the body).

membra: subject of **iacēbant** (15).

15   **sēmimortuus, -a, -um**, *half-dead*.

lectulus, -ī [dim. of **lectus, -ī**, m., *bed*], *little bed*.

16   **iūcunde**: supply **amīce**. In poem 14.2, Catullus addresses Calvus as **iūcundissime Calve**.

poēma, poēmatis [Greek loan word], n., *poem*.

17   **ex quō**: introducing a relative clause of purpose.

perspiciō [**per-**, *through; thoroughly* + **speciō, specere, spexī, spectus**, *to see, observe*], **perspicere, perspexī, perspectus**, *to see clearly*.

dolor, dolōris, m. (see Catullus 2.7), *pain, smart, love-ache*.

18   **audāx, audācis**, *bold; presumptuous, reckless*.

audāx: Thomson translates *over-confident [of my affection]*.

cave: = **cavē** by iambic shortening; the imperative governs the indirect command (**nē**) . . . **sīs**, *beware of being. . . . , make sure you aren't. . . .*

prex, precis, f., *prayer*.

precēs . . . nostrās: = the wishes expressed in line 13.

19   **ōrāmus**: parenthetical.

dēspuō [**dē-**, *down* + **spuō, spuere, spuī, spūtus**, *to spit*] **dēspuere**, *to spit out; to reject, scorn, spurn*.

ocelle: here as a term of endearment, *dearest one*; cf. Catullus 31.2.

20   **Nemesis, Nemeseōs** [Greek loan word], f., *Nemesis* (goddess of retribution).

reposcō, reposcere, *to demand back; exact*.

reposcat: what mood, tense, and construction?

21   **vēmēns, vēmentis** [syncope for **vehemēns, vehementis**], *violent; strong-willed, powerful*.

laedō, laedere, laesī, laesus, *to hurt, harm; to displease, offend*.

hanc: i.e., Nemesis.

cavētō: the formal future imperative, *make sure you do not* + infinitive.

11   sed tōtō indomitus furōre lectō
12   versārer, cupiēns vidēre lūcem,
13   ut tēcum loquerer simulque ut essem.
14   At dēfessa labōre membra postquam
15   sēmimortua lectulō iacēbant,
16   hoc, iūcunde, tibī poēma fēcī,
17   ex quō perspicerēs meum dolōrem.
18   Nunc audāx cave sīs, precēsque nostrās,
19   ōrāmus, cave dēspuās, ocelle,
20   nē poenās Nemesis reposcat ā tē.
21   Est vēmēns dea; laedere hanc cavētō.

Initial Explorations

3.   In what mental condition did Catullus depart from Calvus? (7–8) What re-
      sult did this have for Catullus? (9–13)
4.   When and why did Catullus write the present poem? (14–17)
5.   Of what does Catullus warn Calvus? What are Catullus' **precēs**? (18–19)
6.   With what does Catullus threaten Calvus? (20–21)

Discussion

1.   Catullus describes Calvus and himself with the words **ōtiōsī** (1) and
      dēlicātōs (3). How is their life-style characterized in this poem? What would
      more traditionally-minded Romans such as the **senēs sevēriōrēs** referred to
      in Catullus 5.2 think about Catullus and Calvus' life-style here?
2.   How does the poetic encounter with Calvus affect Catullus? What kind of
      language or what metaphor does Catullus use to describe the effect? Com-
      pare poem 35.

Meter: Sapphic strophe

1   **Ille**: i.e., a man discussed further in lines 3–4.
       mī: take with **vidētur**.
    pār, paris + dat., *equal* (to).
2   **fās**, indeclinable, n., *that which is right or permissible by divine law; that which is
       morally right, fitting, proper; that which is in accordance with natural law.*
       sī fās est: *if it is in accordance with natural law, if it is possible.*
    superō, -āre, -āvī, -ātus, *to overcome, defeat; to be superior to, surpass.*
       superāre: supply **vidētur**.
    dīvus, -ī, m., *god.*
3   **adversus, -a, -um**, *turned towards, facing, opposite.*
       adversus: some editors take this not as an adjective but as an adverb or as a
       preposition governing **tē**.
5   **dulcis, -is, -e**, *sweet.*
       dulce: = **dulciter**.
    miserō: take in agreement with **mihi** (6) as a dative of separation (*from . . .*).
       For the word as a staple of erotic vocabulary, see Catullus 50.9 **miser** and
       8.1 **Miser**.
    quod: *[a thing] that*, subject of **ēripit** in line 6.
    omnīs: = **omnēs**; in early Latin and in many of the poets, the accusative plu-
       ral of i-stem nouns and adjectives often ends in **-īs**.
6   **sēnsus, -ūs**, m., *sensation* (i.e., ability to perceive by the senses).
    simul: supply **ac**, *at the same time as, as soon as.*
7   **aspiciō** [**ad-**, *to, toward* + **speciō, specere, spexī, spectus**, *to see, observe*], **as-
       picere, aspexī, aspectus**, *to catch sight of, behold, look at.*
    est super: = **superest**, *remains, is left.*
       simul tē, / . . . aspexī, nihil est super: *as soon as I [ever] look at you, nothing
       is left. . . .* , perfect tense in the temporal clause and present in the main
       clause = a present-general temporal structure, in which we regularly
       translate the perfect tense with a present tense in English and to which
       we may add the word *ever* to emphasize the generality of the statement.
8   **<vōcis in ōre,>**: this line is missing from the manuscripts. Editors have
       made various suggestions, such as **vōcis in ōre** (supplied in the text here)
       and **Lesbia, vōcis**, with the genitive dependent on **nihil** in line 7.

CATULLUS 51

Lesbia's Devastating Effect on Catullus

This poem may have been the first in the cycle of love poems to Lesbia.

1   Ille mī pār esse deō vidētur,
2   ille, sī fās est, superāre dīvōs,
3   quī sedēns adversus identidem tē
4   spectat et audit

5   dulce rīdentem, miserō quod omnīs
6   ēripit sēnsūs mihi: nam simul tē,
7   Lesbia, aspexī, nihil est super mī
8   <vōcis in ōre,>

continued

Initial Explorations

1. Three people are involved in the first two stanzas of this poem. Who are they? What exactly are we told about the identity of each of them?
2. What rhetorical figure links the first two lines?
3. What does the poet accomplish by adding the second line?
4. Why does the poet add the parenthetical **sī fās est**?
5. What is the man referred to by the word **ille** doing? (3–5)
6. What is the woman doing? (5)
7. To what does **quod** (5) refer?
8. The pronoun **mihi** (6) is modified by **miserō** (5). Is it better to take **miserō** as an attributive adjective (*from miserable/lovesick me*) or to take it proleptically (*from me [and makes me] miserable/lovesick*)? Why is the adjective placed so early, even ahead of the relative pronoun that introduces the clause within which the adjective functions grammatically?
9. How does the word **miserō** (5) set the poet in opposition to the man referred to by the word **ille**?
10. What words in the first stanza are echoed by **simul tē / . . . aspexī** in the second?
11. What contrast is being drawn between Catullus in the second stanza and the man referred to by the word **ille** in the first?

9   **torpeō, torpēre**, *to be numb, be paralyzed.*
     tenuis, -is, -e, *thin, fine.*
     artus, -ūs, m., *joint; limb.*
10   **dēmānō** [dē-, *down* + **mānō, -āre, -āvī, -ātūrus**, *to flow*] **-āre, -āvī, -ātūrus**, *to flow down.*
     suōpte: the suffix **-pte** intensifies the reflexive possessive adjective.
11   **tintinō, -āre**, *to make a ringing sound; to have a ringing sensation, to ring.*
     auris, auris, f., *ear.*
12   **lūmen, lūminis**, n., *light*; pl., *eyes.*
13   **ōtium, -ī**, *spare time; time free from serious occupations; leisure; idleness.*
14   **exsultō** [ex-, *thoroughly* + **saltō, -āre, -āvī, -ātus**, *to dance*], **-āre, -āvī**, *to leap about, dance; to run riot; to rejoice without restraint;* + abl., *to exult/revel* (in).
     nimium, adv., *too much.*
     gestiō [gestus, -ūs, m., *movement* (of the limbs in dancing)], **-īre, -īvī**, *to desire eagerly; to make expressive movements/gestures; to act without restraint, be elated, exult.*
15   **beātus, -a, -um**, *happy, fortunate; wealthy.*
     rēgēs . . . beātās / perdidit urbēs: Catullus may be thinking of the fabulously wealthy and prosperous King Croesus of Lydia, whose city, Sardis, was sacked by the Persian king, Cyrus. Croesus had foolishly lowered his defenses by disbanding his allied army and was intending to wait until the next spring and the arrival of additional allied forces before continuing his war against Cyrus. Cyrus attacked Croesus with his defenses down and captured and sacked his city. See Herodotus 1.77 and 79.

9   lingua sed torpet, tenuis sub artūs

10   flamma dēmānat, sonitū suōpte

11   tintinant aurēs, geminā teguntur

12   lūmina nocte.

13   Ōtium, Catulle, tibī molestum est;

14   ōtiō exsultās nimiumque gestīs;

15   ōtium et rēgēs prius et beātās

16   perdidit urbēs.

Initial Explorations

12. What four more debilitating effects does Catullus describe in lines 9–12?
13. Examine the positions of the nouns and the verbs in the four clauses in lines 9–12 and identify the elements of a chiasmus.
14. What letters in lines 9–12 create a particularly effective alliteration?
15. Find a transferred epithet in lines 9–12.
16. What two words are most effectively juxtaposed in lines 9–12?
17. How does the final clause, geminā ... / ... nocte (11–12), provide a fitting climax for the list of debilitating effects? How is the placement of the word nocte significant?
18. What rhetorical figure is most prominent in the final stanza? (13–16)
19. Point out several ways in which the placement of words and arrangement of clauses in the final stanza parallel the placement of words and arrangement of clauses in the first stanza of the poem.
20. In the second and third stanzas Catullus has listed ways in which he is physically debilitated and devastated whenever he looks at Lesbia. On what does he place blame for this happening to him? (13)
21. How does Catullus rebuke himself for his employment of his leisure (ōtium)? (14)
22. How is the effect that ōtium has had on kings and wealthy cities (15–16) a heightened parallel to the effect that looking at Lesbia has on Catullus?
23. How does Catullus' excessive indulgence in ōtium (14) account for his inability to look at Lesbia and listen to her sweetly laughing the way that the man referred to by the word ille is able to do?

Comparison

Compare this poem with Catullus 50:

Catullus 50

Hesternō, Licinī, diē ōtiōsī
multum lūsimus in meīs tabellīs,
ut convēnerat esse dēlicātōs:
scrībēns versiculōs uterque nostrum
lūdēbat numerō modo hōc modo illōc,
reddēns mūtua per iocum atque vīnum.
Atque illinc abiī tuō lepōre
incēnsus, Licinī, facētiīsque,
ut nec mē miserum cibus iuvāret
nec somnus tegeret quiēte ocellōs,
sed tōtō indomitus furōre lectō
versārer, cupiēns vidēre lūcem,
ut tēcum loquerer simulque ut essem.
At dēfessa labōre membra postquam
sēmimortua lectulō iacēbant,
hoc, iūcunde, tibī poēma fēcī,
ex quō perspicerēs meum dolōrem.
Nunc audāx cave sīs, precēsque nostrās,
ōrāmus, cave dēspuās, ocelle,
nē poenās Nemesis reposcat ā tē.
Est vēmēns dea; laedere hanc cavētō.

Catullus 51

Ille mī pār esse deō vidētur,
ille, sī fās est, superāre dīvōs,
quī sedēns adversus identidem tē
    spectat et audit

dulce rīdentem, miserō quod omnīs
ēripit sēnsūs mihi: nam simul tē,
Lesbia, aspexī, nihil est super mī
    <vōcis in ōre,>

lingua sed torpet, tenuis sub artūs
flamma dēmānat, sonitū suōpte
tintinant aurēs, geminā teguntur
    lūmina nocte.

Ōtium, Catulle, tibī molestum est;
ōtiō exsultās nimiumque gestīs;
ōtium et rēgēs prius et beātās
    perdidit urbēs.

1. In what ways are Catullus' encounters with Calvus and with Lesbia similar? In what ways are they dissimilar?
2. Compare the effects suffered by Catullus from his poetic encounter with Calvus with the effects suffered by Catullus when he looks at Lesbia.
3. What role does **ōtium** play in the two poems?
4. What resolution of his plight does Catullus envision in poem 50? What resolution of his plight in poem 51 does its final stanza hint at?

Another Comparison

The first three stanzas of the poem at the left below by the Greek poetess Sappho of Lesbos (seventh to sixth centuries B.C.) provided a model for Catullus when he wrote the first three stanzas of poem 51. Compare this translation of Sappho's poem (number 31 in modern editions of her work) with Catullus' poem printed next to it. For the Greek text of Sappho's poem, see page 124.

Sappho 31

That man appears to me to be equal
to the gods, who sits opposite
you and listens to your sweet voice
    close at hand

and your lovely laughter, which truly sets
the heart in my breast aflutter,
for when I look at you for a moment, I can
    no longer speak,

but my tongue is tied, a thin
flame has at once run beneath my skin,
I cannot see even one thing with my eyes,
    my ears are buzzing,

sweat pours down me, a trembling
takes hold of all of me, I am paler
than grass, and I seem to myself little
    short of being dead.

But all must be endured. . . .

[The rest of the poem is lost.]

Catullus 51

Ille mī pār esse deō vidētur,
ille, sī fās est, superāre dīvōs,
quī sedēns adversus identidem tē
    spectat et audit

dulce rīdentem, miserō quod omnīs
ēripit sēnsūs mihi: nam simul tē,
Lesbia, aspexī, nihil est super mī
    <vōcis in ōre,>

lingua sed torpet, tenuis sub artūs
flamma dēmānat, sonitū suōpte
tintinant aurēs, geminā teguntur
    lūmina nocte.

Ōtium, Catulle, tibī molestum est;
ōtiō exsultās nimiumque gestīs;
ōtium et rēgēs prius et beātās
    perdidit urbēs.

1. What are the major changes that Catullus has made in adapting the first three stanzas of Sappho's poem?
2. What reasons can you suggest for his having made each of these changes?
3. What is Catullus doing in writing a completely different fourth stanza?

More Comparisons

Sappho 31 again

1   That man appears to me to be equal
2   to the gods, who sits opposite
3   you and listens to your sweet voice
4   close at hand

5   and your lovely laughter, which truly sets
6   the heart in my breast aflutter,
7   for when I look at you for a moment, I can
8   no longer speak,

9   but my tongue is tied, a thin
10   flame has at once run beneath my skin,
12   I cannot see even one thing with my eyes,
13   my ears are buzzing,

14   sweat pours down me, a trembling
15   takes hold of all of me, I am paler
16   than grass, and I seem to myself little
17   short of being dead.

18   But all must be endured. . . .

Sappho's description of her physical symptoms served as a model for later poets when describing women falling in love at first sight. Compare the following description by Apollonius of Rhodes (third century B.C. Hellenistic Greek poet) of Medea falling in love with Jason at first sight when she was shot by the arrow of Eros (Cupid) in *Argonautica*, Book 3. Pay particular attention to the underlined words.

> [Eros] laid the arrow-notch on the cord [of his bow] in the center, and drawing wide apart with both hands he shot at Medea; and speechless amazement seized her soul. . . . and the bolt burnt deep down in the maiden's heart, like a flame; and ever she kept darting bright glances straight at [Jason], and within her breast her heart panted fast with anguish, all remembrance left her, and her soul melted with the sweet pain. . . . so, coiling round her heart, burnt secretly Love the destroyer; and the hue of her soft cheeks went and came, now pale, now red, in her soul's distraction. (3.282–98, trans., R. C. Seaton)

Later, Medea, alone in her bedroom, is wracked by the pangs of her love for Jason:

> And fast did her heart throb within her breast. . . . and ever within anguish tortured her, a smouldering fire through her frame, and about her inner nerves

and deep down beneath the nape of the neck where the pain enters keenest, whenever the unwearied Loves direct against the heart their shafts of agony. (3.755–65, trans., R. C. Seaton)

Her physical symptoms are again catalogued when she has a rendezvous with Jason to give him the magic that will save him from the fire-breathing bulls:

The sight of him brought love-sick care. Her heart fell from out her bosom, and a dark mist came over her eyes, and a hot blush covered her cheeks. And she had no strength to lift her knees backwards or forwards, but her feet beneath were rooted to the ground. (3.961–65, trans., R. C. Seaton)

Another third century B.C. Hellenistic Greek poet, Theocritus, wrote of the love at first sight experienced by a fictional woman named Simaetha for a young man named Delphis. Simaetha describes her love at first sight:

I saw, and madness seized me, and my hapless heart was aflame. My looks faded away. No eyes had I thereafter for that show, nor know how I came home again, but some parching fever shook me, and ten days and ten nights I lay upon my bed. (*Idyll* 2.82–86, trans., A. S. F. Gow)

She then describes her second encounter with Delphis:

Chiller I turned than snow from head to foot, and from my brow, like the damp dews, started the sweat, nor could I speak a word, nay, not so much as babes that whimper in their sleep calling to their mother dear, but all my fair body grew stiff as it were a doll's. (*Idyll* 2.106–10, trans., A. S. F. Gow)

The Latin poet Lucretius, a contemporary of Catullus, borrowed Sappho's imagery to describe the effects on the body of the overwhelming emotion of fear:

But when the intelligence is moved by more vehement fear, we see the whole spirit throughout the frame share in the feeling: sweatings and pallor hence arise over the whole body, the speech falters, the voice dies away, blackness comes before the eyes, a sounding is in the ears, the limbs give way beneath; in a word we often see men fall to the ground for mental terror. (3.152–58, trans., W. H. D. Rouse and M. F. Smith)

Another Latin poet, Valerius Aedituus, writing a little before the time of Catullus, composed an epigram that seems to borrow imagery from Sappho's lyric:

Dīcere cum cōnor cūram tibi, Pamphila, cordis,
    quid mī abs tē quaeram, verba labrīs abeunt,
per pectus mānat subitō mihi sūdor:
    sīc tacitus, subidus, dum pudeō, pereō.

When I try to tell you, Pamphila, the pangs in my heart,
    what I seek from you, the words fail my lips,
sweat suddenly flows over my chest:
    thus in silence, aroused with lust, while ashamed, I perish.

1. Find the words or phrases in the translation of Sappho's poem that one might recall when reading the underlined words and phrases in the passages above. Judging from the translations of Sappho and these later poets provided above, do the descriptions of symptoms in the latter seem to have been written in such a way as to recall Sappho's poem to the reader's mind? If so, what purpose is served by such recall?

2. Sappho's is a female voice, and the descriptions of the catastrophic physical and emotional effects of love at first sight in Apollonius and Theocritus are descriptions of the effects suffered by women. Valerius Aedituus and Catullus adapted these descriptions that had by their time come to be traditionally associated with the physical and emotional suffering of women to describe their own suffering as men overcome by love. What is ironic or paradoxical about Catullus' appropriation to his own situation of Sappho and of her imagery that had become traditional in descriptions of the physical and emotional suffering of *women* falling in love at first sight?

3. How does an understanding of the tradition that lies behind Catullus' portrayal of himself in a female role as victimized by love contribute to an understanding of the unity of his poem 51, including the last stanza?

A Final Comparison

Catullus 51

Ille mī pār esse deō vidētur,
ille, sī fās est, superāre dīvōs,
quī sedēns adversus identidem tē
　　spectat et audit

dulce rīdentem, miserō quod omnīs
ēripit sēnsūs mihi: nam simul tē,
Lesbia, aspexī, nihil est super mī
　　<vōcis in ōre,>

lingua sed torpet, tenuis sub artūs
flamma dēmānat, sonitū suōpte
tintinant aurēs, geminā teguntur
　　lūmina nocte.

Ōtium, Catulle, tibī molestum est;
ōtiō exsultās nimiumque gestīs;
ōtium et rēgēs prius et beātās
　　perdidit urbēs.

Catullus 11

Fūrī et Aurēlī, comitēs Catullī,
sīve in extrēmōs penetrābit Indōs,
lītus ut longē resonante Eōā
　　tunditur undā,

sīve in Hyrcānōs Arabasve mollēs,
seu Sagās sagittiferōsve Parthōs,
sīve quae septemgeminus colōrat
　　aequora Nīlus,

sīve trāns altās gradiētur Alpēs,
Caesaris vīsēns monimenta magnī,
Gallicum Rhēnum horribile aequor ulti-
　　mōsque Brittannōs,

omnia haec, quaecumque feret voluntās
caelitum, temptāre simul parātī,
pauca nūntiāte meae puellae
　　nōn bona dicta.

cum suīs vīvat valeatque moechīs,
quōs simul complexa tenet trecentōs,
nūllum amāns vērē, sed identidem omnium
　　īlia rumpēns;

nec meum respectet, ut ante, amōrem,
quī illius culpā cecidit velut prātī
ultimī flōs, praetereunte postquam
　　tāctus arātrō est.

Gloria S. Duclos compares the two poems as follows:

> There can be no question of the link between c.11 and what was probably the first poem [Catullus] wrote to Lesbia, c.51. There are formal connections: metrical (both are in the Sapphic stanza which Catullus never otherwise used); word usage (the prosaic adverb *identidem* appears only in these two poems, significantly in the same position in the line and verse but in startlingly different contexts); source (c.51 is a partial adaptation of a poem of Sappho and the final stanza of c.11 hinges on a Sapphic image). These seem to be consciously erected signposts for Lesbia that what was begun in *ille mi par esse deo videtur* is now ended in *cecidit velut prati ultimi flos*.
>
> There are more than formal parallels between these two poems. The images of c.51 have been deliberately reversed in the fifth stanza of c.11. The first

stanza of c.51 creates a picture of quiet enchantment yet distance: a . . . figure
sits opposite Lesbia (*qui sedens adversus*, 3) and gazes at her constantly and listens to her sweet laughter; this in contrast to the poet himself who becomes wit-
less when he looks at her, so powerful is her effect upon him. What has happened to this distant enchantment in c.11? Lesbia is now shown in the closest
possible proximity (*quos simul complexa tenet*, 18), not to one . . . admirer, but to
hundreds of adulterers (*moechis . . . trecentos*, 17–18), constantly; (*identidem*, 19)
performing upon them all (*omnium*, 19) sexual acts (*ilia rumpens*, 20). The Lesbia of c.51, who was the passive recipient of the gazes of her admirers, has been
transformed into the voracious fornicator of c.11. The repetition of *identidem*
underlines Catullus' purpose. In 51.3 it describes *te spectat et audit*—a man
watches and listens to you constantly. In 11.19–20, Lesbia has become the subject, not the object, nor does she merely look and listen; she is *ilia rumpens*, and
not of just one but of all her adulterers, and all at the same time and constantly
(*identidem*). Grotesque pornography perhaps, but effective in expressing Catullus' contempt and hatred.

A comparable change has affected the poet too, between c.51 and c.11. The
man who was struck dumb by the sight of Lesbia and was almost on the point
of fainting (*lingua sed torpet . . . gemina teguntur lumina nocte*, 51.9, 11–12) has, in
c.11, revived and found an all too bitter voice. Yet in c.11 he cannot bring himself to talk directly to Lesbia, as he had done in the earlier poem; he employs
the device of intermediaries to convey his message of scorn. The intimate *te* of
c.51 has become a contemptuous third person singular in the last two stanzas of
c.11 and the simple indicatives have been transformed into the scathing com-
mands of lines 17 and 21.

C.11, then, not only recalls c.51 but is in some ways a response to that earlier enthusiasm. . . . Catullus now truly sees Lesbia for what she is, as he had not
when he first gazed on her in c.51. . . .

(Gloria S. Duclos, "Catullus 11: Atque in Perpetuum, Lesbia, Ave atque
Vale," *Arethusa* 9, 1976, 78–79)

1. Study the chiastic arrangement of themes in the two poems when set side by
   side:

Poem 11		Poem 51	
A	B	B	A
negōtium	Final parting of the ways	Love at first sight	**ōtium**
(travel and conquest)	(reminiscence of Sappho)	(adaptation of Sappho)	(destruction of kings and cities)
(lines 1–14)	(lines 21–24)	(lines 1–12)	(lines 13–16)

2. How does the theme of travel developed in lines 1–14 of poem 11 answer the
   poet's self-rebuke for excessive indulgence in **ōtium** in poem 51.13–16?
3. How does the message of Catullus' final parting from Lesbia (11.21–24) echo
   and reverse his description of his original infatuation with her (51.1–12)?

Φαίνεταί μοι κῆνος ἴσος θέοισιν
ἔμμεν' ὤνηρ, ὄττις ἐνάντιός τοι
ἰσδάνει καὶ πλάσιον ἆδυ φωνεί-
σας ὑπακούει

καὶ γελαίσας ἰμέροεν, τό μ' ἦ μὰν
καρδίαν ἐν στήθεσιν ἐπτόαισεν. . . .

That man appears to me to be equal
to the gods, who sits opposite
you and listens to your sweet voice
close at hand

and your lovely laughter, which truly sets
the heart in my breast aflutter. . . .

"Woman with Lyre"
Attic crater, 5th century B.C.
Museo Archeologico
Syracuse, Sicily

Meter: hendecasyllabic

1   **nesciō quis, nesciō quid**, indefinite pronoun [only the **quis, quid** part
    changes form; lit., *I don't know who, I don't know what*], *someone or other, some-*
    thing or other.
        nescio: iambic shortening carries over here into the compound **ne-scio.**
    modo, adv., *just now.*
    corōna, -ae f., *garland; circle* (of people), *audience, crowd* (it was a common
        sight in Rome to see a circle of bystanders gathered in or around a **basilica**,
        a Roman law court, to watch a trial).
2   **mīrificē** [**mīrus, -a, -um**, *extraordinary, remarkable* + **-ficus**, adjectival suffix,
        making, causing + **-ē**, adverbial ending], *in an amazing manner, remarkably*
        well.
    Vatīniānus, -a, -um, *of Vatinius* (Publius Vatinius, whom Calvus prosecuted
        in 58, 56, and 54 B.C.; Vatinius was a tribune of the plebs who sponsored
        bills granting Caesar Cisalpine Gaul and Illyricum, and he served with
        Caesar in Gaul. The trial referred to in Catullus' poem was probably
        Calvus' prosecution of Vatinius in 54 B.C. for illegal electioneering prac-
        tices in his successful bid for the praetorship in 56 B.C. At Caesar's behest,
        Cicero defended Vatinius, and he was acquitted. In two other poems, 14
        and 52 (not in this book), Catullus expresses intense hatred of Vatinius).
3   **crīmen, crīminis**, n., *crime, charge.*
    Vatīniāna (2) . . . **crīmina**: *charges against Vatinius.*
    Calvus, -ī, m., *Gaius Licinius Calvus* (82–ca. 47 B.C., an orator, poet, and close
        friend of Catullus; see Catullus 50 and 96).
    explicō [**ex-**, *out* + **plicō, -āre, -āvī, -ātus**, *to fold; to roll*], **-āre, -āvī, -ātus** (see
        Catullus 1.6), *to unfold, unroll; to make known, explain, give an account of.*
        explicāsset: syncope for **explicāvisset**: what mood, tense, and construc-
        tion?
4   **ait**, *(he) says.*
    haec: *these things, the following words.*
5   **salapūtium, -ī**, n. [etymology and meaning unknown, probably referring to
        a person of short stature], *little runt;* [but probably also obscene, possibly de-
        rived from **salāx, salācis**, *overly sexed, lascivious*], *rake, lecher.*
    disertus, -a, -um, *skilled in speaking, articulate.*
        salapūtium disertum: supply **est**, *the little lecher is. . . .*
            disertum: not as strong a word as **ēloquēns**. Thomson translates, *the little*
            runt can <actually> make a speech!

CATULLUS 53

An Amusing Incident at the Law Court

What is the dramatic situation of this short poem? What did Catullus find humorous?

1 Rīsī nescio quem modo ē corōnā,
2 quī, cum mīrificē Vatīniāna
3 meus crīmina Calvus explicāsset,
4 admīrāns ait haec manūsque tollēns:
5 "Dī magnī, salapūtium disertum!"

Initial Explorations

1. How does the first word of the poem create suspense?
2. Find an example of interlocking order or synchysis in lines 2–3.
3. What word earlier in the poem does line 4 recall?
4. How long is the reader held in suspense before learning what it was that Catullus laughed at?

Discussion

1. Compare this poem with Catullus 50. How do both poems express Catullus' admiration of Calvus? Is the expression of Catullus' admiration diminished in any way by quoting the word **salapūtium**, which may contain a gross obscenity?
2. What does the word **meus** tell us about the relation between Catullus and Calvus? Would it seem that this poem was written before or after Catullus 50?
3. Apart from its meter, what makes Catullus 53 poetic?

Dextrārum iūnctiō

Relief Sculpture from a Roman Sarcophagus
The wedding couple join their right hands in the presence of the **prōnuba**.
The groom holds the marriage contract in his left hand.
British Museum
London, England

A WEDDING: CATULLUS 62

On the morning of the wedding day the auspices are taken and the bride, with her hair arranged in the special style of the *sex crines*, wearing a *tunica recta* bound with a woolen girdle, a flame-coloured veil, matching shoes, and a garland, is escorted by the *pronuba* into the atrium of her parents' house. There the *pronuba* joins the right hands of the bride and groom, perhaps the most significant symbol of the wedding ceremony. Depending on the type of marriage, certain other rites are performed, usually including a sacrifice. The wedding banquet follows and extends until evening. At the sign of the evening star, preparation is made for the *domum deductio*. The bride makes a show of resistance, fleeing to her mother's bosom. She is torn away from her mother and, with two young boys holding her arms and a third preceding them with a pine torch, the procession begins. At the threshold of the groom's house the door is anointed with oil or fat and decked with woolen garlands. The bride makes a final show of resistance and is carried across the threshold into the groom's house. Throughout the day the *pronuba* has been the bride's constant attendant. It is the *pronuba* who leads the girl into the presence of the guests, who joins the right hands of the couple, who accompanies the bride in the procession, and who prepares the bride in the bridal chamber. Also, throughout the day, there are a number of significant moments at which the *pronuba* speaks ritual words or gives the bride advice.

(T. Goud, "Who Speaks the Final Lines? Catullus 62: Structure and Ritual," *Phoenix* 49, 1995, 30–31.)

sex crīnēs:	crīnis, crīnis, m., *lock of hair, tress* (Roman brides had their hair parted into six plaits, and as married women they continued to arrange it this way).
tunica rēcta:	the name of the garment worn by the bride, perhaps so called from the fact that it was woven by a weaver standing upright (**rēctus, -a, -um**) in front of a warp-weighted loom.
prōnuba:	*bride's attendant.*
domum dēductiō:	the escorting of the bride from her parents' home to the home of the groom.

Meter: dactylic hexameter

1   **vesper**, m., **vespera, -ae**, f., *evening;* **Vesper,** *the Evening Star* (Venus).
     cōnsurgō [con-, *together* + **surgō, surgere, surrēxī, surrēctūrus,** *to rise*],
        cōnsurgere, cōnsurrēxī, cōnsurrēctūrus, *to rise up/together.*
     Olympus, -ī, m., *Mount Olympus* (a mountain range in Thessaly and Mace-
        donia); *Olympus* (the home of the gods,); *the sky, the heavens.*
        Olympō: ablative of place where without a preposition.
2   **exspectāta**: *eagerly awaited.*
     lūmen, lūminis, n., *light, radiance;* pl., *rays of light.*
3   **tempus**: supply **est.**
     pinguis, -is, -e, *fat; rich; bountiful.*
     linquere: = **relinquere.**
4   **dīcētur**: here, *will be sung;* **-tur** is scanned long by diastole.
     hymenaeus, -ī, m. [Greek loan word], *refrain* (in the song sung at a wed-
        ding); here, *wedding song* (sung in the procession from the bride's house to
        the groom's).
5   **Hȳmēn** or **Hymēn,** m., *Hymen* (part of the refrain sung at a wedding; per-
        sonified as the god of weddings).
     Hymenaeus, -ī, m., *Hymenaeus* (here personified as the god of weddings).
6   **cernō, cernere, crēvī, crētus,** *to discern, distinguish; to see.*
     innūpta, -ae, f., *unmarried woman, maiden.*
     contrā, adv., *in return; opposite, facing.*
7   **nīmīrum** [**nī-**, negative adverb + **mīrum,** *it would be a wonder if . . . not*], parti-
        cle, *without doubt, clearly.*
     Oetaeus, -a, -um, *of/belonging to Mount Oeta* (a mountain in southern Thes-
        saly).
        Oetaeōs . . . ignēs: an ominous allusion; the great Greek hero Hercules
           was burned to death on Mount Oeta after having put on a cloak given
           to him by his wife, who had soaked the cloak in what she thought was
           a love potion but was actually a phosphorescent poison.   She was try-
           ing to revive his love for her after his affair with Iole.
     Noctifer, Noctiferī, m. [a Catullan coinage from **nox, noctis,** f., *night* + **-fer,**
        -fera, -ferum, adjectival suffix, *bringing*], *the Evening Star.*
8   **certēst**: = **certē est.**
     viden: = **vidēs** + **-ne**; note the iambic shortening; the singular is casually
        used although a group of people is being addressed.
     ut, adv., *how.*
     pernīciter, adv., *quickly, speedily, nimbly.*
     exsiliō [**ex-**, *out, up* + **saliō, salīre, saluī** or **saliī, salitus,** *to jump, leap*],
        exsilīre, exsiluī, *to jump/leap up.*
        exsiluēre: = **exsiluērunt,** indicative used colloquially instead of the sub-
           junctive that would be expected in the indirect question.
9   **temere,** adv., *blindly, heedlessly; without reason, for nothing.*
     pār, paris, *equal.*
        pār est: *is fit, proper, reasonable, likely.*
           quod vincere pār est: *[that] which is likely to win.*

CATULLUS 62

A Glimpse of a Wedding

Choruses of boys and girls here compete at a critical moment in a wedding ceremony. The wedding banquet is over, the evening star is rising, and a chorus of boys and a chorus of girls are about to compete in responsive song. The leader of the chorus of boys notes the rising of the evening star and directs the members of his chorus to rise. The leader of the chorus of girls sees the boys rising and directs the members of her chorus to rise in opposition.

Leader of the Chorus of Boys:

1   Vesper adest; iuvenēs, cōnsurgite; Vesper Olympō
2   exspectāta diū vix tandem lūmina tollit.
3   Surgere iam tempus, iam pinguīs linquere mēnsās;
4   iam veniet virgō, iam dīcētur hymenaeus.

Refrain:

5   Hȳmēn ō Hymenaee, Hymēn ades ō Hymenaee!

Leader of the Chorus of Girls:

6   Cernitis, innūptae, iuvenēs? Cōnsurgite contrā;
7   nīmīrum Oetaeōs ostendit Noctifer ignēs.
8   Sīc certēst; viden ut pernīciter exsiluēre?
9   Nōn temere exsiluēre; canent quod vincere pār est.

Refrain:

10 Hȳmēn ō Hymenaee, Hymēn ades ō Hymenaee!

continued

Explorations

1. What similarities can you detect between the words of the two chorus leaders? How does the leader of the chorus of girls model her words on those of the leader of the chorus of boys? (1–4 and 6–9)
2. What different attitudes do the two chorus leaders take toward the evening star in their descriptions of it? (1–2 and 7)
3. How does the leader of the chorus of girls regard the boys' actions? (6–9)

11 **aequālis, aequālis,** m./f., *a person of the same age, comrade* (of one's own age).
palma, -ae, f., *palm* (of the hand); *palm-tree; palm branch* (awarded for victory in a contest); *victory.*
parātus, -a, -um, *ready, prepared; ready at hand, ready-made, available.*
12 **aspiciō** [ad-, *to, toward* + **speciō, specere, spexī, spectus,** *to see, observe*], **aspicere, aspexī, aspectus,** *to look at; to look.*
ut, adv., *how.*
meditor, -ārī, -ātus sum, *to think about, ponder; to plan, prepare; to rehearse, practice.*
> **meditāta:** *the things they have rehearsed,* the perfect passive participle of this deponent verb is often passive in meaning.

requīrō [re-, *again* + **quaerō, quaerere, quaesīvī, quaesītus,** *to seek, look for*], **requīrere, requīsīvī, requīsītus,** *to ask, inquire; to seek out, look/search for.*
> **requīrunt:** indicative (cf. **exsiluēre** in line 8); the **ut** clause here does not depend grammatically on **aspicite,** but the latter is simply a parenthetical interjection.

13 **memorābilis, -is, -e,** *worthy of being recorded, remarkable, memorable.*
> **memorābile quod sit:** relative clause of characteristic; note the delayed relative pronoun.

14 **nec mīrum:** *and no wonder, it is not surprising;* cf. **nīmīrum** (7).
penitus, adv., *deep within.*
labōrō, -āre, -āvī, -ātus, intransitive, *to work;* transitive, *to work on, labor over.*
> **quae . . . labōrant:** delayed relative pronoun; the relative clause here expresses cause, *since they. . . . ,* and would normally have its verb in the subjunctive.

15 **aliō . . . aliō:** *in one direction . . . in another direction.*
dīvidō, dīvidere, dīvīsī, dīvīsus, *to divide, separate, separate off.*
auris, auris, f., *ear.*
> **aliō mentēs, aliō dīvīsimus aurēs:** in contrast to the girls, who are inwardly concentrating all of their mental effort, the boys' attention is divided between their thoughts and what they hear.

16 **iūs, iūris,** n., *law.*
> **iūre:** abl., *rightly, justifiably.*

17 **saltem,** adv., *at least, anyway.*
convertō [con-, intensive prefix + **vertō, vertere, vertī, versus,** *to turn*], *to turn* (upside down or around); *to direct, concentrate* (one's mind).

Leader of the Chorus of Boys:

11   Nōn facilis nōbīs, aequālēs, palma parāta est;

12   aspicite, innūptae sēcum ut meditāta requīrunt.

13   Nōn frūstrā meditantur: habent memorābile quod sit;

14   nec mīrum, penitus quae tōtā mente labōrant.

15   Nōs aliō mentēs, aliō dīvīsimus aurēs;

16   iūre igitur vincēmur: amat victōria cūram.

17   Quārē nunc animōs saltem convertite vestrōs;

18   dīcere iam incipient, iam respondēre decēbit.

Refrain:

19   Hȳmēn ō Hymenaee, Hymēn ades ō Hymenaee!

continued

Explorations

4.   How do the opening remarks of the leader of the chorus of boys (11–14) relate to what the leader of the chorus of girls has just said?

5.   How does the attitude of the girls toward the singing match differ from that of the boys? (12–17)

20 **Hesperus, -ī**, m., *Hesperus* (the evening star).
quis: interrogative adjective here instead of the usual **quī**; take with **ignis**.
caelō: = **in caelō**.
fertur: *is carried/borne*.

21 **Quī . . . possīs**: relative clause expressing cause, with the subjunctive, as
normal; **possīs**, *have the heart to, can bear to* (Fordyce).
nāta, -ae, f., *daughter*.
complexū: ablative of separation.
āvellō [**ab-**, *away* + **vellō, vellere, vellī** or **vulsī** or **volsī, vulsus** or **volsus**, *to
pull, pluck*], **āvellī** or **āvulsī** or **āvolsī, āvulsus** or **āvolsus**, *to pull/pluck/tear
away*.

22 **retineō** [**re-**, *back* + **teneō, tenēre, tenuī, tentus**, *to hold, grasp*], *to hold back, hold
fast, cling to*.
  retinentem: supply **mātrem** as direct object.

23 **ārdentī**: i.e., with passion or lust.

24 **captā . . . urbe**: ablative absolute expressing time, not comparative ablative
with **crūdēlius**.

26 **caelō**: = **in caelō**.

27 **firmō, -āre, -āvī, -ātus**, *to make strong, reinforce, establish, confirm*.
  Quī . . . firmēs: see note to line 21.
cōnūbium, -ī, n. [**con-**, *together* + **nūbō, nūbere, nūpsī, nūptūrus**, *to marry*],
marriage.

28 **pangō, pangere, pepigī, pactus**, *to set, fix; to arrange* (a matter such as a
wedding).
  pepigēre: = **pepigērunt**.

29 **iūnxēre**: supply **cōnūbia** from line 27 as the object.
prius quam: *earlier than* = **priusquam**, conj., *before*.
ārdor, ārdōris, m. (see Catullus 2.8), *fire; heat*.

30 **dīvus, -ī**, m., *god*.
fēlīx, fēlīcis, *fruitful, productive; lucky, auspicious; blessed, fortunate; happy; having a happy issue, successful; prosperous, wealthy*.
  fēlīcī . . . hōrā: what translation of **fēlīcī** is most appropriate here?
optātus, -a, -um, *desired, welcome*.

The chorus of girls begins the singing match:

20   Hespere, quis caelō fertur crūdēlior ignis?

21   Quī nātam possīs complexū āvellere mātris,

22   complexū mātris retinentem āvellere nātam,

23   et iuvenī ārdentī castam dōnāre puellam.

24   Quid faciunt hostēs captā crūdēlius urbe?

Refrain:

25   Hȳmēn ō Hymenaee, Hymēn ades ō Hymenaee!

The chorus of boys responds:

26   Hespere, quis caelō lūcet iūcundior ignis?

27   Quī dēspōnsa tuā firmēs cōnūbia flammā,

28   quae pepigēre virī, pepigērunt ante parentēs,

29   nec iūnxēre prius quam sē tuus extulit ārdor.

30   Quid datur ā dīvīs fēlīcī optātius hōrā?

Refrain:

31   Hȳmēn ō Hymenaee, Hymēn ades ō Hymenaee!

continued

Explorations

6.   How do the girls' and the boys' conceptions of Hesperus differ, and how does this reflect their different attitudes toward the institution of marriage? (20–24 and 26–30)

7.   What words do the boys repeat from the girls' song in the same metrical positions? (20–24 and 26–30) What phrase of the girls do the boys reflect in their words **fēlīcī optātius hōrā** (30)?

8.   How do the changes that the boys make in lines 26 and 30 reflect their different view of marriage from that of the girls?

9.   Analyze the relationship between word-placement and meaning in lines 21–23.

10.   How does the chorus of boys in lines 27–29 respond to the apprehension and anxiety over marriage expressed by the girls in lines 21–24?

33 **namque**, conj., *for*.
    adventus, -ūs, m., *arrival*.
    custōdia, -ae, f., *protection, defense;* concrete, *a guard, watchman*.
34 **saepe**, adv., *often; many times, time and again*.
    revertor [**re-**, *back* + **vertō, vertere, vertī, versus**, *to turn*], **revertī, reversus sum**, *to turn around; to return*.
35 **mūtō, -āre, -āvī, -ātus**, *to change*.
    comprendō [**con-**, *together* or intensive + **prendō, prendere, prendī, prēnsus**, *to take hold of*], *to take hold of; to catch, find, come upon*.
    Eōus, -ī, m. [**Ēōs**, f. (Greek loan word), *Dawn*], *the Morning Star* (Venus appears in the evening as the Evening Star and in the morning as the Morning Star, thus **īdem**, line 34, but at different times of the year, not one evening and the next morning as implied here).
        Eōus: in apposition with the subject of **comprendis**, *you catch [as] the Morning Star*.
36 **lubet**: archaic for **libet**, impersonal + dat., *(it) is pleasing* (to).
    fictus, -a, -um, *made up, pretended, false*.
    carpō, carpere, carpsī, carptus, *to pluck, pick; to criticize, carp at*.
    questus, -ūs, m., *complaint, protest*.
37 **sī carpunt**: supply **tē**.
    tacitus, -a, -um, *silent, quiet; secret*.

The chorus of girls compares Hesperus to a thief; only the first line of the stanza has survived:

32   Hesperus ē nōbīs, aequālēs, abstulit ūnam.

32b   .   .   .

32c   .   .   .

32d   .   .   .

32e   .   .   .

32f   .   .   .

Refrain:

32g   <Hȳmēn ō Hymenaee, Hymēn ades ō Hymenaee!>

The chorus of boys, in a stanza missing its first line, replies that when evening comes guards are wakeful and that the Evening Star, when appearing as the Morning Star, catches thieves:

32h   .   .

33   namque tuō adventū vigilat custōdia semper.

34   Nocte latent fūrēs, quōs īdem saepe revertēns,

35   Hespere, mūtātō comprendis nōmine Eōus

36   at lubet innūptīs fictō tē carpere questū.

37   Quid tum, sī carpunt, tacitā quem mente requīrunt?

Refrain:

38   Hȳmēn ō Hymenaee, Hymēn ades ō Hymenaee!

continued

Explorations

11. How does the girls' comparison of Hesperus to a thief (32) relate to their earlier description of Hesperus' actions (20–24)?
12. How does the part of the boys' reply preserved in lines 33–35 counter the girls' complaint that Hesperus is a thief?
13. Of what do the boys accuse the girls in lines 36–37?

39 **saepiō, saepīre, saepsī, saeptus,** *to surround, enclose.*
sēcrētus, -a, -um, *set apart; secret, hidden.*
nāscor, nāscī, nātus sum, *to be born; to grow.*
hortus, -ī, m., *garden;* pl., *pleasure-garden.*

40 **ignōtus, -a, -um,** *unknown.*
convellō [con-, intensive prefix + **vellō, vellere, vulsī, vulsus,** *to pull, pluck*], **convellere, convellī, convulsus,** *to pull/tear up, uproot.*
arātrum, -ī, n., *plow.*

41 **mulceō, mulcēre, mulsī, mulsus,** *to caress.*
aura, -ae, f., *breeze.*
firmō, -āre, -āvī, -ātus, *to strengthen.*
ēdūcō [ex-, *out* + **dūcō, dūcere, dūxī, ductus,** *to lead, take, bring*], **-āre, -āvī, -ātus,** *to bring up, nurture, rear.*

41b This line has been lost from the manuscripts; the **iam iam,** *now all but,* is a conjecture based on the beginning of the corresponding line of the next stanza.

42 **optāvēre:** = **optāvērunt**; here and below, the gnomic perfect, a Greek usage, expressing a general truth; translate as present.

43 **tenuis, -is, -e,** *thin.*
dēflōrēscō [dē-, *down* or expressing reversal + **flōreō, -ēre, -uī,** *to bloom* + -scō, inceptive suffix], **dēflōrēscere, dēflōruī,** inceptive, *to lose its blossom.*
unguis, unguis, m., *fingernail.*

45 **dum . . . dum:** *as long as . . . so long,* although the second **dum** need not be translated.
intāctus, -a, -um, *untouched.*

46 **castum . . . flōrem:** = **castitātis flōrem,** *the flower of her chastity.*
āmittō [ab-, *away* + **mittō, mittere, mīsī, missus,** *to send, let go*], **āmittere, āmīsī, āmissus,** *to send away; to lose.*

46 **polluō, polluere, polluī, pollūtus,** *to stain, violate, sully.*

The chorus of girls begins another theme:

39 Ut flōs in saeptīs sēcrētus nāscitur hortīs,

40 ignōtus pecorī, nūllō convulsus arātrō,

41 quem mulcent aurae, firmat sōl, ēducat imber;

41b \<iam iam   .   .   .   \>

42 multī illum puerī, multae optāvēre puellae:

43 īdem cum tenuī carptus dēflōruit unguī,

44 nūllī illum puerī, nūllae optāvēre puellae:

45 sīc virgō, dum intācta manet, dum cāra suīs est;

46 cum castum āmīsit pollūtō corpore flōrem,

47 nec puerīs iūcunda manet, nec cāra puellīs.

Refrain:

48 Hȳmēn ō Hymenaee, Hymēn ades ō Hymenaee!

continued

Explorations

14. What is the final argument against marriage that the girls make? (39–47)
15. The girls develop an elaborate simile comparing virginity or a virgin girl to a flower. How do details of the simile recall objections that the chorus of girls has already leveled against marriage? How do details of the simile counter what the boys have said in defense of the institution of marriage?

Comparison

Some scholars believe that the comparison of the maiden to a flower contained in the lines above may have been suggested to Catullus by the same Sapphic image that is thought to have suggested the image of the flower cut down by the passing plow in Catullus 11.22–24. (See Catullus 11 above, Discussion question 3.) This image is contained in Sappho fragment 105a:

> like the hyacinth that shepherds trample under foot in the mountains, and the purple flower \<lies crushed\> on the ground. . . .

As Gloria S. Duclos explains: "In the Sapphic fragment, the hyacinth trampled by the shepherds is presumably likened to a maiden's virginity. The passage in c.62 explicitly compares the plucked flower to a girl's maidenhood. The image, then, is traditionally used to express the finality of a girl's loss of her virginity."
(Gloria S. Duclos, "Catullus 11: Atque in perpetuum, Lesbia, ave atque vale," *Arethusa* 9, 1976, 86)

49   **viduus, -a, -um**, *lacking a husband/wife; of a grape vine, not trained* (on a prop
      or a tree to support it), *not married* (to a prop or a tree to support it), *unwed.*

      nūdus, -a, -um, *naked; bare, exposed* (i.e., without trees on which grapevines
      could be trained).

      vītis, vītis, f., *grapevine.*

      arvum, -ī, n., *plowed field.*

50   **extollō** [**ex-**, *out* + **tollō, tollere, sustulī, sublātus**, *to lift, raise*], **extollere**, *to lift
      up, raise.*

      mītis, -is, -e, *gentle; of fruit, sweet and juicy.*

51   **tener, tenera, tenerum**, *tender, delicate.*

      prōnus, -a, -um, *leaning forward, bending down, downward leaning.*

      dēflectō [**dē-**, *down* + **flectō, flectere, flexī, flexus**, *to bend*], **dēflectere,
      dēflexī, dēflexus**, *to bend down.*

      pondus, ponderis, n., *weight.*

      prōnō . . . pondere: transferred epithet.

52   **iam iam**: *now [it] all but.*

      contingō [**con-**, intensive + **tangō, tangere, tetigī, tāctus**, *to touch*], **contin-
      gere, contigī, contāctus**, *to touch.*

      rādīx, rādīcis, f., *root.*

      flagellum, -ī, n. [dim. of **flagrum, -ī**, n., *whip*], *whip; young shoot of a grapevine.*

53   **agricola, -ae**, m., *farmer.*

      coluēre: see note on **optāvēre** (42).

      iuvencus, -ī, m., *young bull/ox.*

54   **ulmus, -ī**, f., *elm tree.*

      marītō: noun, *[as] husband*, in apposition with **ulmō** (feminine); the elm tree
      is thought of metaphorically as the husband and the grape-vine as its wife,
      clinging to it. Thomson prints **marītā**, adjective, *married*, modifying **ulmō**
      (feminine)

56   **innūpta**: the manuscripts have **intācta** here, making the word parallel to its
      appearance in line 45, but we may substitute **innūpta** from the fact that the
      ancient writer on education, Quintilian (9.3.16), gives line 45 as **dum in-
      nūpta manet, dum cāra suīs est**, probably quoting from memory and
      confusing lines 45 and 56, putting **innūpta** in line 45 where it does not be-
      long because he remembered the word from line 56 where it does belong.

      incultus, -a, -um, of land or plants, *not cultivated*; of people, *unadorned; un-
      courted; not cultivated/untended* (by relatives, friends, or acquaintances).

      senēscō senēscere, senuī, inceptive, *to grow old.*

57   **pār, paris**, *equal; similar; matching; well-matched.*

      cōnūbium, -ī, n., *marriage; a marriage partner.*

      cōnubium: the first *u* is usually long, but it is scanned as short here; or scan
      the word as three syllables **cōnūbyum** (synaeresis).

      mātūrus, -a, -um, *ripe; fully-grown*; of time, *proper, due.*

      adipīscor, adipīscī, adeptus sum, *to get, obtain.*

58   **invīsus, -a, -um**, *hateful.*

      invīsa parentī: daughters were thought of as burdens on their fathers.

The chorus of boys replies:

49 Ut vidua in nūdō vītis quae nāscitur arvō,

50 numquam sē extollit, numquam mītem ēducat ūvam,

51 sed tenerum prōnō dēflectēns pondere corpus

52 iam iam contingit summum rādīce flagellum;

53 hanc nūllī agricolae, nūllī coluēre iuvencī:

54 at sī forte eadem est ulmō coniūncta marītō,

55 multī illam agricolae, multī coluēre iuvencī:

56 sic virgō, dum innūpta manet, dum inculta senēscit;

57 cum pār cōnubium mātūrō tempore adepta est,

58 cāra virō magis et minus est invīsa parentī.

Refrain:

58b <Hȳmēn ō Hymenaee, Hymēn ades ō Hymenaee!>

continued

Explorations

16. The boys reply by proposing a different simile. To what do they compare an unwed maiden?

17. The boys in their reply repeat many of the words of the girls, usually in the same metrical positions. Locate all such repetitions. In a number of cases the boys echo words, phrases, and lines from the song of the girls but vary them by substituting different words. Locate all such echoes.

18. How does the simile of the vine reverse the implications of the simile of the flower to present a positive rather than a negative conception of marriage?

59   **nē pugnā**: an archaic form of negative imperative.
60   **aequus, -a, -um**, *level; equal; fair, right.*
      aequum est, idiom, *it is right.*
      pater cui: delayed relative, lacking an antecedent; expand the line as follows: **Nōn aequum est pugnāre [eī] cui pater [tē] trādidit ipse**. The verb **pugnāre** can take a dative as suggested here and as in line 64 below, or it can take a prepositional phrase (**cum** + abl.).
62   **virginitās, virginitātis**, f., *virginity.*
      parentum est: possessive genitive, *belongs to your parents.*
63   **patrīst**: = **patrī est**, dative of the possessor; Thomson prints **patris est**.
65   **gener, generī**, m., *son-in-law.*
      iūs, iūris, n., *law; claims; rights.*
      dōs, dōtis, f., *dowry* (wealth brought by a bride to her husband at marriage).

The leader of the girls' chorus addresses the bride*:

58c   .   .   .

59   Et tū nē pugnā cum tālī coniuge, virgō.

60   Nōn aequum est pugnāre, pater cui trādidit ipse,

61   ipse pater cum mātre, quibus parēre necesse est.

62   Virginitās nōn tōta tua est, ex parte parentum est,

63   tertia pars patrīst, pars est data tertia mātrī,

64   tertia sōla tua est: nōlī pugnāre duōbus,

65   quī generō sua iūra simul cum dōte dedērunt.

Refrain:

66   Hȳmēn ō Hymenaee, Hymēn ades ō Hymenaee!

*See Initial Exploration question 19 below.

Explorations

19. It is not certain to whom the last stanza should be assigned. In the past it was usually assigned to the chorus of boys, but Goud in a recent analysis of the structure of the poem as a whole concludes that it should be assigned to the leader of the chorus of girls, thus balancing the stanza comprised of lines 11–18, spoken by the leader of the chorus of boys. If this is so, then how should the structure of the entire poem be diagrammed?

20. How does the stanza above correspond to the stanza spoken by the leader of the chorus of boys in lines 11–18? Which side of the singing match does the leader of the chorus of girls appear to favor here? Is there a winner and a loser?

21. What explanation does the leader of the chorus of girls give for why the bride should not fight against marriage but should obey her parents?

22. What relationship does the explanation that the leader of the chorus of girls gives to the bride have to concerns expressed by the choruses in the singing match?

23. Situate the action of the poem in the sequence of events in a wedding as described in the paragraph preceding this poem.

Meter: elegiac couplet

1   **Nūllī**: substantive = **Nēminī**, *No one*, dative with **nūbere**.
    dīcit . . . mulier mea: the verb of the main clause of the sentence (**dīcit**) and
      its subject (**mulier mea**) are embedded in the indirect statement, **Nūllī sē
      . . . nūbere mālle**. Explain the construction of each infinitive in this line.
2   **nōn sī**: *not [even] if.*
    Iuppiter, Iovis, m., *Jupiter, Jove* (king of the gods).
    petat: what mood and tense? This is the first half (protasis) of a future-less-
      vivid condition. How is the protasis of this type of conditional sentence
      translated?
3   **mulier . . . quod dīcit**: delayed relative without an antecedent, *[that]
      which/what a woman says. . . .* This clause is the object of **scrībere** in line 4.
    cupidus, -a, -um [**cupiō, cupere, cupīvī, cupītus**, *to desire, want* + **-idus, -a,
      -um**, adjectival suffix], *passionately longing, desirous, eager.*
    amāns, amantis, m., *lover.*
4   **rapidus, -a, -um** [**rapiō, rapere, rapuī, raptus**, *to snatch, seize* + **-idus, -a,
      -um**, adjectival suffix], *flowing so violently as to carry anything along in its
      path, strong flowing, swiftly moving.*
    scrībere oportet: the infinitive with its object clause is the grammatical sub-
      ject of the impersonal verb, *to write what a woman says . . . is fitting = one ought
      to write. . . .* The language is proverbial; the Greek tragedian Sophocles (ca.
      496–406 B.C.) wrote: "I write the oath of a woman onto water." Other ex-
      amples of the proverb speak of writing on water (as here) and of letting
      winds *carry words away* rather than of *writing on the wind* (as here).

CATULLUS 70

Words, Words, Words!

This is one of several poems in which Catullus tries to analyze the failure of his love affair with Lesbia. Here he adapts an epigram from the Greek poet Callimachus.

1   Nūllī sē dīcit mulier mea nūbere mālle
2   quam mihi, nōn sī sē Iuppiter ipse petat.
3   Dīcit; sed mulier cupidō quod dīcit amantī,
4   in ventō et rapidā scrībere oportet aquā.

Comparison

Catullus adapted this epigram from an epigram of the Greek poet Callimachus (ca. 305–ca. 240 B.C.). Here is a translation of Callimachus' epigram:

1   Callignotus swore to Ionis that he would hold
2   neither man nor woman dearer than her.
3   He swore: the truth is that lovers' oaths
4   do not enter the ears of the immortals.
5   Now he burns for a man, while of the poor girl,
6   as of the Megarians, there is no word or record.
                                  —*Palatine Anthology* 5.6

The names Callignotus and Ionis are purely fictional. The Megarians were proverbial for being of no account whatsoever.

Explorations

1. Which lines of Callimachus' poem has Catullus used?
2. What are the similarities between Catullus' epigram and the first two couplets of Callimachus'?
3. Of what significance are the following differences between Catullus' epigram and the first two couplets of Callimachus'?
    a. Callimachus is writing about fictional characters, while Catullus is writing about himself and his **mulier**.
    b. In Callimachus' epigram it is a man who swears the oath, while in Catullus it is a woman who makes the statement.
    c. Catullus has introduced the idea of marriage and the possibility of marriage with Jupiter.
4. Why do you suppose Catullus did not use Callimachus' third couplet?

Meter: elegiac couplet

1   **quondam**, adv., *formerly.*
    sōlum: modifying **Catullum**.
    nōscō, nōscere, nōvī, nōtus, inceptive, *to get to know, learn;* perfect, *to know*
        (a person or thing).
        nōsse: syncope for **nōvisse**.
            sōlum tē nōsse Catullum: ambiguous, *that you knew only Catullus*
                (with **tē** as subject of the infinitive) or *that only Catullus knew you*
                (with **tē** as object of the infinitive).
2   **prae**, prep. + abl., *instead of, before.*
    Iuppiter, Iovis, m., *Jupiter, Jove* (king of the gods).
        nec prae mē velle tenēre Iovem: supply **tē** from line 1 as the subject of
            velle; now the ambiguity of line 1 is eliminated and **tē** must be taken as
            the subject of the infinitive there.
3   **nōn tantum**: *not only,* picked up in the next line by **sed**; the usual idiom
        would have **sed etiam**, *but also.*
    vulgus, -ī, n., *the common people, general public.*
        ut vulgus amicam: supply **dīligit**; **amīcam** here = *courtesan, prostitute.*
4   **gnātus** (= **nātus**), **-ī**, m., *son.*
    gener, generī, m., *son-in-law.*
5   **cognōscō** [**con-**, intensive prefix + **nōscō**, see above], **cognōscere,**
        cognōvī, cognitus, inceptive, *to get to know, learn, become acquainted with;*
        perfect, *to have come to understand, to know* (a person or thing).
    etsī, conj., *even if, although.*
    impēnsē, adv.; comparative **impēnsius** [perhaps from perfect passive par-
        ticiple of **impendō, impendere, impendī, impēnsus**, *to pay out, disburse,*
        spend; to spend to no purpose, waste], *to an immoderate degree, without stint, lav-*
        ishly; comparative, *to a more immoderate degree, more heavily; more lavishly, at*
        greater expense, more earnestly.
    ūrō, ūrere, ūssī, ūstus, *to destroy by fire, burn; to heat by fire, roast; to inflame*
        with desire.
6   **vīlis, -is, -e**, *costing little, cheap; worthless; contemptible; of low rank, common, or-*
        dinary.
    levis, -is, -e, *light in weight; of little worth, insignificant, trivial; unreliable, in-*
        constant, fickle.
7   **quī**, adv. [old ablative form], *how.*
    potis or **pote**, indeclinable adjective + infinitive (see Catullus 45.5), *having the*
        power (to), *able* (to).
        potis est: = **potest**; supply **fierī**.
    amāns, amantis, m., *lover.*
    iniūria, -ae, f., *unlawful conduct; a wrong, an injustice* (here specifically of un-
        faithfulness, which a husband would punish in a wife by divorcing her, but
        which a lover must put up with).
8   **bene velle**, idiom, *to wish* (a person) *well* (used of normal friendly feelings be-
        tween two people).

CATULLUS 72

Now I know you!

In this poem Catullus probes deeper into his complex feelings for Lesbia.

1 Dīcēbās quondam sōlum tē nōsse Catullum,
2   Lesbia, nec prae mē velle tenēre Iovem.
3 Dīlēxī tum tē nōn tantum ut vulgus amīcam,
4   sed pater ut gnātōs dīligit et generōs.
5 Nunc tē cognōvī; quārē, etsī impēnsius ūror,
6   multō mī tamen es vīlior et levior.
7 Quī potis est, inquis? Quod amantem iniūria tālis
8   cōgit amāre magis, sed bene velle minus.

Explorations

1. Compare this poem with Catullus 70. What are the similarities and differences?
2. What has Catullus borrowed in this poem from Callimachus' epigram (see Catullus 70) that he did not borrow in poem 70?
3. How is what Lesbia is reported to have said in lines 1 and 2 of poem 72 different from what the **mulier** is reported to say in the first two lines of poem 70?
4. How does Catullus define his love for Lesbia in lines 3–4?
5. What has Catullus come to know (5) and what effect has that knowledge had on him (5–6)?
6. What is accomplished by the addition of the final couplet, introduced by Lesbia's reported question?
7. Examine the relationship between the sentences and clauses in this epigram and the metrical structures of the hexameter and the pentameter lines. How do the grammatical and metrical structures enhance the meaning expressed in each of the couplets?
8. Locate significant placement of words and repetition of words, rhythms, and sounds in the epigram. How do they enhance the meaning?

Meter: elegiac couplet

1 **quisquam, quisquam, quicquam**, indefinite pronoun, *anyone, anything.*
   quicquam: adverbial, *in any way* (at all).
  velle . . . / . . . putāre (2): complementary infinitives dependent on **dēsine**.
   Explain the use of the infinitives **merērī, fierī**, and **posse** (1–2).
  mereor, -ērī, -itus sum, *to deserve.*
    bene merērī + dē + abl., *to deserve well* (of someone), *to have a claim on some-*
     one's gratitude.

2 **pius, -a, -um**, *faithful to one's moral, religious, or social obligations that are sanc-*
   tioned by the gods; dutiful, devout, loyal.

3 **ingrātus, -a, -um**, *ungrateful, thankless; not received with gratitude, unappreci-*
   ated.
    omnia . . . ingrāta: **omnia** could mean *the whole world*, in which case **in-**
     grāta would have the first of its meanings given above, or it could
     mean *all the things one does*, in which case **ingrāta** would have the sec-
     ond of its meanings given above.
  nihil: with **prōdest** (4).
  benignē, adv., *with friendliness, kindly, generously.*

4 **prōsum, prōdesse, prōfuī**, *to be of use; to help; to be beneficial.*
    nihil (3) . . . / **prōdest**: **nihil** is adverbial; the infinitive phrase **fēcisse be-**
     nignē (3) is the subject. See below for a different version of lines 3–4.
  immō, particle serving to correct a previous statement, *rather.*
  obsum, obesse, obfuī + dat., *to get in the way* (of), *be harmful* (to).
    taedet obestque: the infinitive phrase **fēcisse benignē** is still the subject.
  magis, adv., *more; rather, instead.*

5 **ut mihi**: take as dative with **obest** (4).
  quem nēmō . . . quam (6) **. . . quī**: *whom no one . . . than . . . [he] who. . . .*
  acerbus, -a, -um, *bitter; cruel; distressing.*
    gravius . . . acerbius: what does the ending on these words indicate?
  urgeō, urgēre, ursī, *to press, weigh down, oppress.*

6 **modo**, adv., *just now.*
  ūnicus, -a, -um, *only, sole.*
  habeō, habēre, habuī, habitus, *to have, hold; to consider;* here with double
   predicate, *to regard/treat X as Y.*

Text

3–4 The word **prōdest** at the beginning of line 4 is not in the manuscripts but has
   been supplied by modern editors to fill out the metrical pattern of the line.
   Thomson proposes a different reading for lines 3 and 4 as follows, supply-
   ing the words in brackets:
     3   Omnia sunt ingrāta, nihil fēcisse benignē <est>;
     4   immō etiam taedet, <taedet> obestque magis;
   The verb **est** and the second **taedet** have been supplied; **nihil . . . est**
   means *is no good*, and the subject of **est** is **fēcisse benignē**, which is also the
   subject of **taedet, <taedet> obestque.**

CATULLUS 73

Ingratitude Everywhere

The poet complains that no good deed goes unpunished.

1   Dēsine dē quōquam quicquam bene velle merērī
2   aut aliquem fierī posse putāre pium.
3   Omnia sunt ingrāta, nihil fēcisse benignē
4   <prōdest,> immō etiam taedet obestque magis;
5   ut mihi, quem nēmō gravius nec acerbius urget
6   quam modo quī mē ūnum atque ūnicum amīcum habuit.

Explorations

1.   How does the large number of infinitives (five of them) in lines 1–2 affect your ability to comprehend what is being expressed in these lines? Does the similarity of sound of the words **quōquam**, **quicquam**, and **aliquem** help or hinder your understanding of the meaning of the lines? How does alliteration bind the words together? What is the tone of the lines?
2.   Which version of lines 3–4 is more effective?
3.   What is the logical relationship of the second couplet to the first?
4.   The words **merērī** (1), **pium** (2), **ingrāta** (3), **benignē** (3), and **prōdest** (4) refer to traditional values in Roman society. These values put great store in a network of mutual loyalties, favors, and gratitude between individuals, between individuals and the state, and between individuals and the gods. What view does Catullus urge that the reader take of these mutual interrelationships in the first two couplets of this poem?
5.   What is the effect of the elisions in the last line of the poem?
6.   What imagery (use of descriptive language to represent people or objects, often appealing to our senses) does Catullus use in this poem, if any? How many nouns can you find? Of what significance are your findings? From what does this poem draw its power?
7.   Some scholars believe that Catullus arranged his poems in essentially the order in which they are preserved in the manuscripts; others believe that the arrangement is due to an editor who collected Catullus' poems after his death. Why would either Catullus or an editor put poem 73 after poem 72?

Meter: elegiac couplet

1   dēdūcō [dē-, *down, from, away* + dūcō, dūcere, dūxī, ductus, *to lead, take,*
      bring], dēdūcere, dēdūxī, dēductus, *to lead down; to lead off/along* (to a cer-
      tain destination); *to bring down, reduce* (to a certain state or condition).
     culpa, -ae, f., *fault, blame; wrongdoing;* (of sexual misconduct) *infidelity.*
        culpā: ablative of cause; see Catullus 11.22.
2   officium, -ī, n., *a helpful/beneficial act* (done to someone to whom one owes an
        obligation); *duty, obligation, commitment, devotion* (to a person, to the state);
        function, job (i.e., what one does to fulfill one's role).
        officiō . . . suō: *by its own function/job; by its own commitment/devotion.*
     ipsa: i.e., mēns.
3   ut: does this introduce a purpose or result clause here? How do you know?
     bene velle: see Catullus 72.8.
     queō, quīre, quīvī or quiī, *to be able.*
     tibi: dative with bene velle.
     sī optima fīās: what type of conditional clause?
4   dēsistō [dē-, *down, from, away* + sistō, sistere, stetī, status, *to cause* (a person
        or thing) *to stand*], dēsistere, dēstitī, *to cease.*
     omnia: [*anything and*] *everything* = the worst things possible.

Text

1   mea: Thomson takes this as modifying **Lesbia** instead of **mēns** and places
      the comma after **tuā**, thus:
             1   Hūc est mēns dēducta tuā, mea Lesbia, culpā

CATULLUS 75

The Love-Hate Deepens.

Catullus admits in this short poem that personal reflection and analysis have worsened his condition.

1   Hūc est mēns dēducta tuā mea, Lesbia, culpā
2   atque ita sē officiō perdidit ipsa suō,
3   ut iam nec bene velle queat tibi, sī optima fīās,
4   nec dēsistere amāre, omnia sī faciās.

Explorations

1. Catullus has put strong emphasis on the opening word, **Hūc**. To what state of mind does **Hūc** refer? How does the compound verb **est . . . dēducta** color the assertion?
2. In lines 1–2, what is Catullus claiming he did and that Lesbia did not do? Consider the words **culpā** (1) and **officiō** (2) in your answer. What is the consequence of Catullus' actions according to line 2?
3. In your own words state what the last two lines say. The phrase **bene velle** (3) clearly relates this poem to Catullus 72, where the same phrase is used in the final line. What are the similarities and the differences between the two poems?
4. Specific words in Catullus 73 highlight traditional Roman values based on mutual loyalties, favors, and gratitude between individuals. What words in Catullus 75 highlight these values? Are any words of this sort found in Catullus 72?
5. Read the poem in meter. Where do you feel that the first comma should go in line 1? Find a chiastic arrangement of words in lines 1 and 2. Analyze the parallel structure of lines 3 and 4. How many elisions do you find? Why are the ones in line 4 so effective?

Meter: elegiac couplet

1 **quī, qua, quod**, indefinite adjective after **sī**, *any*.
   qua: sometimes written together with the **sī** as one word, **sīqua**; the indef-
     inite adjective modifies **voluptās**.
  recordor [re-, *back, again* + **cor, cordis**, n., *heart, mind*], **-ārī, -ātus sum**, *to call*
  to mind, recollect.
  recordantī . . . hominī (2): dative of possession.
  benefactum, -ī, n., *kindness, good deed*.
   benefacta: one's own good deeds. See Catullus 73.3, **fēcisse benignē**.
2 **esse**: not simply *is*, but *has been and still is*.
  pium: see Catullus 73.2.
3 **nec . . . nec**: *and not . . . and not*.
  violō, -āre, -āvī, -ātus, *to violate, break*.
   violāsse: syncope for **violāvisse**.
  nec . . . nūllō: double negative, *and not in any*. Thomson prints **in ūllō**, elim-
    inating the double negative.
  foedus, foederis, n., *formal agreement, treaty; compact*.
   fidēs . . . foedere: note the alliteration of **fid- . . . foed-** in these key
    words.
4 **dīvus, -ī**, m., *god*.
   dīvum: syncope for **dīvōrum**; take with **nūmine**.
  fallō, fallere, fefellī, falsus, *to deceive*.
   ad fallendōs . . . hominēs: what form is **fallendōs**? How do you trans-
    late it with **ad**?
  nūmen, nūminis, n., *divinity, power*.
   nūmine: what case and why?
  abūtor, abūtī, abūsus sum + abl., *to abuse, misuse*.
   abūsum: supply **esse**.
5 **parō, -āre, -āvī, -ātus**, *to prepare, get ready; to produce, bring about; to win, earn*.
   multa parāta: with **gaudia** (6).
  aetās, aetātis, f., *age* (the years of one's life).
   in longā aetāte: *in the long years ahead, for the remainder of your life, over a*
    long life.
6 **ingrātō**: see the meanings given at Catullus 73.3.
7 **quīcumque, quaecumque, quodcumque**, indefinite relative pronoun, *who-*
  ever, whatever.
  bene: take with **dīcere** and **facere** (8).
  quisquam, quisquam, quicquam, indefinite pronoun, *anyone, anything*.
   cuiquam: *to any single person*.

CATULLUS 76

An Urgent Plea for a "Quid pro Quo"

Catullus appeals to the gods for salvation.

1	Sī qua recordantī benefacta priōra voluptās
2	est hominī, cum sē cōgitat esse pium,
3	nec sānctam violāsse fidem, nec foedere nūllō
4	dīvum ad fallendōs nūmine abūsum hominēs,
5	multa parāta manent in longā aetāte, Catulle,
6	ex hōc ingrātō gaudia amōre tibi.
7	Nam quaecumque hominēs bene cuiquam aut dīcere possunt
8	aut facere, haec ā tē dictaque factaque sunt,

continued

Explorations

1. When doing what might a person experience pleasure (**voluptās**)? (1–4)
2. What lies in store for Catullus? (5–6) Why is this so? (7–8)
3. A syllogism consists of a major and a minor premise and a conclusion. Identify the elements of a syllogism in the thoughts contained in lines 1–8 (the elements of the syllogism are there, but not in the usual order).
4. It was a philosophical commonplace in antiquity "that the recollection of past good deeds is a source of pleasure," as Powell remarks. He continues: "One of the chief problems in ancient moral philosophy was the need to show that virtue is profitable to those who practise it. One of the arguments employed to this end was that virtuous deeds are a source of pleasurable memories and that the enjoyment of a good conscience has a greater value than more mundane pleasures" (Powell, 199). Powell quotes the following example of this thinking from Cicero's *De senectute* (9): **cōnscientia bene āctae vītae multōrumque benefactōrum recordātiō iūcundissima est,** *knowledge of a life well lived and memory of many good deeds is most pleasant.* Compare Cicero's statement with lines 1–5 of Catullus 76.
5. Is there anything in lines 1–5 that would lead you to expect that this poem will deal with a love affair?
6. Are lines 5–6 straightforward? That is, is Catullus flooded with **voluptās** and **gaudia** at the thought of his good deeds and clean conscience? If not, why not? What words in line 6 undercut the optimism of lines 1–5?
7. The truth or falsity of the conclusion of a syllogism depends on the truth or falsity of each of its premises. Which premise (1–4, 7–8) when applied to Catullus' situation may be false here?

9   **omnia quae**: delayed relative. Other editors make line 9 an independent
     sentence with **quae** a connecting relative introducing a main clause.
     crēdō, crēdere, crēdidī, crēditus + dat., *to trust; to believe; to commit, entrust.*
     periērunt crēdita: as if they were bad investments, yielding no return.
10   **tētē**: emphatic **tē**.
     amplius, comparative adv., *more, further.*
     excruciō [**ex-**, *thoroughly* + **cruciō, -āre, -āvī, -ātus**, *to crucify; to torture;* from
     crux, crucis, f., *cross* (on which slaves could be punished by being impaled
     and allowed to die)], **-āre, -āvī, -ātus**, *to crucify; to torture, torment.*
        excruciēs: deliberative subjunctive.
        Quārē ... excruciēs: this is Thomson's reading; other texts give
        Quārē iam tē cūr amplius excruciēs?
11   **quīn**, interrogative adv., *why ... not?*
     animō: = **in animō**.
     offirmō [**ob-**, *against* + **firmō, -āre, -āvī, -ātus**, *to make strong*] **-āre, -āvī,**
     -ātus, *to make firm;* intransitive, *to be determined.*
     istinc, adv., *from where you are, from the state you are in.*
     tē ipse: this is Thomson's reading; other texts have **tēque**, with an unneeded
     connective.
12   **dīs**: = **deīs**.
     dīs invītīs: *because/since the gods are unwilling* (i.e., that she love you in re-
     turn).
     dēsinis esse miser: compare Catullus 8.1.
13   **longum subitō**: note the effective juxtaposition of words.
14   **vērum**, conj., *but.*
     quā lubet = **quā libet** [**quā**, *in any way* + **libet**, impersonal, *(it) pleases*], *in any*
     way it pleases, no matter how, somehow or other.
     efficiō [**ex-**, *thoroughly* + **faciō, facere, fēcī, factus**, *to make, do*], **efficere, ef-**
     fēcī, effectus, *to accomplish, carry out.*
        efficiās: jussive subjunctive, *you must. . . .* ; cf. Catullus 8.1, **dēsinās**.
15   **salūs, salūtis**, f., *safety; health; salvation.*
     haec: feminine singular in place of the neuter **hoc,** by attraction to the gen-
     der of **salūs**.
     hōc: neuter nominative singular; sometimes, as here, the *o* is regarded as
     long. The four demonstratives in lines 14–16 (**hoc, haec, hōc,** and **hoc;**
     note the anaphora) refer to **longum subitō dēpōnere amōrem** (13).
     pervincō [**per-**, *thoroughly* + **vincō, vincere, vīcī, victus**, *to conquer, win*],
     pervincere, pervīcī, pervictus, *to prevail over; to overcome; to bring about, ac-*
     complish.
        est ... pervincendum: note the effect of the spondaic fifth foot.
16   **sīve ... sīve**, conj., *whether ... or.*
     potis or **pote**, indeclinable adjective + infinitive (see Catullus 45.5 and 72.7),
     having the power (to), *able* (to).
        pote: supply **est**, = **potest**, and **fierī**.

9   omnia quae ingrātae periērunt crēdita mentī.

10   Quārē cūr tētē iam amplius excruciēs?

11   Quīn tū animō offirmās atque istinc tē ipse redūcis

12   et dīs invītīs dēsinis esse miser?

13   Difficile est longum subitō dēpōnere amōrem.

14   Difficile est, vērum hoc quā lubet efficiās;

15   ūna salūs haec est, hōc est tibi pervincendum,

16   hoc faciās, sīve id nōn pote sīve pote.

continued

Explorations

8. Explain the commercial connotations of the words **periērunt** and **crēdita** (9).
9. Compare the idea expressed in lines 8–9 with line 3 of Catullus 73. What specific example of ingratitude does the poet give in poem 76?
10. What is the relationship between the question in line 10 and what has preceded it in the poem?
11. What answer does Catullus give in lines 11–12 to the question he asks of himself in line 10?
12. Lines 13–14 stand in the exact middle of the poem. Explain them as an internal dialogue.
13. What devices of rhetoric, grammar, and meter does Catullus use in lines 15–16 to emphasize the necessity of accomplishing the task? Does he think he can accomplish it?

17   dī: = deī.

vestrum est + infinitive, *is characteristic of you, is within you.*

    vestrum: genitive of **vōs**.

misereor, -ērī, -itus sum, *to have pity, have mercy.*

    miserērī: the infinitive serves as the subject of **vestrum est**.

quis, qua/quae, quid, indefinite pronoun after **sī**, *anyone, anything.*

18   **extrēmus, -a, -um**, *last, final, last-minute.*

ops, opis, f., *power; aid, help.*

19   **aspiciō** [ad- + **speciō, specere, spexī, spectus**, *to see, observe*], **aspicere, as-**
        pexī, aspectus, *to look at.*

pūriter [**pūrus, -a, -um**, *clean* + **-ter**], adv. [a formal, archaic formation for the
    later and more usual **pūrē**], *in a clean manner; without moral blemish.*

20   **pestis, pestis**, f., *disease, plague.*

perniciēs, -ēī, f., *destruction, ruin.*

    pestem perniciemque: alliteration and hendiadys, = *destructive disease* or
       ruinous plague.

mihi: dative of separation.

21   **mihi**: dative of reference, indicating possession, with **īmōs . . . in artūs**.

subrēpō [sub-, *under* + **rēpō, rēpere, rēpsī**, *to crawl, creep*], **subrēpere, sub-**
    rēpsī, subrēptūrus, *to creep under; to steal upon.*

īmus, -a, -um, *deepest, innermost.*

torpor, torpōris, m., *numbness, paralysis.*

artus, -ūs, m., *joint; limb.*

22   **laetitia, -ae**, f., *gladness, joy.*

23   **illud . . . ut . . . illa**: *the following . . . that she.*

contrā, adv., *in return.*

    contrā: take with **dīligat**.

        contrā ut mē, this is Thomson's reading replacing **contrā mē ut** of other
          editions; it avoids delaying the conjunction and obviates the tempta-
          tion to take **contrā** as a preposition governing **mē**.

24   **quod**: *[something] that.*

    quod nōn potis est: supply **fierī**, *[something] that is not able to happen* or
        supply **facere**, *[something] that [she] is not able to do.*

pudīcus, -a, -um, *virtuous, honorable, chaste.*

velit: what mood and tense?

25   **ipse**: over against **illa** (23).

taeter, taetra, taetrum, *offensive, revolting, foul.*

26   **prō**, prep. + abl., *for, in return for.*

pietās, pietātis, f., *dutifulness, devotion, loyalty.*

17   Ō dī, sī vestrum est miserērī, aut sī quibus umquam
18   extrēmam iam ipsā in morte tulistis opem,
19   mē miserum aspicite et, sī vītam pūriter ēgī,
20   ēripite hanc pestem perniciemque mihi,
21   quae mihi subrēpēns īmōs ut torpor in artūs
22   expulit ex omnī pectore laetitiās.
23   Nōn iam illud quaerō, contrā ut mē dīligat illa,
24   aut, quod nōn potis est, esse pudīca velit;
25   ipse valēre optō et taetrum hunc dēpōnere morbum.
26   Ō dī, reddite mī hoc prō pietāte meā.

Explorations

14. To whom does Catullus turn in his helplessness?
15. Catullus incorporates standard elements of ancient prayers to the gods, such as the if-clauses in lines 17–18, but how are these two clauses particularly relevant to Catullus' condition?
16. What lines at the beginning of the poem do the words **sī vītam pūriter ēgī** (19) recall?
17. For what does Catullus pray? (20–22)
18. With what kind of imagery does the poet now describe his love? (20) What words in the remaining lines of the poem develop this imagery?
19. What words in lines 19–21 recall words in Catullus 51, which may have been the first poem that Catullus addressed to Lesbia?
20. What two words in the first part of the poem are recalled by the word **laetitiās** (22)?
21. What does Catullus no longer seek, and why? (23–24)
22. What line earlier in the poem is echoed by line 25 and to what effect?
23. How does the last line of the poem round out the prayer to the gods and the poem as a whole?

Comparisons

How does Catullus 76 compare with Catullus 8 in theme and in tone?

Compare the following translations by William Walsh and Horace Gregory both with each other and with Catullus 76.

William Walsh (1663–1708)

Is there a pious pleasure that proceeds
From contemplation of our virtuous deeds?
That all mean sordid action we despise,
And scorn to gain a throne by cheats and lies?
Thyrsis, thou hast sure blessings laid in store
From thy just dealing in this curst amour.
What honour can in words or deeds be shown
Which to the fair thou hast not said and done?
On her false heart they all are thrown away:
She only swears more easily to betray.
Ye powers that know the many vows she broke,
Free my just soul from this unequal yoke.
My love boils up, and like a raging flood
Runs through my veins and taints my vital blood.
I do not vainly beg she may grow chaste,
Or with an equal passion burn at last—
The one she cannot practise, though she would,
And I contemn the other, though she should—:
Nor ask I vengeance on the perjured jilt;
'Tis punishment enough to have her guilt.
I beg but balsam for my bleeding breast,
Cure for my wounds and from my labours rest.

Horace Gregory

IF man can find rich consolation, remembering his good deeds
    and all he has done,
if he remembers his loyalty to others, nor abuses his religion
    by heartless betrayal
of friends to the anger of powerful gods,
then, my Catullus, the long years before you shall not sink
    in darkness with all hope gone,
wandering, dismayed, through the ruins of love.

All the devotion that man gives to man, you have given,
Catullus,
your heart and your brain flowed into a love that was desolate, wasted, nor can it return.
But why, why do you crucify love and yourself through the
years?
Take what the gods have to offer and standing serene, rise
forth as a rock against darkening skies;
and yet you do nothing but grieve, sunken deep in your
sorrow, Catullus,
for it is hard, hard to throw aside years lived in poisonous
love that has tainted your brain
and must end.
If this seems impossible now, you must rise
to salvation. O gods of pity and mercy, descend and witness
my sorrow, if ever
you have looked upon man in his hour of death, see me now
in despair.
Tear this loathsome disease from my brain. Look, a subtle
corruption has entered my bones,
no longer shall happiness flow through my veins like a river.
No longer I pray
that she love me again, that her body be chaste, mine forever.
Cleanse my soul of this sickness of love, give me power to
rise, resurrected, to thrust love aside,
I have given my heart to the gods, O hear me, omnipotent
heaven
and ease me of love and its pain.

Meter: Elegiac couplet

1   **Rūfus, -ī**, m., *Rufus* (perhaps M. Caelius Rufus, the lover of Clodia defended by Cicero).
    mihi: take with **amīce**, *my friend*, or with **crēdite**, *believed by me*, or with both.
    frūstrā ac nēquīquam: near synonyms, meaning *in vain*, the former emphasizing disappointment, the latter failure (Fordyce).
2   **immō**, particle serving to correct a previous statement, *rather*.
    malum, -ī, n., *trouble; distress, pain; damage*.
3   **sīcine**: = **sīc + -ne**.
    subrēpō [**sub-**, *under* + **rēpō, rēpere, rēpsī**, *to crawl, creep*], **subrēpere, subrēpsī, subrēptūrus** + dat. (see Catullus 76.21), *to creep under; to steal upon*.
        subrēpstī: syncope for **subrēpsistī**.
    intestīna, -ōrum, n. pl., *intestines, guts*.
    perūrō [**per-**, *thoroughly* + **ūrō, ūrere, ūssī, ūstus**, *to burn*], **perūrere, perūssī, perūstus**, *to consume, burn up*.
4   **ei**, interj., *alas!*
    miserō: supply **mihi**, dative of separation with **ēripuistī**.
    bona: neuter plural, but translate with a singular abstract noun such as *happiness*.
5   **heu heu**: Thomson prints **ēheu** instead of **heu heu** here and in line 6.
    venēnum, -ī, n., *poison*.
        venēnum: vocative.
6   **pestis, pestis**, f. (see Catullus 76.20), *disease, plague; blight* (often applied to a person as an agent in destroying something).
        pestis: vocative.
    amīcitia, -ae, f., *friendship*.
        nostrae . . . amīcitiae: *of our friendship*; i.e., of Catullus' friendship with Rufus, cf. **amīce** (1).

CATULLUS 77

Friend?

No, betrayal!

1   Rūfe mihi frūstrā ac nēquīquam crēdite amīce
2   (frūstrā? immō magnō cum pretiō atque malō),
3   sīcine subrēpstī mī atque intestīna perūrēns
4   ei miserō ēripuistī omnia nostra bona?
5   Ēripuistī, heu heu nostrae crūdēle venēnum
6   vītae, heu heu nostrae pestis amīcitiae.

Explorations

1. Compare the theme of this poem with that of Catullus 73. What are the similarities? What are the differences?
2. Poems 73 and 77 both find echoes in poem 76. What lines in poems 73 and 76 express the futility of behaving toward anyone with the kindness and generosity that would engender friendship? What lines in poem 76 are recalled by words, phrases, and clauses in poem 77?
3. Locate four nouns in the vocative case.
4. In lines 1–2 locate an ascending triad of two adverbs and a prepositional phrase.
5. In lines 3–6 locate the members of an ascending tricolon.
6. Study the pattern of *m-*, *s-*, and *ō*-sounds in the poem. How do they enhance its effectiveness?
7. Locate all repeated words. How does repetition emphasize the forward movement of the rhetorical structures in the poem?
8. The Rufus of this poem is sometimes identified with M. Caelius Rufus, a lover of Clodia Metelli, the woman who is often identified as Catullus' Lesbia. If these two identifications were to be made, how would this affect your interpretation of this poem? How would your interpretation of the poem be different if these two identifications were not made?

Meter: elegiac couplet

1   **praesēns, praesentis**, *being in the same place, present.*

        praesente virō: if Lesbia is equated with Clodia Metelli, then this will refer to Clodia's husband Quintus Metellus Celer, who died in 59 B.C.

        mala . . . dīcit: tmesis for **maledīcit**, from **maledīcō** [**male**, *badly* + **dīcō, dīcere, dīxī, dictus**, *to say*], **maledīcere, maledīxī, maledictus** + dat., *to curse, heap abuse* (upon).

2   **haec**: i.e., the verbal abuse mentioned in line 1. Explain why **haec**, not **hoc**, is used here. Compare the use of **haec** in line 15 of Catullus 76.

        fatuus, -a, -um, *mentally lacking, foolish.*

        illī fatuō: i.e., Lesbia's husband.

        laetitia, -ae, f., *happiness.*

        laetitia: predicate nominative.

3   **mūlus, -ī**, m., *mule.*

        nostrī: genitive of **nōs**, perhaps in the sense of *the relationship between us;* or plural for singular, = **meī**.

        oblītus, -a, -um + gen., *forgetful* (of).

        tacēret: the subject is Lesbia. What mood and tense are **tacēret** here and **esset** in line 4? What type of conditional sentence is this?

4   **sānus, -a, -um**, *sane, rational, in one's right mind, normal* (i.e., not dominated by overpowering emotions).

        ganniō, gannīre, (often of dogs) *to snarl, growl; to grumble.*

        obloquor [**ob-**, *against* + **loquor, loquī, locūtus sum**, *to speak*], **obloquī, oblocūtus sum**, *to break in* (on a speaker), *interrupt.*

          obloquitur: some translate *reproaches/abuses/reviles.*

            quod gannit et obloquitur: adverbial **quod** clause, *in as much as/in that.* . . .

5   **meminit**: supply **nostrī** from line 3.

        quae . . . rēs: the antecedent **rēs** is included in the relative clause, translate, *a matter that.* . . .

        ācer, ācris, ācre, *keen, sharp; serious, critical, dangerous.*

6   **Hōc est**: *That is [to say].*

        Hōc: nominative singular, with the *o* pronounced as a long vowel.

        ūrō, ūrere, ūssī, ūstus, *to burn;* passive (cf. Catullus 72.5), *to be inflamed* (with desire or passion).

        loquitur: some editors suggest that **loquitur** is meant to have the same meaning as **obloquitur** in line 4, not just *talks* but *interrupts,* = keeps talking and won't let anyone else talk; Thomson prints **coquitur**, from **coquō, coquere, coxī, coctus**, *to cook;* of emotions, *to stir up, excite, agitate.*

CATULLUS 83

Lesbia's stinging words are not what they seem. Or are they?

What does Lesbia's behavior mean?

1 Lesbia mī praesente virō mala plūrima dīcit;
2   haec illī fatuō maxima laetitia est.
3 Mūle, nihil sentīs? Sī nostrī oblīta tacēret,
4   sāna esset; nunc quod gannit et obloquitur,
5 nōn sōlum meminit, sed, quae multō ācrior est rēs,
6   īrāta est. Hōc est, ūritur et loquitur.

Explorations

1. What is the situation described in this poem? Some commentators identify Lesbia with Clodia Metelli and believe that the reader is to imagine Catullus as being with Lesbia/Clodia and her husband, Q. Metellus Celer. Others, noting the words **nostrī oblīta** (3) and **meminit** (5), maintain that Catullus cannot be imagined as being present. Others deny the identification of Lesbia with Clodia Metelli. Which interpretation makes greater sense for the poem as a whole?
2. Why does Catullus call the husband a mule in the second couplet?
3. How will your translation of **obloquitur** (4) depend on your answer to question 1 above?
4. What word in line 6 corresponds to **sāna** in line 4?
5. If the reading **loquitur** is kept in line 6, how should the word be translated here? Thomson prints **coquitur**. Can that reading be defended? What words in line 3 might suggest that **loquitur** should be retained in line 6?
6. Propertius, a love poet of the Augustan age, had Catullus 83 in mind when he wrote a poem on "the theme that an angry tongue is a proof of love" (Quinn, 418). The following lines are extracts from Propertius' poem (3.8.3–4, 9–12, 27–28). Does Propertius' imitation help you interpret Catullus' poem?
   When, crazed with wine, you knock over the table and fling full cups at me with frenzied hand, you are without question giving me tokens of true ardor: for no woman smarts unless hers is a serious passion. She whose raging tongue spits out insults is groveling at the feet of mighty Venus. . . . I should always wish to be the wan lover of an angry mistress (**semper in īrātā pallidus esse velim**). (trans., G. P. Goold)
7. Some see in lines 3–6 "a deliberate evasion of the unpleasant conclusions that might be drawn from the situation described in lines 1–2" (Holoka, 119). Is this view defensible?

Meter: elegiac couplet

1   **chommoda**: = **commoda**, n. pl., *advantages*. This is the first of three words in
    the poem that Arrius mispronounces by aspirating the initial letter, i.e., by
    adding a rough breathing sound equivalent to the letter *h*, so that here *c*
    becomes *ch*. *Ch, ph,* and *th* sounds were not native to Latin, but they were
    frequent in Greek and in the parent language from which both Greek and
    Latin evolved. When Latin began borrowing words from Greek that con-
    tained aspirated consonants, it did not borrow the aspiration, so that Greek
    theatron, "theater," originally became Latin **teātrum**. By Catullus' time,
    however, Latin had begun to incorporate the aspirated consonants in
    Greek loan words, thus giving **theātrum**, and there was a tendency to
    overdo this Greek influence by incorporating aspiration into Latin words
    where it did not belong, hence **pulcher** instead of **pulcer** and **phius** instead
    of **pius**. This practice bothered Cicero (*Orator* 160), and it was a source of
    amusement for Catullus, as this poem shows. (See Fordyce, 373–74.)
    sī quandō, here with the imperfect subjunctive instead of the usual pluper-
    fect indicative, *if ever, whenever.*
    vellet: from what verb? What is the tense of the subjunctive here?
2   **īnsidiae, -ārum**, f. pl., *ambush*.
    īnsidiās Arrius hīnsidiās: ellipsis, implying repetition of the earlier
    clauses, only in reverse order, i.e., **sī quandō Arrius vellet īnsidiās
    dīcere, hīnsidiās dīcēbat**. Aspiration (an *h* sound) before an initial
    vowel was native to Latin, but in popular speech it tended to disappear,
    thus **arēna** instead of **harēna**, *sand; arena,* and **ortus** instead of **hortus**,
    garden. Conversely, it was sometimes added where it did not belong,
    giving **hūmidus** instead of **ūmidus**, *wet, moist,* and **have** instead of **ave**,
    greetings! Arrius makes the latter mistake. (See Fordyce, 374.)
    Arrius, -ī, m., *Arrius* (possibly Quintus Arrius, an orator of whom Cicero
    thought very little, describing him as a man of low birth who though lack-
    ing education and native talent managed to gain political office, wealth,
    and the favor of powerful patrons, including Marcus Crassus; see Cicero,
    Brutus 242).
3   **mīrificē** [**mīrus, -a, -um**, *extraordinary, remarkable* + **-ficus**, adjectival suffix,
    making, causing + **-ē**, adverbial ending] (see Catullus 53.2), *in an amazing
    manner, remarkably well.*
    mīrificē: take with **esse locūtum**.
    spērō, -āre, -āvī, -ātus, *to look forward to, hope for; to hope; to flatter oneself* (that +
    acc. and infin.).
    spērābat . . . / . . . dīxerat (4): past general, with imperfect indicative in
    the main clause and pluperfect indicative in the temporal clause;
    translate the temporal clause *whenever he said. . . .*
4   **quantum poterat**: *with as much effort as he could, as loudly as he could.*
5   **līber, lībera, līberum**, *free*.
6   **māternus, -a, -um**, *maternal*.
    avus, -ī, m., *grandfather*.
    avia, -ae f., *grandmother*.

CATULLUS 84

Aspirations reveal aspirations.

The affected pronunciation of a social climber doesn't impress Catullus.

1 Chommoda dīcēbat, sī quandō commoda vellet
2 dīcere, et īnsidiās Arrius hīnsidiās,
3 et tum mīrificē spērābat sē esse locūtum,
4 cum quantum poterat dīxerat hīnsidiās.
5 Crēdō, sīc māter, sīc līber avunculus eius,
6 sīc māternus avus dīxerat atque avia.

continued

Text

5 **līber:** it is difficult to explain why Catullus would describe the uncle as **līber**, and R. G. M. Nisbet has suggested that **semper** is what Catullus wrote here.

Explorations

1. How does Catullus use word placement and chiasmus to highlight Arrius' humorous mispronunciations? (1–2)
2. What do we learn about Arrius in lines 3–4? Compare this behavior to that of Suffenus described in lines 15–17 of Catullus 22. What is the similarity? What is the poet's attitude toward this behavior?
3. Arrius' mispronunciations are often explained as misguided attempts on the part of someone of lower class to imitate the speech of the upper classes. Explain this in the light of the information on aspiration supplied in the notes on lines 1 and 2 and in the light of what Cicero says about Quintus Arrius (see note on line 2), assuming that he is the Arrius of this poem.
4. Why does Catullus mention Arrius' family in lines 5–6? Is **līber** to be taken literally or sarcastically? What is implied about the social status of Arrius' maternal relatives?

7   **Hōc**: i.e., Arrius. What construction is **Hōc missō**? If Arrius is the Quintus
     Arrius described by Cicero in his *Brutus*, he may have been sent to Syria
     by Crassus on a diplomatic mission in conjunction with Crassus' military
     expedition to Parthia in 55 B.C.
     requiēscō (**re-**, expressing reversal + **quiēscō, quiēscere, quiēvī,**
     quiētūrus, inceptive, *to fall asleep; to take rest*], **requiēscere, requiēvī, re-**
     quiētūrus, inceptive, *to rest; to find relief.*
          requiērant: syncope for **requiēverant**.
     omnibus: dative of reference, *for all concerned.*
     auris, auris, f., *ear.*
8   **audībant**: syncope for **audiēbant**.
     eadem haec: supply **verba** (i.e., the words **commoda** and **īnsidiae**).
     lēniter, adv., *gently; with a smooth breathing* (i.e., without the rough breathing
          or aspiration, the *h*-sound of Greek aspirated vowels and consonants), *with-*
          out aspiration.
     leviter, adv., *lightly, gently, softly.*
9   **sibi**: dative of reference, *for themselves.*
     postillā, adv., *afterwards, after that time.*
     metuō, metuere, metuī, metūtus, *to fear.*
10   **affertur**: historical present.
     nūntius: sometimes an indirect statement is introduced through a reference
          to speech, as here; i.e., *a message is brought, that. . . .*
     horribilis, -is, -e, *inspiring fear/horror; dreadful, horrible.*
11   **Īonius, -a, -um**, *Ionian* (referring to the Ionian Sea off the west coast of
          Greece).
     flūctus, -ūs, m., *wave.*
     īsset: relative and temporal clauses inside indirect statements take the sub-
          junctive. From what verb is **īsset**, and what tense is it?

Comparison

Here is an Anglicized version of Arrius. What is the particularly British mistake in
pronunciation that Sir 'Arry makes? Which of the two poems do you prefer? Why?

Sir 'Arry, though lately created a knight,
Is unable to order his h's aright.
He expounds the wise views of a man of haffairs
Or explains 'ow 'e 'ates haristocracy's hairs.
(To his mother, nee 'Awkins, he owes, I expect,
This unpleasant, invincible vocal defect.)
His victims had looked for a respite at least
While Sir 'Arry is occupied doin' the Heast.
But alas for our hopes! You've not heard the news? What?
Sir 'Arry finds Hindia 'ellishly 'ot.

                                                        Anonymous

7   Hōc missō in Syriam requiērant omnibus aurēs:
8   audībant eadem haec lēniter et leviter,
9   nec sibi postillā metuēbant tālia verba,
10   cum subitō affertur nūntius horribilis,
11   Īoniōs flūctūs, postquam illūc Arrius īsset,
12   iam nōn Īoniōs esse sed Hīoniōs.

Explorations

5. What do the words **Hōc missō in Syriam** (7) and **requiērant <u>omnibus</u> au-rēs** (7) imply about the social status of Arrius at this time?
6. How do the words **lēniter** and **leviter** (8) correspond to descriptions of Arrius' speech in lines 1–4?
7. Explain the point of the final couplet.

Chommoda dīcēbat. . . .

Meter: elegiac couplet

1   **ōdī, ōdisse**, perfect in form, present in meaning, *to hate.*
     quārē, interrogative adv., *why, for what reason.*
        Quārē id faciam: indirect question dependent on **requīris**.
     requīrō [re-, prefix here perhaps expressing repeated action + **quaerō,**
        quaerere, quaesīvī, quaesītus, *to ask*], **requīrere, requīsīvī, requīsītus**, *to*
        ask, inquire.
           requīris?: Thomson prints a period instead of a question mark here.
2   **Nescio**: see note on Catullus 2.6.
     fierī: infinitive in an indirect statement dependent on **sentiō**; supply **id** as
        subject of the infinitive and **mihi** as dative of reference, *that [it] is being done*
        [to me].
     excruciō [ex-, *thoroughly* + **crucio, -āre, -āvī, -ātus**, *to crucify; to torture;* from
        crux, crucis, f., *cross* (on which slaves could be punished by being impaled
        and allowed to die)] (see Catullus 76.10), **-āre, -āvī, -ātus**, *to crucify; to tor-*
        ture, torment.

Comparisons

Grade these versions for their faithfulness to the original, their success in convey-
ing its tone and sentiment, and their simplicity of expression.

I hate, and yet I love thee too;
How can that be? I know not how;
Only that so it is I know;
And feel with torment that 'tis so.

                                                    —Abraham Cowley, 1667

I hate and love. Why? You may ask but
It beats me. I feel it done to me, and ache.

                                                    —Ezra Pound

I hate and I love. And if you ask me how,
I do not know: I only feel it, and I'm torn in two.

                                                    —Peter Whigham

I HATE and love.
And if you ask me why,
I have no answer, but I discern,
can feel, my senses rooted in eternal torture.

                                                    —Horace Gregory

Of course I hate what I love, and can't explain, for how is one to syllogize
    his pain?

                                                    —Gary Wills

CATULLUS 85

I Hate and I Love.

How does Catullus' analysis of his predicament differ now from what it was in poems 72 and 75?

1   Ōdī et amō. Quārē id faciam, fortasse requīris?
2   Nescio, sed fierī sentiō et excrucior.

Explorations

1. How many verbs are there in this couplet? How many nouns and adjectives can you find? On what does the poet focus in poem 85?
2. Read the poem aloud and in meter. How many elisions can you find and what is the effect of the first and of the last elision?
3. Identify the members of an ascending tricolon in the poem. What word does the ascending tricolon highlight?
4. Locate two caesuras in the first line and two diaereses in the second line.
5. Divide the poem into segments based on the pauses (caesuras, diaereses, and sentence-ends).
6. Using these divisions of the poem into segments, label each of the segments as members of a ring composition or chiasmus consisting of ABCCBA.
7. Label the members of the ring composition or chiasmus as (A) feelings felt by an active agent, (B) action performed by an active agent, (C) inquiry by an active agent, (C) response by an active agent, (B) suffering experienced by a passive victim, and (A) feelings felt by a passive victim. What pattern do you detect?
8. How does the final word of the poem relate to the first three words?
9. How do the words that immediately precede the second pause in each line (labeled B in the ring composition or chiasmus) relate to one another?
10. What are the main oppositions or antitheses in the poem?
11. Who is the *you* of **requīris**?
12. Compare this poem with Catullus 72 and 75. How does it carry to its logical conclusion and crystallize the basic antithesis expressed in those poems?
13. Catullus 72 contains elements of a dialogue. How does the implied dialogue in Catullus 85 lead the poet to a different conclusion and to a different state of mind?
14. In poem 72 the clause **Nunc tē cognōvī** (5) shows the poet fully in command of his rational faculties, and with these rational faculties he clearly describes his emotional situation twice over, first in the second half of line 5 and line 6 and then in answer to Lesbia's reported question, in the second half of line 7 and line 8. What word in Catullus 85 reverses this sense of intellectual knowledge expressed in Catullus 72?

Meter: elegiac couplet

1   **Quīntia, -ae** f., *Quintia* (a woman whom Catullus is comparing to Lesbia).
     fōrmōsus, -a, -um, *beautiful, gorgeous.*
       fōrmōsa: the word occurs in Catullus only in this poem.
     multīs: *in the eyes of many*, dative of reference or dative of the person judging.
     candidus, -a, -um (see Catullus 13.4), *white, fair-skinned, pretty.*
     longus, -a, -um, *long, tall.*

2   **rēctus, -a, -um** (see Catullus 10.20), *straight, tall;* of posture, *upright, stately.*
     haec: substantive, *these [characteristics].*
     singulī, -ae, -a, *taken separately, individual.*
     cōnfiteor [con-, intensive + **fateor, fatērī, fassus sum**, *to accept as true, admit*], **cōnfitērī, cōnfessus sum**, *to admit* (a fact).

3   **Tōtum illud fōrmōsa negō**: the phrase **Tōtum illud fōrmōsa** as a whole is
     the object of **negō**, *I deny/disavow.* The word **fōrmōsa** is quoted from line 1
     and remains in the nominative case instead of becoming accusative to
     match the words with which it is in apposition (**tōtum illud**); translate, *that*
     [expression/description] fōrmōsa as a whole I deny/disavow.
     venustās, venustātis (see Catullus 3.2, 10.4, 12.5, 13.6, 22.2, 31.12, 35.17, 36.17),
       f., *charm, attractiveness.*

4   **in tam magnō . . . corpore**: a complimentary phrase in itself; the ancients
     admired stature in both men and women.
     mīca, -ae f., *particle, grain.*
     sal, salis, m., *salt;* by metonymy, *wit, "spice."*
       salis: compare Catullus 13.5, **sale**, 10.33, **īnsulsa male**, and 12.4, **salsum**;
       here in 86.4 the word refers less to verbal wit or intellectual sophistica
       tion than to sexual charm and appeal.

5   **cum . . . tum** (6), *both . . . and, not only . . . but also.*
     pulcerrima: = **pulcherrima**.

6   **omnibus**: *from all women.*
     omnīs: = **omnēs**.
     surripiō [sub-, *from below* + **rapiō, rapere, rapuī, raptus**, *to snatch, seize*], **surripere, surripuī, surreptus**, *to steal.*
     Venerēs: for the plural, see Catullus 3.1; some editors print the word with a
       small *v* here; in either case it refers to the qualities of a woman that excite
       sexual desire in men, *charms, graces*, the sources of a woman's sex appeal.

CATULLUS 86

A Beauty Contest

Catullus displays his high standards and flatters Lesbia in the process.

1 Quīntia fōrmōsa est multīs. Mihi candida, longa,
2   rēcta est: haec ego sīc singula cōnfiteor.
3 Tōtum illud "fōrmōsa" negō: nam nūlla venustās,
4   nūlla in tam magnō est corpore mīca salis.
5 Lesbia fōrmōsa est, quae cum pulcerrima tōta est,
6   tum omnibus ūna omnīs surripuit Venerēs.

Explorations

1. Where in the first line does Catullus deliberately place words next to each other in order to set himself and his values against society and its values?
2. Examine the placement of the word **fōrmōsa** in each of the three couplets. What do you discover?
3. What qualities does Catullus admit that Quintia has? (1–2)
4. Why does Catullus refuse to admit that Quintia measures up to the full definition of the word **fōrmōsa**? (3–4)
5. What does Lesbia have that Quintia does not? (5–6)
6. What does Catullus mean by the phrase **omnīs . . . Venerēs** (6)?

Lesbia . . . omnibus ūna omnīs surripuit Venerēs.

"Aphrodite from Melos," c. 200 B.C.
Louvre
Paris, France

Meter: elegiac couplet

1   **tantum ... quantum** (2), *as much ... as, to the extent that.*
      tantum: modifying **amātam (esse)**.
         amātam (esse): why is an infinitive used here? What tense and voice is
           it?
2   **vērē**: modifying **dīcere** (1).
3   **foedus, foederis**, n., *formal agreement, treaty; compact; bond, tie* (of friendship).
      ūllō ... foedere: = **in ūllō foedere**.
         fidēs ... foedere: note the alliteration of **fid- ... foed-** in these key
           words here as in Catullus 76.3. For **foedus**, see also Catullus 109.6.
      tanta ... quanta (4): *as great ... as.*
4   **in amōre tuō**: conceivably either *in your love [for me]* or *in [my] love for you.*
      reperiō [re-, *back* + **pariō, parere, peperī, partus**, *to give birth to, produce; to*
         get], **reperīre, repperī, repertus**, *to find.*
      reperta ... est: the subject is **fidēs**.

Text

2   **est**: Thomson prints **es**, removing the awkward shift from third person in the
      first couplet to second person in the next; the words **Lesbia ... mea** then
      become vocative, and the line could be punctuated as follows:
         vērē, quantum ā mē, Lesbia, amāta, mea, es.

3   **ūllō ... foedere**: Thomson prints **ūllō ... in foedere**, thus:
         Nūlla fidēs ūllō fuit umquam in foedere tanta,

CATULLUS 87

A Love Unparalleled but Flawed

Find the sting in the final words of this epigram.

1   Nūlla potest mulier tantum sē dīcere amātam
2   vērē, quantum ā mē Lesbia amāta mea est.
3   Nūlla fidēs ūllō fuit umquam foedere tanta,
4   quanta in amōre tuō ex parte reperta meā est.

Explorations

1. What words establish a parallelism between the two couplets of this poem?
2. What is gained and what is lost by reading **es** instead of **est** in line 2?
3. How does alliteration enhance the diction in line 3?
4. Thomson remarks, "The sting of this epigram lies, of course, in *ex parte mea*." Explain how this could be true. What is the flaw in this unparalleled love?
5. Compare the reciprocity of love and faithfulness expressed in the dialogue between Septimius and Acme in Catullus 45 with the one-sided declaration of love and faithfulness in Catullus 87.

Comparison

With what other poem(s) of Catullus has Walter Savage Landor (1775–1864) joined poem 87 in the following translation? Why did Landor join the poems together?

Love's Madness

None could ever say that she,
Lesbia! was so loved by me;
Never, all the world around,
Faith so true as mine was found.
If no longer it endures,
(Would it did!) the fault is yours.
I can never think again
Well of you: I try in vain.
But, be false, do what you will,
Lesbia! I must love you still.

Meter: elegiac couplet

1   **dīcit . . . male**: see Catullus 83.1.

2   **dispereō** [**dis-** *apart* or with intensive force + **pereō, perīre, periī, peritūrus,** *to perish, die*], **disperīre, disperiī,** *to be ruined; to perish, die.*

        dispeream nisi amat: optative subjunctive expressing a colloquial wish, *may I perish if she doesn't. . . .*

            dispeream: embedded in the subordinate clause dependent on it, **Lesbia mē . . . nisi amat = nisi Lesbia mē amat.**

3   **Quo signo?**: *By what sign [do I know that she loves me]?*

    quia, conj., *because.*

    totidem [**tot**, indeclinable adjective, *as many (as)* + **īdem, eadem, idem,** *the same*], indeclinable adjective, *as many (as), the same.*

    sunt totidem mea: colloquial, *the same things/symptoms are mine,* = *it's the same with me.*

    dēprecor [**dē-**, *down, away* + **precor, -ārī, -ātus sum,** *to pray*], **-ārī, -ātus sum,** *to try to avert by prayer; to entreat relief from, pray to be rid of; to express disapproval of, deprecate* (Aulus Gellius, second century A.D. author of *Noctes Atticae*, cites the following words to give a sense of what Catullus means by **dēprecor**: **dētestor,** *to call down a solemn curse upon; to ward off by entreaty; to detest, loathe,* **exsecror,** *to utter curses against; to detest, abhor,* **dēpellō,** *to drive/push away, drive off, repel,* **abominor,** *to seek to avert by prayer; to loathe, abhor, detest* [Gellius 7.16.5–6]).

4   **assiduē** [**ad-**, *to, near* + **sedeō, sedēre, sēdī, sessūrus,** *to sit*], adv., *continually, all the time.*

    vērum, conj., *but.*

CATULLUS 92

How do I know she loves me?

In this poem, as in poem 83, Catullus manages to read Lesbia's behavior in a paradoxical or contradictory way. Is he deceiving himself again?

1 Lesbia mī dīcit semper male nec tacet umquam
2   dē mē: Lesbia mē dispeream nisi amat.
3 Quō signō? Quia sunt totidem mea: dēprecor illam
4   assiduē, vērum dispeream nisi amō.

Explorations

1. What examples of parallel wording do you find in this poem?
2. What is unusual about the word order of the two clauses contained in the words **Lesbia mē dispeream nisi amat** (2)?
3. What is the structural and logical point of the phrase **Quō signō** (3)?
4. How would you best translate **dēprecor** in line 3?
5. Compare the theme of this poem with that of Catullus 83.
6. Compare poem 104, given below in Latin and a very literal English translation. Does Catullus' denial there that he was ever able to heap abuse upon Lesbia suggest a flaw in the argument of poem 92?

Comparison

Catullus 104

Crēdis mē potuisse meae maledīcere vītae,
    ambōbus mihi quae cārior est oculīs?
nōn potuī, nec, sī possem, tam perditē amārem:
    sed tū cum Tappōne omnia mōnstra facis.

Do you believe that I was capable of heaping abuse upon the light of my
    life,
    who is more dear to me than my two eyes?
I was not capable [of this], and, if I were, I would not be loving [her] as
    desperately [as I do]:
    but you and that clownish friend of yours exaggerate everything.

Meter: elegiac couplet

1   **Zmyrna, -ae**, f. [Greek word], *Zmyrna* or *Smyrna* (the name of a short epic
    poem, a so-called epyllion, written by C. Helvius Cinna, see Catullus 10.30,
    about the passion of a young woman, Zmyrna/Smyrna, sometimes called
    Myrrha, for her father, her transformation into a tree, and the birth of her
    son, the ill-fated Adonis, from the trunk of the tree; see Ovid, *Metamor-
    phoses* 10.298–528).

  Zmyrna . . . ēdita (2) . . . Zmyrna . . . mittētur (5): the noun **Zmyrna**
  (1), the subject of the sentence, modified by **ēdita (2)**, is repeated at the
  beginning of line 5 after the interruption of the subordinate clause in
  lines 3–4 and then finds its main verb **mittētur (5)**. Or, less likely, supply **est** with **ēdita** to constitute the main verb; line 5 will then be a new
  main clause.

  nōnam post . . . messem / . . . nōnamque . . . post hiemem: prepositional
  phrases modifying **ēdita (2)**, *published after the ninth . . . / and after the
  ninth. . . .*

  dēnique, adv., *finally, at last.*

  messis, messis, f., *harvest.*

2   **coepī, coepisse, coeptus**, perfect stem only, *to begin.*

  post (1) . . . quam coepta est: *after it was begun*: **post (1** and repeated in **2)**
  serves as both a preposition with the accusatives and as part of the conjunction **postquam**.

  ēdō [ex-, *out* **+ dō, dare, dedī, datus,** *to give*], **ēdere, ēdidī, ēditus,** *to give out;
  to give forth* (offspring), *give birth to; to publish.*

3   **cum**, conj. + indicative, *when, while.*

  intereā, adv., *meanwhile, in the meantime;* with adversative force, *nevertheless,
  however, anyhow, at any rate.*

  intereā: Thomson translates not *in the meantime,* but, *for his part.*

  Hatriēnsis, -is, -e, *of/belonging to Hatria;* here, *the [man] of Hatria, Volusius*
  (Hatria, a town in northern Italy on the Adriatic coast, the modern Adria, is
  presumably the birthplace of Volusius, the author of the *Annals* scathingly
  criticized by Catullus in poem 36; the word **Hatriēnsis** is A. E. Housman's
  conjectural correction of the manuscript reading, **Hortēnsius**, which most
  commentators find problematic because of poem 65, in which Catullus dedicates a translation he has made of a poem of Callimachus to Hortensius,
  who had requested it—the two men seem to have very similar literary
  tastes; here in poem 95 the person described in lines 3–4 is the diametric
  opposite of what Catullus admires in a poet and can scarcely be Hortensius).

4   Line 4 has been lost from the manuscripts and what is printed here is a con-
    jecture; other conjectures have been suggested, including **versiculōrum
    annō quōlibet ēdiderit** [**quōlibet** = *any*].

  versiculī, -ōrum, m. pl., *light verse.*

  pūtidus, -a, -um, *rotten, foul.*

  ēvomō [ex-, *out* **+ vomō, vomere, vomuī, vomitus,** *to vomit, spew out*],
  ēvomere, ēvomuī, ēvomitus, *to vomit; to emit* (from the mouth).

CATULLUS 95

Cinna's *Zmyrna* is born.

*Catullus stakes out his poetics with reference to such Latin and Greek poets as
Cinna, Volusius, Philetas, and Antimachus.*

1   Zmyrna meī Cinnae nōnam post dēnique messem
2   quam coepta est nōnamque ēdita post hiemem,
3   mīlia cum intereā quīngenta Hatriēnsis in ūnō
4   <versiculōrum annō pūtidus ēvomuit,>

continued

Explorations

1. What contrast is being made between Cinna's production of poetry as described in the first couplet and Volusius' production of poetry as described in the second couplet?
2. What words in the first couplet mirror the time frame of a human pregnancy?
3. What word in the second couplet suggests that Volusius' production of poetry can best be described with vocabulary describing a bodily function? How does it contrast with the vocabulary of the first couplet?
4. What words are highlighted by their placement in line 3?
5. In what other poem does Catullus castigate a poet for writing too many verses?

5   **cavus, -a, -um**, *hollow, deep-channeled.*
    cavās: transferred epithet.
  Satrachus, -ī, m., *Satrachus* (a river in Cyprus, related to the myth of Adonis, the son of Zmyrna).
  penitus, adv., *to a remote distance, far off.*
6   **cānus, -a, -um**, *gray.*
  saeculum, -ī, n. (see Catullus 1.10), *age; lifetime; generation; century.*
    cāna . . . saecula: *gray-haired generations of men*, subject of **pervoluent**.
  pervolvō [per-, *through, continuously* + **volvō, volvere, volvī, volūtus**, *to roll*], **pervolvere**, *to go on unrolling* (a papyrus roll for reading).
    pervoluent: scanned as four syllables = **pervolvent**.
7   **Volusī annālēs**: see Catullus 36.1.
  Padua, -ae, f., *Padua* (one of the mouths of the Po river in northern Italy).
    Paduam . . . ad ipsam: delayed preposition; **ad** = *at* here.
8   **laxus, -a, -um**, *loose.*
  scomber, scombrī, m., *scomber* (a fish, possibly mackerel).
  tunica, -ae, f., *tunic; covering, wrapping.*
    laxās scombrīs saepe dabunt tunicās: some think Catullus means that the papyrus sheets on which Volusius' *Annals* are written will be used to wrap fish at the fish-market; Thomson argues persuasively that they will be used as wrappers within which the fish will be cooked. In either case there will be plenty of papyrus from Volusius' *Annals* to use often (**saepe**) for either purpose, with no need to wrap the fish tightly (cf. **laxās**), in spite of the fact that papyrus was very expensive.
9   **Parva . . . Antimachō** (10): it is uncertain whether lines 9 and 10 belong to poem 95 or not; some editors make them a separate poem labeled 95b.
  meī: the genitive of a noun or proper name is missing from the manuscripts at the end of the line; editors have supplied various possibilities, such as **sodālis**, *comrade*, and **poētae**, *poet*. In any case, the reference should be to Cinna, e.g., **meī . . . poētae**, *of my poet* would mean *of the poet I have been speaking of*, namely Cinna. Solodow's conjecture, **Philītae** (for which, see below), is printed in the text here.
  mihi sint cordī: optative subjunctive in idiom with double dative, *may . . . be to/for the heart to me, may . . . be dear/pleasing to me.*
  monimentum, -ī, n., *monument*; pl., *literary works, writings.*
  Philētās (Philētās), -ae, m., *Philetas* (of Cos in the Eastern Mediterranean; a Greek poet of the early third century B.C., the founder of the Alexandrian school of scholar-poets, the most famous of whom was Callimachus).
    Philītae: by metonymy for **Cinnae**, as **Antimachō** (10) is for **Volusiō**.
10   **tumidus, -a, -um**, *swollen, bloated*; of literary works, *inflated, pretentious.*
  gaudeat: jussive subjunctive. What case does this verb take?
  Antimachus, -ī, m., *Antimachus* (of Colophon; a Greek scholar and poet of the late fifth/early fourth centuries B.C., author of a famous epic poem, the *Thebais*, dealing with the first expedition against Thebes, and an elegiac poem titled *Lyde*, perhaps written after the death of his wife or mistress of the same name; Callimachus condemned him for his verbose style).

5   Zmyrna cavās Satrachī penitus mittētur ad undās,
6   Zmyrnam cāna diū saecula pervoluent.
7   At Volusī annālēs Paduam morientur ad ipsam
8   et laxās scombrīs saepe dabunt tunicās.
9   Parva meī mihi sint cordī monimenta <Philītae>,
10   at populus tumidō gaudeat Antimachō.

Explorations

6.   What rhetorical device is used in lines 5 and 6?
7.   How do lines 5 and 7 contrast the fate of Cinna's poem with the fate of Volusius' verses?
8.   How do lines 6 and 8 contrast the fate of Cinna's poetry with the fate of Volusius' verses in a different way from that seen in lines 5 and 7?
9.   The production and publication of Cinna's *Zmyrna* were described in the first couplet in language suggesting child-birthing. How do lines 6 and 7 continue the metaphor of poetry as a living creature?
10. What is the poet's wish for himself in line 9? What does he order the vulgar crowd to do in line 10? What contrasts are established?
11. What is accomplished by Catullus' referring to Cinna with the phrase **meī . . . Philītae** and by his referring to Volusius as Antimachus?
12. How is this poem structured?
13. What is Catullus saying in this poem about good poetry and bad poetry, and how does what he says compare with what Callimachus says about poetry in the passage for comparison?

Comparison

Callimachus in his *Hymn to Apollo*, 108–12, has Apollo, the god of poetry, express his poetic preferences through metaphors of the Assyrian river (the Euphrates) and a trickling spring:

The stream of the Assyrian river is great, but it carries
much filth of the earth and refuse on its waters.
The Bees do not carry water to Demeter from every source
but whatever springs up pure and undefiled,
a trickling spring from a holy fountain, the choicest, the flower of its kind.

Meter: elegiac couplet

1   **quisquam, quisquam, quicquam**, indefinite pronoun, *anyone, anything.*
     mūtus, -a, -um, *mute, silent.*
         mūtīs . . . sepulcrīs: dative with **grātum** and **acceptum**. The adjective is
             described as a transferred epithet by Thomson since it is really the silent
             ashes of the dead that are on the speaker's mind.
     grātus, -a, -um, *grateful, appreciative; received with gratitude or appreciation;* +
         dat., *welcome, pleasing.*
     acceptus, -a, -um + dat., *acceptable, pleasing, welcome.*
     -ve, enclitic conj., *or.*
2   **accidō** [**ad-**, *to* + **cadō, cadere, cecidī, cāsūrus**, *to fall*], **accidere, accidī**, *to
         fall down, descend; to happen, occur.*
     Calvus, -ī, m., *Calvus* (a close friend of Catullus—see Catullus 50 and 53—
         whose wife or mistress, Quintilia, has died).
     dolor, dolōris, m. (see Catullus 2.7 and 50.17), *pain, smart, love-ache; grief.*
3   **dēsīderium, -ī**, n. (see Catullus 2.5), *something longed for, object of desire; sweet-
         heart; desire, longing* (for a lost person or thing).
         quō dēsīderiō: the antecedent of **quō** is **dolōre** (2), and that antecedent
             is picked up and repeated in the more specific word **dēsīderiō** in the
             relative clause itself; in line 3 translate **quō dēsīderiō** as ablative of in-
             strument or means, *by means of which desire/longing*; repeat the phrase
             at the beginning of line 4 but now translate it as ablative of cause, *be-
             cause of which desire/longing.*
4   **ōlim**, adv., *once, of old.*
         ōlim missās: *long sent away/rejected/abandoned,* or (Davis) *long since bidden
             farewell, long departed/gone.*
     amīcitia, -ae, f., *friendship.*
5   **nōn tantō . . . dolōrī est / Quīntiliae** (6): double dative, *is not a matter of such
         great grief to Quintilia = does not cause as much grief for Quintilia.*
     mors: i.e., Quintilia's.
     immātūrus, -a, -um, *premature, untimely.*
6   **quantum**, relative adv., *to the extent to which, as much as, as.*

CATULLUS 96

To Calvus, on the Sad Occasion of His Wife's or Mistress's Death

Catullus tries to console Calvus with the thought that death may not be a final break between the living and the dead, and he redefines Calvus' grief as an expression of his continuing love for and friendship with the departed.

1   Sī quicquam mūtīs grātum acceptumve sepulcrīs
2   accidere ā nostrō, Calve, dolōre potest,
3   quō dēsīderiō veterēs renovāmus amōrēs
4   atque ōlim missās flēmus amīcitiās,
5   certē nōn tantō mors immātūra dolōrī est
6   Quīntiliae, quantum gaudet amōre tuō.

Explorations

1. What is the grammatical structure of the single sentence of which this poem is composed?
2. What proposition does the poet put forth in the first and the third couplets?
3. What words in the third couplet recall a specific word and a specific phrase in the first couplet? What central thematic contrast in the poem do these words and this phrase define?
4. How does the relative clause that makes up the second couplet define its antecedent, **dolōre** (2)?
5. What are the similarities and what are the differences between the two clauses in lines 3 and 4?
6. What words suggest that Catullus is generalizing about the human condition in lines 1–5?
7. How do lines 3 and 4 lead to the conclusion expressed in the final couplet?

Comparison

Sulpicius, a friend of Cicero's, wrote to him, reproving his excessive grieving over the death of his beloved daughter, Tullia, as follows (*Epistulae ad familiares*, 4.5.6):

There is no grief that the passage of time does not lessen and soothe. For you to await this time rather than to use your wisdom to take care of the grief is shameful of you. But if any consciousness belongs to the inhabitants of the underworld, such was your daughter's love for you and devotion to her family that certainly this is not what she wants you to do.

Meter: elegiac couplet

1   **vectus**, *having been carried, having traveled.*

2   **frāter**: the word occurs in the vocative three times in the poem, here and in lines 6 and 10, always at the same metrical position. It was a customary part of funeral rites to call upon the deceased three times.

    ad, prep. + acc., *to; at;* here, *for the purpose of.*

    īnferiae, -ārum, f. pl. [**in-**, *in, into* + **ferō**, *I carry;* but thought by the ancients to be related to **īnferī, -ōrum**, m. pl., *the inhabitants of the underworld*], *offerings for the dead, funeral rites* (such offerings at the site of the grave might have included milk, honey, wine, and flowers).

        miserās . . . īnferiās: the rites are so described because they evoke sadness in those who perform them.

3   **dōnō, -āre, -āvī, -ātus**, *to give; to present* (somebody, acc., with something, abl.).

        dōnārem: an imperfect subjunctive is used here and in line 4 in spite of the fact that the main verb of the sentence, **adveniō** (2) is present tense. Some explain the secondary sequence as dependent on the perfect passive participle, **vectus** (1).

    mūnus, mūneris, n., *task; duty; gift, offering* (given as a duty).

        mūnere mortis: the word in the genitive is adjectival, *offering associated with death.*

4   **mūtus, -a, -um**, *mute, silent.*

    nēquīquam, adv., *in vain.*

    alloquor [**ad-**, *to* + **loquor, loquī, locūtus sum**, *to speak*], **alloquī, allocūtus sum**, *to address, speak to.*

        alloquerer: imperfect subjunctive; see note on line 3 above.

    cinis, cineris, m., here f., *ash.*

5   **quandoquidem**, conj., *since, seeing that.*

    fortūna, -ae, f., *fortune.*

    mihī: dative of separation here and in line 6.

    tētē: emphatic **tē.**

6   **indignē**, adv., *undeservedly; outrageously;* here more specifically, *prematurely.*

        indignē: translate with **adēmpte.**

    adēmpte: what case?

        heu miser indignē frāter adēmpte mihi: apostrophe. Thomson (followed in this edition) punctuates with a period after this line instead of the comma in most editions and with a comma instead of the period in most editions at the end of line 4, making line 6 a "climactic outburst" that concludes the first six lines of the poem.

CATULLUS 101

Here rests his head upon the lap of Earth
A youth to Fortune and to Fame unknown.

(Thomas Gray, 1716–71)

Catullus' brother has died in Asia Minor near Troy. How does Catullus stress the distance he has traveled to the site of the grave? What must he do there?

1   Multās per gentēs et multa per aequora vectus
2   adveniō hās miserās, frāter, ad īnferiās,
3   ut tē postrēmō dōnārem mūnere mortis
4   et mūtam nēquīquam alloquerer cinerem,
5   quandoquidem fortūna mihī tētē abstulit ipsum,
6   heu miser indignē frāter adēmpte mihi.

continued

Explorations

1. What letters and sounds predominate in lines 1–4?
2. Read lines 1–4 aloud. How does Catullus use dactyls and spondees effectively here?
3. How does Catullus effectively position words in lines 3 and 4 to highlight the verbs?
4. How does the poet evoke sympathy for his task in the first four lines?
5. Observe the placement of the words in line 4: **et mūtam nēquīquam alloquerer cinerem**. What would be expressed by taking **nēquīquam** as modifying **mūtam**?
6   What feelings are expressed in lines 5–6? Look closely at the individual words in this couplet. What is the point of using **tētē** and **ipsum** in combination? What is the force of the words **abstulit** and **adēmpte**? How do the three words **heu miser indignē** build on each other? Why is **mihi** repeated?

7   **intereā**, adv., *meanwhile, in the meantime;* with adversative force, *nevertheless,*
     however, anyhow, at any rate.
     haec: i.e., the traditional offerings for the dead. **Haec** is the antecedent of
     quae and the object of **accipe** in line 9.
     prīscus, -a, -um, *ancient, old.*
     quae . . . trādita sunt . . . ad īnferiās: *which have been handed over/given [by*
     me] for. . . . Others take **trādita sunt** to mean *have been handed down.*
       mōre parentum: = **mōre maiōrum**, *in the manner of. . . .*
8   **trīstī mūnere**: ablative of manner, *as a sad duty/offering.*
9   **frāternus, -a, -um**, *of/belonging to a brother, a brother's.*
     multum, adv., *much, abundantly.*
     mānō, -āre, -āvī, -ātūrus, *to flow;* + abl., *to drip (with), be wet (with).*
     flētus, -ūs, m., *crying, tears.*
10   **perpetuus, -a, -um**, *everlasting, continuous, uninterrupted.*
       in perpetuum: *forever.*
     avē: *hail!*

Adveniō hās miserās, frāter, ad īnferiās. . . .

"Lament at the Grave"
Lekythos, late fifth century B.C.
National Museum
Athens, Greece

7   Nunc tamen intereā haec, prīscō quae mōre parentum
8   trādita sunt trīstī mūnere ad īnferiās,
9   accipe frāternō multum mānantia flētū,
10   atque in perpetuum, frāter, avē atque valē.

Explorations

7.   What is the structure of the poem?
8.   What is the effect of the threefold repetition of **frāter** in the poem?
9.   Comment on alliteration and assonance in the last four lines.
10. This poem speaks of last rites performed by the poet for his brother. How
     does the poem itself enact and become part of the ritual?

Comparison

Compare the following epigram by the Hellenistic Greek poet Meleager, who was
writing about 100 B.C. What similarities do you find between Meleager's epigram
and Catullus 101, 96, and 3?

Tears I bestow upon you, Heliodora, even down
    through the earth to Hades, the last gift of my love,
tears sorely wept; and on your tomb, much wept over, I pour them
    as an offering, a memorial of longing, a memorial of affection.
For piteously, piteously do I Meleager mourn for you
    even among the dead, a useless favor to Acheron.
Alas, where is the lovely blossom I desire? Hades has snatched
    her away, snatched her away; the dust has desecrated the flower in
        bloom.
But I implore you, Earth nurturer of all, enfold gently in your bosom,
    mother, the girl who is mourned by all.

    —*Palatine Anthology* 7.476

Meter: elegiac couplet

1   **Sī quicquam ... optigit ... / ... hōc est grātum. ...:** perfect indicative
in the if-clause and present indicative in the main clause constituting a
present-general condition, *If anything [ever] happens ... / ... this is [always]
pleasing. ...*

      quisquam, quisquam, quicquam, indefinite pronoun, *anyone, anything.*

      cupidus, -a, -um [cupiō, cupere, cupīvī, cupītus, *to desire, want* + **-idus, -a,
-um,** adjectival suffix], *passionately longing, desirous, eager.*

        cupidō optantīque: supply the pronoun **cuiquam,** *to anyone,* for these
two adjectives to modify. Hiatus occurs between the two adjectives; do
not elide.

      optingō [ob-, *against* + **tangō, tangere, tetigī, tāctus,** *to touch*] **optingere,
optigī** + dat., *to fall* (to as one's lot), *to happen* (to someone to his/her advan-
tage or disadvantage).

2   **īnspērāns, īnspērantis,** *not hoping/expecting.*

      īnspērantī: predicative to **(cuiquam) cupidō optantīque** in line 1, translate
when he is not hoping [for it]/expecting [it].

      hōc: nominative (here and in line 3 the *o* is long), referring to **quicquam** (1).

      grātus, -a, -um (see Catullus 96.1), *grateful, appreciative; received with gratitude
or appreciation;* + dat., *welcome, pleasing.*

      propriē, adv., *on one's own account, privately, personally; properly, strictly speak-
ing, rightly.*

        propriē: *in the true sense of the word,* take with **grātum** (in the third sense
above).

3   **hōc:** nominative, referring to the good news expressed in the relative clause,
quod. ... (4), *[the fact] that. ...*

      nōbīs: here and in line 6 = **mihi.**

      cārus, -a, -um, *dear, precious.*

      et cārius aurō: this is Heyworth's emendation.

4   **restituō [re-,** *back, again* + **statuō, statuere, statuī, statūtus,** *to set; to stand up;
to place*], **restituere, restituī, restitūtus,** *to set up again; to restore; to bring back;*
+ dat., *to bring oneself back into favor* (with).

5   **restituis:** supply **tē mihi.**

      ipsa: *yourself* or *of your own accord.*

6   **lūx, lūcis,** f., *light; day.*

      candidus, -a, -um, *white, bright, dazzling; cheerful, favorable, happy.*

      nota, -ae, f., *mark* (here, to indicate a lucky day on a calendar).

        candidiōre notā: ablative of description; for the idea, compare Catullus 8.3
candidī sōlēs.

7   **mē ūnō:** *than I alone, than I myself.*

      vīvit: = **est** (cf 8.10 and 10.33).

      aut magis umquam / optandam vītam dūcere quis poterit: this is Lyne's
emendation.

8   **quis:** note the postponement of the interrogative pronoun.

CATULLUS 107

Lesbia returns!

Catullus expresses his ecstatic joy when the unexpected happens.

1 Sī quicquam cupidō optantīque optigit umquam
2   īnspērantī, hōc est grātum animō propriē.
3 Quārē hōc est grātum nōbīs, et cārius aurō,
4   quod tē restituis, Lesbia, mī cupidō,
5 restituis cupidō atque īnspērantī, ipsa refers tē
6   nōbīs. Ō lūcem candidiōre notā!
7 Quis mē ūnō vīvit fēlīcior, aut magis umquam
8   optandam vītam dūcere quis poterit?

Text

The Oxford Classical Text prints lines 3 and 7–8 as follows:

3 quārē hōc est grātum †nōbīs quoque† cārius aurō

7 Quis mē ūnō vīvit fēlīcior, aut magis †hāc est
8   †optandus vītā dīcere quis poterit?

The †s indicate textual corruptions. Compare the lines carefully with the text given above, which contains emendations suggested by Heyworth and Lyne.

Explorations

1. What is the logical structure of thought in this poem?
2. Catullus has created an extraordinarily elaborate verbal mosaic in this poem. What words are repeated from the first couplet in the last couplet?
3. What words are repeated from the first couplet in the central second and third couplets?
4. What words are repeated within the central two couplets?
5. Are any words repeated in the final couplet from the central second and third couplets?
6. Analyze the example of conduplicatio that is at the exact center of the poem.
7. Identify the members of a tricolon in the central second and third couplets.
8. Comment on the placement of the name Lesbia in line 4.
9. What words in lines 3 and 6 highlight how welcome what has happened is?
10. What is unusual about this poem when you compare it with the rest of the short elegiac poems you have read?

Meter: elegiac couplet

1   **Iūcundum**: *a pleasant thing*, direct object of **prōpōnis**.
     mea vīta: cf. 45.13.
     prōpōnō [**pro-**, *forward* + **pōnō, pōnere, posuī, positus**, *to put, place*],
         prōpōnere, prōposuī, prōpositus, *to set forth, state, declare; to propose.*
     amōrem: modified by **hunc nostrum** (2).
2   **perpetuus, -a, -um**, *everlasting, continuous, uninterrupted.*
     usque, adv., *continuously, to the end.*
     fore: = **futūrum esse**, future infinitive in indirect statement. The text of
         lines 1–2 as given here is that of Thomson. The text as given in the Oxford
         Classical Text edition and by Quinn and Fordyce is printed below, with
         notes on attempts to make sense of it.
3   **facite ut** + subjunctive, *bring it about that, see to it that.* The verb **facere** may be
         used to introduce a subjunctive clause of result, particularly in situations
         that imply effort. Point out the two subjunctives that are introduced by
         facite ut.
4   **sincērē**, adv., *faithfully, truly.*
5   **ut liceat**: a result clause.
     tōtā . . . vītā: ablative instead of accusative of extent of time (here for the first
         time in extant Latin literature) = **per tōtam vītam**.
     perdūcō [**per-**, *through* + **dūcō, dūcere, dūxī, ductus**, *to lead, take, bring*],
         perdūcere, perdūxī, perductus, *to protract, prolong, carry through, extend.*
6   **aeternus, -a, -um**, *eternal, everlasting;* in a weakened sense, *enduring, life-
         long.*
     sānctae: cf. Catullus 76.3.
     foedus, foederis, n., *formal agreement, treaty; compact; bond, tie* (of friendship).
         foedus: cf. Catullus 76.3 and 87.3.
     amīcitia, -ae, f., *friendship.*

Text

The text of lines 1–2 is given as follows in the Oxford Classical Text:
    1 Iūcundum, mea vīta, mihi prōpōnis amōrem
    2   hunc nostrum inter nōs perpetuumque fore.
fore: = **futūrum esse**, future infinitive in indirect statement introduced by
prōpōnis (1), with **amōrem / hunc nostrum inter nōs** as the subject of the indirect statement and **Iūcundum . . . perpetuumque** as predicate adjectives.
Alternatively, Quinn suggests taking **Iūcundum . . . amōrem** as a simple direct object of **prōpōnis**, *you propose a pleasant love*, with **hunc nostrum inter nōs**
in apposition with **iūcundum amōrem** and **perpetuum fore** as a further ex-
pansion, *[and] that it will last forever.*

CATULLUS 109

More Promises

What does Lesbia promise Catullus in the opening lines of this poem? What is Catullus' response?

1 Iūcundum, mea vīta, mihi prōpōnis: amōrem
2   hunc nostrum inter nōs perpetuum usque fore.
3 Dī magnī, facite ut vērē prōmittere possit,
4   atque id sincērē dīcat et ex animō,
5 ut liceat nōbīs tōtā perdūcere vītā
6   aeternum hoc sānctae foedus amīcitiae.

Explorations

1. Compare Thomson's version of the first couplet printed in the text above with the traditional version printed below the notes on the opposite page. Do you find any problems with the traditional version? Is Thomson's version an improvement?
2. What is the relationship between the first couplet and the remainder of the poem? Compare the structures of Catullus 70 and 72.
3. In poem 70 Catullus is skeptical of Lesbia's protestations, and in poem 72 he has caught her lying. Through his prayer to the gods in lines 3–4 of poem 109, what attitude does Catullus reveal toward Lesbia's proposal in lines 1–2?
4. What result does Catullus envision in the third couplet as coming from the gods' enabling Lesbia to promise *truly, sincerely,* and *from the heart*?
5. The two major themes of this poem are (1) life-long continuance of love/friendship and (2) sincerity. How are the themes allocated to couplets?
6. Consider the final line of the poem. Locate its interlocked word order. Are there examples of transferred epithets here? If so, what are their implications? What kind of relationship is described in these words?
7. What is the relationship between **amōrem** (end of line 1) and **amīcitiae** (end of line 6)? With the concepts and words here, compare Catullus 72.3–4 and Catullus 96.3–4.

FORMS

The following charts show the forms of typical Latin nouns, adjectives, pronouns, and verbs. As an aid in pronunciation, markings of long vowels and of word stress are included.

I. Nouns

Number Case	1st Declension Fem.	2nd Declension Masc.	Masc.	Masc.	Neut.	3rd Declension Masc.	Fem.	Neut.
Singular								
Nominative	puélla	sérvus	púer	áger	báculum	páter	vōx	nómen
Genitive	puéllae	sérvī	púerī	ágrī	báculī	pátris	vócis	nóminis
Dative	puéllae	sérvō	púerō	ágrō	báculō	pátrī	vócī	nóminī
Accusative	puéllam	sérvum	púerum	ágrum	báculum	pátrem	vócem	nómen
Ablative	puéllā	sérvō	púerō	ágrō	báculō	pátre	vóce	nómine
Vocative	puélla	sérve	púer	áger	báculum	páter	vōx	nómen
Plural								
Nominative	puéllae	sérvī	púerī	ágrī	bácula	pátrēs	vócēs	nómina
Genitive	puellárum	servórum	puerórum	agrórum	baculórum	pátrum	vócum	nóminum
Dative	puéllīs	sérvīs	púerīs	ágrīs	báculīs	pátribus	vócibus	nóminibus
Accusative	puéllās	sérvōs	púerōs	ágrōs	bácula	pátrēs	vócēs	nómina
Ablative	puéllīs	sérvīs	púerīs	ágrīs	báculīs	pátribus	vócibus	nóminibus
Vocative	puéllae	sérvī	púerī	ágrī	bácula	pátrēs	vócēs	nómina

Number Case	4th Declension Masc.	Neut.	5th Declension Masc.	Fem.
Singular				
Nominative	árcus	génū	díēs	rēs
Genitive	árcūs	génūs	diéī	réī
Dative	árcuī	génū	diéī	réī
Accusative	árcum	génū	díem	rem
Ablative	árcū	génū	díē	rē
Vocative	árcus	génū	díēs	rēs
Plural				
Nominative	árcūs	génua	díēs	rēs
Genitive	árcuum	génuum	diérum	rérum
Dative	árcibus	génibus	diébus	rébus
Accusative	árcūs	génua	díēs	rēs
Ablative	árcibus	génibus	diébus	rébus
Vocative	árcūs	génua	díēs	rēs

II. Adjectives

Number Case	1st and 2nd Declension			3rd Declension		
	Masc.	Fem.	Neut.	Masc.	Fem.	Neut.
Singular						
Nominative	mágn*us*	mágn*a*	mágn*um*	ómn*is*	ómn*is*	ómn*e*
Genitive	mágn*ī*	mágn*ae*	mágn*ī*	ómn*is*	ómn*is*	ómn*is*
Dative	mágn*ō*	mágn*ae*	mágn*ō*	ómn*ī*	ómn*ī*	ómn*ī*
Accusative	mágn*um*	mágn*am*	mágn*um*	ómn*em*	ómn*em*	ómn*e*
Ablative	mágn*ō*	mágn*ā*	mágn*ō*	ómn*ī*	ómn*ī*	ómn*ī*
Vocative	mágn*e*	mágn*a*	mágn*um*	ómn*is*	ómn*is*	ómn*e*
Plural						
Nominative	mágn*ī*	mágn*ae*	mágn*a*	ómn*ēs*	ómn*ēs*	ómn*ia*
Genitive	magn*órum*	magn*árum*	magn*órum*	ómn*ium*	ómn*ium*	ómn*ium*
Dative	mágn*īs*	mágn*īs*	mágn*īs*	ómn*ibus*	ómn*ibus*	ómn*ibus*
Accusative	mágn*ōs*	mágn*ās*	mágn*a*	ómn*ēs*	ómn*ēs*	ómn*ia*
Ablative	mágn*īs*	mágn*īs*	mágn*īs*	ómn*ibus*	ómn*ibus*	ómn*ibus*
Vocative	mágn*ī*	mágn*ae*	mágn*a*	ómn*ēs*	ómn*ēs*	ómn*ia*

III. Comparative Adjectives

Case	Masc.	Fem.	Neut.
Singular			
Nominative	púlchrior	púlchrior	púlchrius
Genitive	pulchriór*is*	pulchriór*is*	pulchriór*is*
Dative	pulchriór*ī*	pulchriór*ī*	pulchriór*ī*
Accusative	pulchriór*em*	pulchriór*em*	púlchrius
Ablative	pulchriór*e*	pulchriór*e*	pulchriór*e*
Vocative	púlchrior	púlchrior	púlchrius
Plural			
Nominative	pulchriór*ēs*	pulchriór*ēs*	pulchriór*a*
Genitive	pulchriór*um*	pulchriór*um*	pulchriór*um*
Dative	pulchriór*ibus*	pulchriór*ibus*	pulchriór*ibus*
Accusative	pulchriór*ēs*	pulchriór*ēs*	pulchriór*a*
Ablative	pulchriór*ibus*	pulchriór*ibus*	pulchriór*ibus*
Vocative	pulchriór*ēs*	pulchriór*ēs*	pulchriór*a*

Adjectives have *positive*, *comparative*, and *superlative* forms. You can usually recognize the comparative by the letters **-ior(-)** and the superlative by **-issimus**, **-errimus**, or **-illimus**:

ignávus, -a, -um, *lazy*	ignávior, ignávius	ignávíssimus, -a, -um
púlcher, púlchra, púlchrum, *beautiful*	púlchrior, púlchrius	pulchérrimus, -a, -um
fácilis, -is, -e, *easy*	facílior, facílius	facíllimus, -a, -um

Some very common adjectives are irregular in the comparative and superlative:

Positive	Comparative	Superlative
bónus, -a, -um, *good*	mélior, mélius, *better*	óptimus, -a, -um, *best*
málus, -a, -um, *bad*	péior, péius, *worse*	péssimus, -a, -um, *worst*
mágnus, -a, -um, *big*	máior, máius, *bigger*	máximus, -a, -um, *biggest*
párvus, -a, -um, *small*	mínor, mínus, *smaller*	mínimus, -a, -um, *smallest*
múltus, -a, -um, *much*	plūs,* *more*	plúrimus, -a, -um, *most, very much*
múltī, -ae, -a, *many*	plúrēs, plúra, *more*	plúrimī, -ae, -a, *most, very many*

*Note that **plūs** is not an adjective but a neuter substantive, usually found with a partitive genitive, e.g., Titus **plūs vīnī** bibit. *Titus drank **more (of the) wine**.*

IV.   Present Participles

Number Case	Masc.	Fem.	Neut.
Singular			
Nominative	párāns	párāns	párāns
Genitive	parántis	parántis	parántis
Dative	parántī	parántī	parántī
Accusative	parántem	parántem	párāns
Ablative	parántī/e	parántī/e	parántī/e
Plural			
Nominative	parántēs	parántēs	parántia
Genitive	parántium	parántium	parántium
Dative	parántibus	parántibus	parántibus
Accusative	parántēs	parántēs	parántia
Ablative	parántibus	parántibus	parántibus

V. Numbers

Case	Masc.	Fem.	Neut.	Masc.	Fem.	Neut.	Masc.	Fem.	Neut.
Nom.	únus	úna	únum	dúo	dúae	dúo	trēs	trēs	tría
Gen.	ūníus	ūníus	ūníus	duórum	duárum	duórum	tríum	tríum	tríum
Dat.	únī	únī	únī	duóbus	duábus	duóbus	tríbus	tríbus	tríbus
Acc.	únum	únam	únum	dúōs	dúās	dúo	trēs	trēs	tría
Abl.	únō	únā	únō	duóbus	duábus	duóbus	tríbus	tríbus	tríbus

	Cardinal	**Ordinal**
I	únus, -a, -um, *one*	prímus, -a, -um, *first*
II	dúo, -ae, -o, *two*	secúndus, -a, -um, *second*
III	trēs, trēs, tría, *three*	tértius, -a, -um, *third*
IV	quáttuor, *four*	quártus, -a, -um
V	quínque, *five*	quíntus, -a, -um
VI	sex, *six*	séxtus, -a, -um
VII	séptem, *seven*	séptimus, -a, -um
VIII	óctō, *eight*	octávus, -a, -um
IX	nóvem, *nine*	nónus, -a, -um
X	décem, *ten*	décimus, -a, -um
XI	úndecim, *eleven*	ūndécimus, -a, -um
XII	duódecim, *twelve*	duodécimus, -a, -um
XIII	trédecim, *thirteen*	tértius décimus, -a, -um
XIV	quattuórdecim, *fourteen*	quártus décimus, -a, -um
XV	quíndecim, *fifteen*	quíntus décimus, -a, -um
XVI	sédecim, *sixteen*	séxtus décimus, -a, -um
XVII	septéndecim, *seventeen*	séptimus décimus, -a, -um
XVIII	duodēvīgíntī, *eighteen,*	duodēvīcésimus, -a, -um
XIX	ūndēvīgíntī, *nineteen,*	ūndēvīcésimus, -a, -um
XX	vīgíntī, *twenty*	vīcésimus, -a, -um
L	quīnquāgíntā, *fifty*	quīnquāgésimus, -a, -um
C	céntum, *a hundred*	centésimus, -a, -um
D	quīngéntī, -ae, -a, *five hundred*	quīngentésimus, -a, -um
M	mílle, *a thousand*	mīllésimus, -a, -um

N.B. The cardinal numbers from **quattuor** to **centum** do not change their form to indicate case and gender.

VI. Personal Pronouns

Number Case	1st Person	2nd Person	3rd Person		
			Masc.	Fem.	Neut.
Singular					
Nominative	égo	tū	is	éa	id
Genitive	méī	túī	éius	éius	éius
Dative	míhi	tíbi	éī	éī	éī
Accusative	mē	tē	éum	éam	id
Ablative	mē	tē	éō	éā	éō
Plural					
Nominative	nōs	vōs	éī	éae	éa
Genitive	nóstrī	véstrī	eórum	eárum	eórum
	nóstrum	véstrum			
Dative	nóbīs	vóbīs	éīs	éīs	éīs
Accusative	nōs	vōs	éōs	éās	éa
Ablative	nóbīs	vóbīs	éīs	éīs	éīs

Note: The forms of **is, ea, id** may also serve as demonstrative adjectives.

VII. Reflexive Pronoun

Singular	
Nominative	——
Genitive	súī
Dative	síbi
Accusative	sē
Ablative	sē
Plural	
Nominative	——
Genitive	súī
Dative	síbi
Accusative	sē
Ablative	sē

VIII. Relative Pronoun

	Masc.	Fem.	Neut.
Singular			
Nominative	quī	quae	quod
Genitive	cúius	cúius	cúius
Dative	cui	cui	cui
Accusative	quem	quam	quod
Ablative	quō	quā	quō
Plural			
Nominative	quī	quae	quae
Genitive	quórum	quárum	quórum
Dative	quíbus	quíbus	quíbus
Accusative	quōs	quās	quae
Ablative	quíbus	quíbus	quíbus

IX. Interrogative Pronoun

Number Case	Masc.	Fem.	Neut.
Singular			
Nominative	quis	quis	quid
Genitive	cúius	cúius	cúius
Dative	cui	cui	cui
Accusative	quem	quem	quid
Ablative	quō	quō	quō
Plural	Same as the plural of the relative pronoun on page 175.		

X. Indefinite Adjective and Pronouns

Number Case	Masc.	Fem.	Neut.	Masc.	Fem.	Neut.
Singular						
Nominative	quídam	quaédam	quóddam	áliquī	áliqua	áliquod
Genitive	cuiúsdam	cuiúsdam	cuiúsdam	álicuius	álicuius	álicuius
Dative	cúidam	cúidam	cúidam	álicui	álicui	álicui
Accusative	quéndam	quándam	quóddam	áliquem	áliquam	áliquod
Ablative	quódam	quádam	quódam	áliquō	áliqua	áliquō
Plural						
Nominative	quídam	quaédam	quaédam	áliquī	áliquae	áliqua
Genitive	quōrúndam	quārúndam	quōrúndam	aliquốrum	aliquárum	aliquốrum
Dative	quibúsdam	quibúsdam	quibúsdam	aliquíbus	aliquíbus	aliquíbus
Accusative	quốsdam	quásdam	quaédam	áliquōs	áliquās	áliqua
Ablative	quibúsdam	quibúsdam	quibúsdam	aliquíbus	aliquíbus	aliquíbus

The indefinite pronoun **quīdam, quaedam, quiddam** has the same forms as the indefinite adjective, except for **quiddam** in the neuter nominative and accusative singular. The indefinite pronoun **aliquis, aliquis, aliquid** has the regular forms of the interrogative adjective **quis, quis, quid**, as do the indefinite pronouns **quisque, quisque, quidque** and **quisquam, quisquam, quidquam (quicquam)**. The indefinite adjective **quisque, quaeque, quodque** has the same forms as the relative pronoun **quī, quae, quod** except for **quis-** in the masculine nominative singular.

XI. Demonstrative Adjectives and Pronouns

Number Case	Masc.	Fem.	Neut.	Masc.	Fem.	Neut.
Singular						
Nominative	hic	haec	hoc	ílle	illa	íllud
Genitive	húius	húius	húius	illíus	illíus	illíus
Dative	húic	húic	húic	íllī	íllī	íllī
Accusative	hunc	hanc	hoc	íllum	íllam	íllud
Ablative	hōc	hāc	hōc	íllō	íllā	íllō
Plural						
Nominative	hī	hae	haec	íllī	íllae	ílla
Genitive	hórum	hárum	hórum	illórum	illárum	illórum
Dative	hīs	hīs	hīs	íllīs	íllīs	íllīs
Accusative	hōs	hās	haec	íllōs	íllās	ílla
Ablative	hīs	hīs	hīs	íllīs	íllīs	íllīs

Number Case	Masculine	Feminine	Neuter
Singular			
Nominative	ípse	ípsa	ípsum
Genitive	ipsíus	ipsíus	ipsíus
Dative	ípsī	ípsī	ípsī
Accusative	ípsum	ípsam	ípsum
Ablative	ípsō	ípsā	ípsō
Plural			
Nominative	ípsī	ípsae	ípsa
Genitive	ipsórum	ipsárum	ipsórum
Dative	ípsīs	ípsīs	ípsīs
Accusative	ípsōs	ípsās	ípsa
Ablative	ípsīs	ípsīs	ípsīs

Number Case	Masc.	Fem.	Neut.	Masc.	Fem.	Neut.
Singular						
Nominative	is	éa	id	ídem	éadem	ídem
Genitive	éius	éius	éius	eiúsdem	eiúsdem	eiúsdem
Dative	éī	éī	éī	eídem	eídem	eídem
Accusative	éum	éam	id	eúndem	eándem	ídem
Ablative	éō	éā	éō	eódem	eádem	eódem
Plural						
Nominative	éī	éae	éa	eídem	eaédem	éadem
Genitive	eórum	eárum	eórum	eōrúndem	eārúndem	eōrúndem
Dative	éīs	éīs	éīs	eísdem	eísdem	eísdem
Accusative	éōs	éās	éa	eósdem	eásdem	éadem
Ablative	éīs	éīs	éīs	eísdem	eísdem	eísdem

XII. Adverbs

Latin adverbs may be formed from adjectives of the 1st and 2nd declensions by adding *-ē* to the base of the adjective, e.g., **strēnuē**, *strenuously*, from **strēnuus, -a, -um.** To form an adverb from a 3rd declension adjective, add *-iter* to the base of the adjective or *-er* to bases ending in **-nt-**, e.g., **breviter**, *briefly*, from **brevis, -is, -e**, and **prūdenter**, *wisely*, from **prūdēns, prūdentis.**

laétē, *happily*	**laétius**	**laetíssimē**
fēlíciter, *luckily*	**fēlícius**	**fēlīcíssimē**
celériter, *quickly*	**celérius**	**celérrimē**
prūdénter, *wisely*	**prūdéntius**	**prūdentíssimē**

Note the following as well:

díū, *for a long time*	**diútius**	**diūtíssimē**
saépe, *often*	**saépius**	**saepíssimē**
sérō, *late*	**sérius**	**sēríssimē**

Some adverbs are irregular:

béne, *well*	**mélius,** *better*	**óptimē,** *best*
mále, *badly*	**péius,** *worse*	**péssimē,** *worst*
fácile, *easily*	**facílius,** *more easily*	**facíllimē,** *most easily*
magnópere, *greatly*	**mágis,** *more*	**máximē,** *most*
paúlum, *little*	**mínus,** *less*	**mínimē,** *least*
múltum, *much*	**plūs,** *more*	**plúrimum,** *most*

XIII. Regular Verbs Active: Infinitive, Imperative, Indicative

			1st Conjugation	2nd Conjugation	3rd Conjugation		4th Conjugation
	Infinitive		par*áre*	hab*ére*	mítt*ere*	iác*ere (-iō)*	aud*íre*
	Imperative		pár*á*	háb*é*	mítt*e*	iác*e*	aúd*í*
			par*áte*	hab*éte*	mítt*ite*	iác*ite*	aud*íte*
Present	Singular	1	pár*ō*	hábe*ō*	mítt*ō*	iáci*ō*	aúdi*ō*
		2	pár*ās*	hábē*s*	mítti*s*	iáci*s*	aúdī*s*
		3	pára*t*	hábe*t*	mítti*t*	iáci*t*	aúdi*t*
	Plural	1	par*ámus*	habé*mus*	mítti*mus*	iáci*mus*	audí*mus*
		2	par*átis*	habé*tis*	mítti*tis*	iáci*tis*	audí*tis*
		3	pára*nt*	hábe*nt*	míttu*nt*	iáciu*nt*	aúdiu*nt*
Imperfect	Singular	1	para*bam*	habé*bam*	mittē*bam*	iaciē*bam*	audiē*bam*
		2	para*bās*	habé*bās*	mittē*bās*	iaciē*bās*	audiē*bās*
		3	para*bat*	habé*bat*	mittē*bat*	iaciē*bat*	audiē*bat*
	Plural	1	parā*bámus*	habē*bámus*	mittē*bámus*	iaciē*bámus*	audiē*bámus*
		2	parā*bátis*	habē*bátis*	mittē*bátis*	iaciē*bátis*	audiē*bátis*
		3	para*bant*	habé*bant*	mittē*bant*	iaciē*bant*	audiē*bant*
Future	Singular	1	para*bō*	habé*bō*	mítt*am*	iáci*am*	aúdi*am*
		2	para*bis*	habé*bis*	mítt*ēs*	iáci*ēs*	aúdi*ēs*
		3	para*bit*	habé*bit*	mítt*et*	iáci*et*	aúdi*et*
	Plural	1	para*bimus*	habé*bimus*	mitt*émus*	iaci*émus*	audi*émus*
		2	para*bitis*	habé*bitis*	mitt*étis*	iaci*étis*	audi*étis*
		3	para*bunt*	habé*bunt*	mítt*ent*	iáci*ent*	aúdi*ent*
Perfect	Singular	1	paráv*ī*	hábu*ī*	mís*ī*	iéc*ī*	audív*ī*
		2	parāv*ístī*	habu*ístī*	mis*ístī*	iēc*ístī*	audiv*ístī*
		3	paráv*it*	hábu*it*	mís*it*	iéc*it*	audív*it*
	Plural	1	paráv*imus*	habú*imus*	mís*imus*	iéc*imus*	audív*imus*
		2	paráv*istis*	habu*ístis*	mis*ístis*	iēc*ístis*	audiv*ístis*
		3	paráv*érunt*	habu*érunt*	mís*érunt*	iēc*érunt*	audiv*érunt*
Pluperfect	Singular	1	paráv*eram*	habú*eram*	mís*eram*	iéc*eram*	audív*eram*
		2	paráv*erās*	habú*erās*	mís*erās*	iéc*erās*	audív*erās*
		3	paráv*erat*	habú*erat*	mís*erat*	iéc*erat*	audív*erat*
	Plural	1	parāv*erámus*	habu*erámus*	mis*erámus*	iēc*erámus*	audiv*erámus*
		2	parāv*erátis*	habu*erátis*	mis*erátis*	iēc*erátis*	audiv*erátis*
		3	paráv*erant*	habú*erant*	mís*erant*	iéc*erant*	audív*erant*
Future Perfect	Singular	1	paráv*erō*	habú*erō*	mís*erō*	iéc*erō*	audív*erō*
		2	paráv*eris*	habú*eris*	mís*eris*	iéc*eris*	audív*eris*
		3	paráv*erit*	habú*erit*	mís*erit*	iéc*erit*	audív*erit*
	Plural	1	parāv*érimus*	habu*érimus*	mis*érimus*	iēc*érimus*	audiv*érimus*
		2	parāv*éritis*	habu*éritis*	mis*éritis*	iēc*éritis*	audiv*éritis*
		3	paráv*erint*	habú*erint*	mís*erint*	iéc*erint*	audív*erint*

XIV. Regular Verbs Passive: Infinitive, Imperative, Indicative

			1st Conjugation	2nd Conjugation	3rd Conjugation		4th Conjugation
	Infinitive	1	port*ā́rī*	mov*ḗrī*	mítt*ī*	iác*ī*	aud*ī́rī*
	Imperative	1	port*ā́re*	mov*ḗre*	mítt*ere*	iác*ere*	aud*ī́re*
		2	port*ā́minī*	mov*ḗminī*	mítt*iminī*	iac*íminī*	aud*ī́minī*
Present	Singular	1	pórto*r*	móveo*r*	mítto*r*	iácio*r*	aúdio*r*
		2	port*ā́ris*	mov*ḗris*	mítte*ris*	iáce*ris*	aud*ī́ris*
		3	port*ā́tur*	mov*ḗtur*	mítti*tur*	iáci*tur*	aud*ī́tur*
	Plural	1	port*ā́mur*	mov*ḗmur*	mítti*mur*	iáci*mur*	aud*ī́mur*
		2	port*ā́minī*	mov*ḗminī*	mittí*minī*	iac*íminī*	aud*ī́minī*
		3	port*ā́ntur*	mov*ḗntur*	mittú*ntur*	iaci*úntur*	audi*úntur*
Imperfect	Singular	1	portā*bar*	movē*bar*	mittē*bar*	iaciē*bar*	audiē*bar*
		2	portā*bā́ris*	movē*bā́ris*	mittē*bā́ris*	iaciē*bā́ris*	audiē*bā́ris*
		3	portā*bā́tur*	movē*bā́tur*	mittē*bā́tur*	iaciē*bā́tur*	audiē*bā́tur*
	Plural	1	portā*bā́mur*	movē*bā́mur*	mittē*bā́mur*	iaciē*bā́mur*	audiē*bā́mur*
		2	portā*bā́minī*	movē*bā́minī*	mittē*bā́minī*	iaciē*bā́minī*	audiē*bā́minī*
		3	portā*bántur*	movē*bántur*	mittē*bántur*	iaciē*bántur*	audiē*bántur*
Future	Singular	1	portā*bor*	movē*bor*	mítta*r*	iácia*r*	aúdia*r*
		2	portā*beris*	movē*beris*	mittē*ris*	iaci*ḗris*	audi*ḗris*
		3	portā*bitur*	movē*bitur*	mittḗ*tur*	iaci*ḗtur*	audi*ḗtur*
	Plural	1	portā*bimur*	movē*bimur*	mittḗ*mur*	iaci*ḗmur*	audi*ḗmur*
		2	portā*bíminī*	movē*bíminī*	mittḗ*minī*	iaci*ḗminī*	audi*ḗminī*
		3	portā*búntur*	movē*búntur*	mittḗ*ntur*	iaci*ḗntur*	audi*ḗntur*

		Perfect Passive		Pluperfect Passive		Future Perfect Passive	
Singular	1	portā́tus, -a	sum	portā́tus, -a	éram	portā́tus, -a	érō
	2	portā́tus, -a	es	portā́tus, -a	érās	portā́tus, -a	éris
	3	portā́tus, -a, -um	est	portā́tus, -a, -um	érat	portā́tus, -a, -um	érit
Plural	1	portā́tī, -ae	súmus	portā́tī, -ae	erā́mus	portā́tī, -ae	érimus
	2	portā́tī, -ae	éstis	portā́tī, -ae	erā́tis	portā́tī, -ae	éritis
	3	portā́tī, -ae, -a	sunt	portā́tī, -ae, -a	érant	portā́tī, -ae, -a	érunt

XV. Regular Verbs Active: Subjunctive

			1st Conjugation	2nd Conjugation	3rd Conjugation		4th Conjugation
Present	Singular	1	pórt*em*	móve*am*	mítt*am*	iáci*am*	aúdi*am*
		2	pórt*ēs*	móve*ās*	mítt*ās*	iáci*ās*	aúdi*ās*
		3	pórt*et*	móve*at*	mítt*at*	iáci*at*	aúdi*at*
	Plural	1	port*émus*	move*ámus*	mitt*ámus*	iaci*ámus*	audi*ámus*
		2	port*étis*	move*átis*	mitt*átis*	iac*átis*	audi*átis*
		3	pórt*ent*	móve*ant*	mítt*ant*	iáci*ant*	aúdi*ant*
Imperfect	Singular	1	portá*rem*	mové*rem*	mítte*rem*	iáce*rem*	audí*rem*
		2	portá*rēs*	mové*rēs*	mítte*rēs*	iáce*rēs*	audí*rēs*
		3	portá*ret*	mové*ret*	mítte*ret*	iáce*ret*	audí*ret*
	Plural	1	portārḗ*mus*	movērḗ*mus*	mitterḗ*mus*	iacerḗ*mus*	audīrḗ*mus*
		2	portārḗ*tis*	movērḗ*tis*	mitterḗ*tis*	iacerḗ*tis*	audīrḗ*tis*
		3	portá*rent*	mové*rent*	mítte*rent*	iáce*rent*	audí*rent*
Perfect	Singular	1	portáv*erim*	móv*erim*	mís*erim*	iéc*erim*	audív*erim*
		2	portáv*eris*	móv*eris*	mís*eris*	iéc*eris*	audív*eris*
		3	portáv*erit*	móv*erit*	mís*erit*	iéc*erit*	audív*erit*
	Plural	1	portāv*érimus*	mōv*érimus*	mīs*érimus*	iēc*érimus*	audīv*érimus*
		2	portāv*éritis*	mōv*éritis*	mīs*éritis*	iēc*éritis*	audīv*éritis*
		3	portáv*erint*	móv*erint*	mís*erint*	iéc*erint*	audív*erint*
Pluperfect	Singular	1	portāvís*sem*	mōvís*sem*	mīsís*sem*	iēcís*sem*	audīvís*sem*
		2	portāvís*sēs*	mōvís*sēs*	mīsís*sēs*	iēcís*sēs*	audīvís*sēs*
		3	portāvís*set*	mōvís*set*	mīsís*set*	iēcís*set*	audīvís*set*
	Plural	1	portāvissḗ*mus*	mōvissḗ*mus*	mīsissḗ*mus*	iēcissḗ*mus*	audīvissḗ*mus*
		2	portāvissḗ*tis*	mōvissḗ*tis*	mīsissḗ*tis*	iēcissḗ*tis*	audīvissḗ*tis*
		3	portāvís*sent*	mōvís*sent*	mīsís*sent*	iēcís*sent*	audīvís*sent*

XVI. Regular Verbs Passive: Subjunctive

			1st Conjugation	2nd Conjugation	3rd Conjugation		4th Conjugation
Present	Singular	1	pórt*er*	móve*ar*	mítt*ar*	iáci*ar*	aúdi*ar*
		2	pórt*ēris*	move*áris*	mítt*āris*	iaci*áris*	audi*áris*
		3	pórt*ētur*	move*átur*	mítt*ātur*	iaci*átur*	audi*átur*
	Plural	1	port*émur*	move*ámur*	mitt*ámur*	iaci*ámur*	audi*ámur*
		2	port*éminī*	move*áminī*	mitt*áminī*	iaci*áminī*	audi*áminī*
		3	port*éntur*	move*ántur*	mitt*ántur*	iaci*ántur*	audi*ántur*
Imperfect	Singular	1	portá*rer*	mové*rer*	mítte*rer*	iáce*rer*	audí*rer*
		2	portārḗ*ris*	movērḗ*ris*	mitte*réris*	iace*réris*	audīrḗ*ris*
		3	portārḗ*tur*	movērḗ*tur*	mitterḗ*tur*	iacerḗ*tur*	audīrḗ*tur*
	Plural	1	portārḗ*mur*	movērḗ*mur*	mitterḗ*mur*	iacerḗ*mur*	audīrḗ*mur*
		2	portārḗ*minī*	movērḗ*minī*	mitterḗ*minī*	iacerḗ*minī*	audīrḗ*minī*
		3	portārḗ*ntur*	movērḗ*ntur*	mitterḗ*ntur*	iacerḗ*ntur*	audīrḗ*ntur*
Perfect	1		portátus sim	mótus sim	míssus sim	iáctus sim	audítus sim
			etc.	etc.	etc.	etc.	etc.
Pluperfect	1		portátus éssem	mótus éssem	míssus éssem	iáctus éssem	audítus éssem
			etc.	etc.	etc.	etc.	etc.

XVII.   Deponent Verbs: Infinitive, Imperative, Indicative

			1st Conjugation	2nd Conjugation	3rd Conjugation		4th Conjugation
Present Infinitive			cōn*ā́rī*	ver*ḗrī*	lóqu*ī*	régred*ī*	exper*írī*
Imperative			cōn*ā́re*	ver*ére*	lóqu*ere*	regréd*ere*	exper*íre*
			cōn*ā́minī*	ver*émini*	loqu*íminī*	regred*íminī*	exper*íminī*
Present	Singular	1	cón*or*	vére*or*	lóqu*or*	regrédi*or*	expéri*or*
		2	cōn*ā́ris*	ver*éris*	lóque*ris*	regréde*ris*	experí*ris*
		3	cōn*ā́tur*	ver*étur*	lóqui*tur*	regrédi*tur*	experí*tur*
	Plural	1	cōn*ā́mur*	ver*émur*	lóqui*mur*	regrédi*mur*	experí*mur*
		2	cōn*ā́minī*	ver*éminī*	loquí*minī*	regredí*minī*	experí*minī*
		3	cōn*ántur*	ver*éntur*	loquú*ntur*	regrediú*ntur*	experiú*ntur*
Imperfect	Singular	1	cōn*ā́bar*	ver*ébar*	loqu*ébar*	regredi*ébar*	experi*ébar*
		2	cōn*ābā́ris*	ver*ēbā́ris*	loqu*ēbā́ris*	regredi*ēbā́ris*	experi*ēbā́ris*
		3	cōn*ābátur*	ver*ēbátur*	loqu*ēbátur*	regredi*ēbátur*	experi*ēbátur*
Future	Singular	1	cōn*ā́bor*	ver*ábor*	lóqu*ar*	regréd*iar*	expéri*ar*
		2	cōn*ā́beris*	ver*éberis*	loqu*éris*	regredi*éris*	experi*éris*
		3	cōn*ā́bitur*	ver*ébitur*	loqu*étur*	regredi*étur*	experi*étur*
Perfect	1		cōn*ā́tus* sum	vér*itus* sum	loc*ū́tus* sum	regréssus sum	expértus sum
Pluperfect	1		cōn*ā́tus* éram	vér*itus* éram	loc*ū́tus* éram	regréssus éram	expértus éram
Future Perfect	1		cōn*ā́tus* érō	vér*itus* érō	loc*ū́tus* érō	regréssus érō	expértus érō

XVIII.   Deponent Verbs: Subjunctive

			1st Conjugation	2nd Conjugation	3rd Conjugation		4th Conjugation
Present	Singular	1	cón*er*	vére*ar*	lóqu*ar*	regrédi*ar*	expéri*ar*
		2	cōn*éris*	vere*áris*	loqu*áris*	regredi*áris*	experi*áris*
		3	cōn*étur*	vere*átur*	loqu*átur*	regredi*átur*	experi*átur*
	Plural	1	cōn*émur*	vere*ámur*	loqu*ámur*	regredi*ámur*	experi*ámur*
		2	cōn*éminī*	vere*áminī*	loqu*áminī*	regredi*áminī*	experi*áminī*
		3	cōn*éntur*	vere*ántur*	loqu*ántur*	regredi*ántur*	experi*ántur*
Imperfect	Singular	1	cōn*ā́rer*	ver*érer*	lóqu*erer*	regréd*erer*	exper*írer*
		2	cōn*ārḗris*	ver*ērḗris*	loqu*erḗris*	regred*erḗris*	experī*rḗris*
		3	cōn*ārḗtur*	ver*ērḗtur*	loqu*erḗtur*	regred*erḗtur*	experī*rḗtur*
	Plural	1	cōn*ārḗmur*	ver*ērḗmur*	loqu*erḗmur*	regred*erḗmur*	experī*rḗmur*
		2	cōn*ārḗminī*	ver*ērḗminī*	loqu*erḗminī*	regred*erḗminī*	experī*rḗminī*
		3	cōn*ārḗntur*	ver*ērḗntur*	loqu*eréntur*	regred*eréntur*	experī*réntur*
Perfect	1		cōn*ā́tus* sim	vér*itus* sim	loc*ū́tus* sim	regréssus sim	expértus sim
Pluperfect	1		cōn*ā́tus* éssem	vér*itus* éssem	loc*ū́tus* éssem	regréssus éssem	expértus éssem

XIX. Irregular Verbs: Infinitive, Imperative, Indicative

Infinitive			ésse	pósse	vélle	nólle	málle
Imperative			es	——	——	nólī	——
			éste	——	——	nólíte	——
Present	Singular	1	sum	póssum	vólō	nólō	málō
		2	es	pótes	vīs	nōn vīs	mávīs
		3	est	pótest	vult	nōn vult	mávult
	Plural	1	súmus	póssumus	vólumus	nólumus	málumus
		2	éstis	potéstis	vúltis	nōn vúltis	māvúltis
		3	sunt	póssunt	vólunt	nólunt	málunt
Imperfect	Singular	1	éram	póteram	volébam	nōlébam	mālébam
		2	erās	póterās	volébās	nōlébās	mālébās
		3	érat	póterat	volébat	nōlébat	mālébat
	Plural	1	erámus	poterámus	volebámus	nōlēbámus	mālēbámus
		2	erátis	poterátis	volebátis	nōlēbátis	mālēbátis
		3	érant	póterant	volébant	nōlébant	mālébant
Future	Singular	1	érō	póterō	vólam	nólam	málam
		2	éris	póteris	vólēs	nólēs	málēs
		3	érit	póterit	vólet	nólet	málet
	Plural	1	érimus	potérimus	volémus	nōlémus	mālémus
		2	éritis	potéritis	volétis	nōlétis	mālétis
		3	érunt	póterunt	vólent	nólent	málent

Infinitive			férre	férrī	fíerī	íre
Imperative			fer	férre	——	ī
			férte	feríminī	——	íte
Present	Singular	1	férō	féror	fíō	éō
		2	fers	férris	fīs	īs
		3	fert	fértur	fit	it
	Plural	1	férimus	férimur	fímus	ímus
		2	fértis	feríminī	fítis	ítis
		3	férunt	ferúntur	fíunt	éunt
Imperfect	Singular	1	ferébam	ferébar	fiébam	íbam
		2	ferébās	ferébáris	fiébās	íbās
		3	ferébat	ferébátur	fiébat	íbat
	Plural	1	ferēbámus	ferēbámur	fiēbámus	íbámus
		2	ferēbátis	ferēbáminī	fiēbátis	íbátis
		3	ferébant	ferēbántur	fiébant	íbant
Future	Singular	1	féram	férar	fíam	íbō
		2	férēs	feréris	fíēs	íbis
		3	féret	férétur	fíet	íbit
	Plural	1	ferémus	ferémur	fiémus	íbimus
		2	ferétis	feréminī	fiétis	íbitis
		3	férent	feréntur	fíent	íbunt

XX. Irregular Verbs: Perfect, Pluperfect, Future Perfect Indicative

Full charts are not supplied for these forms because (except for the perfect of **eō**, for which see below) they are not irregular in any way. They are made in the same way as the perfect, pluperfect, and future perfect tenses of regular verbs, by adding the perfect, pluperfect and future perfect endings to the perfect stem. The perfect stem is found by dropping the *-ī* from the third principal part. The first three principal parts of the irregular verbs are as follows:

> sum, esse, <u>fuī</u>
> possum, posse, <u>potuī</u>
> volō, velle, <u>voluī</u>
> nōlō, nōlle, <u>nōluī</u>
> mālō, mālle, <u>māluī</u>
> ferō, ferre, <u>tulī</u>
> eō, īre, <u>iī</u> or <u>īvī</u>

Examples:

> Perfect: fuistī, voluērunt, tulimus
> Pluperfect: fueram, potuerant, nōluerāmus
> Future Perfect: fuerō, volueris, tulerimus

The perfect forms of **eō** made from the stem i- are as follows:

> Singular: iī, īstī, iit
> Plural: iimus, īstis, iērunt

Note that the stem vowel (**i-**) contracts with the *-i* of the endings *-istī* and *-istis* to give **ī-** (**īstī, īstis**). Thus also the perfect infinitive: **īsse** (for **iisse**).

The perfect forms of **eō** made from the stem **īv-** are regular, as follows:

> Singular: īvī, īvistī, īvit
> Plural: īvimus, īvistis, īvērunt

XXI. Irregular Verbs: Subjunctive

Present	Singular	1	s*im*	póss*im*	vél*im*	nól*im*	mál*im*
		2	s*īs*	póss*īs*	vél*īs*	nól*īs*	mál*īs*
		3	s*it*	póss*it*	vél*it*	nól*it*	mál*it*
	Plural	1	s*ímus*	poss*ímus*	vel*ímus*	nōl*ímus*	māl*ímus*
		2	s*ítis*	poss*ítis*	vel*ítis*	nōl*ítis*	māl*ítis*
		3	s*int*	póss*int*	vél*int*	nōl*int*	māl*int*
Imperfect	Singular	1	éss*em*	póss*em*	vél*lem*	nól*lem*	mál*lem*
		2	éss*ēs*	póss*ēs*	vél*lēs*	nól*lēs*	mál*lēs*
		3	éss*et*	póss*et*	vél*let*	nól*let*	mál*let*
	Plural	1	ess*émus*	poss*émus*	vel*lémus*	nōl*lémus*	māl*lémus*
		2	ess*étis*	poss*étis*	vel*létis*	nōl*létis*	māl*létis*
		3	éss*ent*	póss*ent*	vél*lent*	nól*lent*	mál*lent*
Perfect	Singular	1	fú*erim*	potú*erim*	volú*erim*	nōlú*erim*	mālú*erim*
		2	fú*eris*	potú*eris*	volú*eris*	nōlú*eris*	mālú*eris*
		3	fú*erit*	potú*erit*	volú*erit*	nōlú*erit*	mālú*erit*
	Plural	1	fu*érimus*	potu*érimus*	volu*érimus*	nōlu*érimus*	mālu*érimus*
		2	fu*éritis*	potu*éritis*	volu*éritis*	nōlu*éritis*	mālu*éritis*
		3	fú*erint*	potú*erint*	volú*erint*	nōlú*erint*	mālú*erint*
Pluperfect	Singular	1	fuíss*em*	potuíss*em*	voluíss*em*	nōluíss*em*	māluíss*em*
		2	fuíss*ēs*	posuíss*ēs*	voluíss*ēs*	nōluíss*ēs*	māluíss*ēs*
		3	fuíss*et*	potuíss*et*	voluíss*et*	nōluíss*et*	māluíss*et*
	Plural	1	fuiss*émus*	potuiss*émus*	voluiss*émus*	nōluiss*émus*	māluiss*émus*
		2	fuiss*étis*	potuiss*étis*	voluiss*étis*	nōluiss*étis*	māluiss*étis*
		3	fuíss*ent*	potuíss*ent*	voluíss*ent*	nōluíss*ent*	māluíss*ent*

Present	Singular	1	fér*am*	fér*ar*	fí*am*	é*am*
		2	fér*ās*	fer*áris*	fí*ās*	é*ās*
		3	fér*at*	fer*átur*	fí*at*	é*at*
	Plural	1	fer*ámus*	fer*ámur*	fi*ámus*	e*ámus*
		2	fer*átis*	fer*áminī*	fi*átis*	e*átis*
		3	fér*ant*	fer*ántur*	fí*ant*	é*ant*
Imperfect	Singular	1	férr*em*	férr*er*	fíer*em*	īr*em*
		2	férr*ēs*	ferr*éris*	fíer*ēs*	īr*ēs*
		3	férr*et*	ferr*étur*	fíer*et*	īr*et*
	Plural	1	ferr*émus*	ferr*émur*	fier*émus*	īr*émus*
		2	ferr*étis*	ferr*éminī*	fier*étis*	īr*étis*
		3	férr*ent*	ferr*éntur*	fíer*ent*	īr*ent*
Perfect	Singular	1	túl*erim*	lát*us sim*	fáct*us sim*	í*erim*
		2	túl*eris*	lát*us sīs*	fáct*us sīs*	í*eris*
		3	túl*erit*	lát*us sit*	fáct*us sit*	í*erit*
	Plural	1	tul*érimus*	lát*ī símus*	fáct*ī símus*	i*érimus*
		2	tul*éritis*	lát*ī sítis*	fáct*ī sítis*	i*éritis*
		3	túl*erint*	lát*ī sint*	fáct*ī sint*	í*erint*
Pluperfect	Singular	1	tulíss*em*	lát*us éssem*	fáct*us éssem*	íss*em*
		2	tulíss*ēs*	lát*us éssēs*	fáct*us éssēs*	íss*ēs*
		3	tulíss*et*	lát*us ésset*	fáct*us ésset*	íss*et*
	Plural	1	tulíss*émus*	lát*ī essémus*	fáct*ī essémus*	īss*émus*
		2	tulíss*étis*	lát*ī essétis*	fáct*ī essétis*	īss*étis*
		3	tulíss*ent*	lát*ī éssent*	fáct*ī éssent*	íss*ent*

Note: the perfect subjunctive of **eō** may be **ierim**, etc., as above, or **īverim**.
The pluperfect subjunctive of **eō** may be **īssem**, etc., as above, or **īvissem**.

XXII. Participles of Non-deponent Verbs

		Active	Passive
Present	1	párāns, parántis	
	2	hábēns, habéntis	
	3	míttēns, mitténtis	
	-*iō*	iáciēns, iaciéntis	
	4	aúdiēns, audiéntis	
Perfect	1		parátus, -a, -um
	2		hábitus, -a, -um
	3		míssus, -a, -um
	-*iō*		iáctus, -a, -um
	4		audítus, -a, -um
Future	1	parātúrus, -a, -um	parándus, -a, -um
	2	habitúrus, -a, -um	habéndus, -a, -um
	3	missúrus, -a, -um	mitténdus, -a, -um
	-*iō*	iactúrus, -a, -um	iaciéndus, -a, -um
	4	audītúrus, -a, -um	audiéndus, -a, -um

Note: the future passive participle is also known as the gerundive.

XXIII. Participles of Deponent Verbs

		Active	Passive
Present	1	cónāns, cōnántis	
	2	vérēns, veréntis	
	3	lóquēns, loquéntis	
	-*iō*	ēgrédiēns, ēgrediéntis	
	4	expériēns, experiéntis	
Perfect	1	cōnátus, -a, -um	
	2	véritus, -a, -um	
	3	locútus, -a, -um	
	-*iō*	ēgréssus, -a, -um	
	4	expértus, -a, -um	
Future	1	cōnātúrus, -a, -um	cōnándus, -a, -um
	2	veritúrus, -a, -um	veréndus, -a, -um
	3	locūtúrus, -a, -um	loquéndus, -a, -um
	-*iō*	ēgressúrus, -a, -um	ēgrediéndus, -a, -um
	4	expertúrus, -a, -um	experiéndus, -a, -um

XXIV.   Infinitives of Non-deponent Verbs

		Active	Passive
Present	1	paráre	parárī
	2	habére	habérī
	3	míttere	míttī
	-iō	iácere	iácī
	4	audíre	audírī
Perfect	1	parāvísse	parátus, -a, -um ésse
	2	habuísse	hábitus, -a, -um ésse
	3	mīsísse	míssus, -a, -um ésse
	-iō	iēcísse	iáctus, -a, -um ésse
	4	audīvísse	audítus, -a, -um ésse
Future	1	parātúrus, -a, -um ésse	
	2	habitúrus, -a, -um ésse	
	3	missúrus, -a, -um ésse	
	-iō	iactúrus, -a, -um ésse	
	4	audītúrus, -a, -um ésse	

XXV.   Infinitives of Deponent Verbs

Present	1	cōnárī
	2	verérī
	3	lóquī
	-iō	égredī
	4	experírī
Perfect	1	cōnátus, -a, -um ésse
	2	véritus, -a, -um ésse
	3	locútus, -a, -um ésse
	-iō	ēgréssus, -a, -um ésse
	4	expértus, -a, -um ésse
Future	1	cōnātúrus, -a, -um ésse
	2	veritúrus, -a, -um ésse
	3	locūtúrus, -a, -um ésse
	-iō	ēgressúrus, -a, -um ésse
	4	expertúrus, -a, -um ésse

XXVI. Gerunds of Non-deponent Verbs

Case	1st Conjugation	2nd Conjugation	3rd Conjugation	3rd -iō Conjugation	4th Conjugation
Genitive	pará*ndī*	habé*ndī*	mitté*ndī*	iacié*ndī*	audié*ndī*
Dative	pará*ndō*	habé*ndō*	mitté*ndō*	iacié*ndō*	audié*ndō*
Accusative	pará*ndum*	habé*ndum*	mitté*ndum*	iacié*ndum*	audié*ndum*
Ablative	pará*ndō*	habé*ndō*	mitté*ndō*	iacié*ndō*	audié*ndō*

XXVII. Gerunds of Deponent Verbs

Case	1st Conjugation	2nd Conjugation	3rd Conjugation	3rd -iō Conjugation	4th Conjugation
Genitive	cōná*ndī*	veré*ndī*	loqué*ndī*	ēgredié*ndī*	experié*ndī*
Dative	cōná*ndō*	veré*ndō*	loqué*ndō*	ēgredié*ndō*	experié*ndō*
Accusative	cōná*ndum*	veré*ndum*	loqué*ndum*	ēgredié*ndum*	experié*ndum*
Ablative	cōná*ndō*	veré*ndō*	loqué*ndō*	ēgredié*ndō*	experié*ndō*

VOCABULARY

A

ā or **ab**, prep. + abl., *from, by*

ac, conj., *and*

accipiō [**ad-**, *to* + **capiō, capere, cēpī, captus**, *to take*], **accipere, accēpī, acceptus**, *to accept, get, receive*

ad, prep. + acc., *to; expressing purpose, for*

adēmpte: from **adēmptus**, see **adimō**

adeō [**ad-**, *to* + **eō, īre, iī, itūrus**, *to go*], **adīre, adiī, aditus**, *to come to, approach*

adimō [**ad-**, *to* + **emō, emere, ēmī, ēmptus**, *to take*], **adimere, adēmī, adēmptus** + dat., *to take away* (from)

admīror [**ad-**, *to* + **mīror, -ārī, -ātus sum**, *to be surprised*] **-ārī, -ātus sum**, *to wonder (at)*

adsum [**ad-**, *to* + **sum, esse, fuī futūrus**, *to be*], **adesse, adfuī, adfutūrus**, *to be present, be near*

adveniō [**ad-**, *to* + **veniō, venīre, vēnī, ventūrus**, *to come*], **advenīre, advēnī, adventūrus**, *to reach, arrive*

aequor, aequoris, n. (see 11.8), *sea*

afferō [**ad-**, *to* + **ferō, ferre, tulī, lātus**, *to carry*], **afferre, attulī, allātus**, *to bring*

ager, agrī, m., *field, territory, land*

agō, agere, ēgī, āctus, *to do, drive*
    grātiās/grātēs agere + dat., *to thank*

agricola, -ae, m., *farmer*

aliquī, -ae, -a, indefinite adjective, *some*

aliquis, aliquis, aliquid, indefinite pronoun, *someone, anyone, something, anything*

alius, alia, aliud, *other*

Alpēs, Alpium, f. pl., *the Alps*

alter, altera, alterum, *another*

altus, -a, -um, *tall, high*

ambō, ambae, ambō, *both*

amīca, -ae, f., *friend*

amīcus, -ī, m., *friend*

amō, -āre, -āvī, -ātus, *to love*

amor, amōris, m. (see 6.16, 7.8, 13.9), *love*

animus, -ī, m. (see 45.20), *mind*

annus, -ī, m., *year*

ante, adv., *previously, before*

anteā, adv., *previously, before*

apud, prep. + acc., *with, at the house of*

aqua, -ae, f., *water*

ārdeō, ārdēre, ārsī, ārsūrus, *to burn, blaze*

at, conj., *but*

atque, conj., *and, also*

attineō [**ad-**, *to* + **teneō, tenēre, tenuī, tentus**, *to hold*], **attinēre, attinuī, attentus**, *to hold back;* + **ad** + acc., *to be of concern (to)*

audeō, audēre, ausus sum + infin., *to dare (to)*

audiō, -īre, -īvī, -ītus, *to hear, listen to*

auferō [**ab-**, *from* + **ferō, ferre, tulī, lātus**, *to carry*], **auferre, abstulī, ablātus**, *to carry away, take away*

aurum, -ī, n., *gold*

aut, conj., *or*
    aut . . . aut, conj., *either . . . or*

avunculus, -ī, m., *maternal uncle*

B

bene, adv., *well*

bonus, -a, -um, *good*

brevis, -is, -e, *short*

Britannī, -ōrum, m. pl., *inhabitants of Britain, Britons*

C

cadō, cadere, cecidī, cāsūrus, *to fall*

caelum, -ī, n., *sky, heaven*

campus, -ī, m., *plain, field*

canō, canere, cecinī, cantus (see 34.4), *to sing*

capiō, capere, cēpī, captus, *to take, catch, capture, seize*

caput, capitis, n., *head*

cārus, -a, -um, *dear*

castus, -a, -um, *virtuous, chaste*

caveō, cavēre, cāvī, cautus, *to be careful, watch out for, beware* celer, celeris, celere, *swift*

cēna, -ae, f., *dinner*

cēnō, -āre, -āvī, -ātus, *to dine, eat dinner*

centum, indeclinable adjective, *a hundred*

certē, adv., *certainly*

cibus, -ī, m., *food*

clāmō, -āre, -āvī, -ātūrus, *to shout*

cōgitō, -āre, -āvī, -ātus, *to think*

cōgō [con-, intensive + agō, agere, ēgī, āctus, *to do, drive*], cōgere, cōēgī, cōāctus, *to compel, force*

colō, colere, coluī, cultus (see 36.14), *to cultivate*

comes, comitis, m./f., *companion , comrade*

comparō, -āre, -āvī, -ātus, *to buy, obtain,*

complexus, -ūs, m., *embrace*

coniungō [con-, *with, together* + iungō, iungere, iūnxī, iūnctus, *to join*], coniungere, coniūnxī, coniūnctus, *to join*

coniūnx, coniugis, m./f., *husband, wife, spouse*

convīva, -ae, m., *guest (at a banquet)*

cor, cordis, n., *heart*

corpus, corporis, n., *body*

crēdō, crēdere, crēdidī, crēditus + *dat.*, *to trust; to believe*

creō, -āre, -āvī, -ātus, *to create*

crūdēlis, -is, -e, *cruel*

culpa, -ae, f. (see 11.22, 73.1), *fault, blame*

cum, prep. + abl., *with*

cum, conj., *when, whenever; since; although*

Cupīdō, Cupīdinis, m. (see 3.1), *Cupid (son of Venus and god of love)*

cupiō, cupere, cupīvī, cupītus, *to desire, want*

cūr, adv., *why*

cūra, -ae, f. (see 2.10), *care, distress*

D

dē, prep. + abl., *down from, concerning, about*

dea, -ae, f., *goddess*

decem, indeclinable adjective, *ten*

decet, decēre, decuit, impersonal, *(it) is becoming, fitting; should*

dēdicō [dē-, *thoroughly, completely* + dicō, -āre, -āvī, -ātus, *to indicate; to dedicate*], -āre, -āvī, -ātus, *to dedicate*

dēferō [dē-, *down* + ferō, ferre, tulī, lātus, *to carry*], dēferre, dētulī, dēlātus, *to carry down*

dēfessus, -a, -um, *tired*

deinde, adv., *then, next*

dēpōnō [dē-, *down* + pōnō, pōnere, posuī, positus, *to put*], dēpōnere, dēposuī, dēpositus, *to lay down, put aside, set down*

dēsīderō, -āre, -āvī, -ātus, *to long for, desire, miss*

dēsinō [dē-, *thoroughly, completely* + sinō, sinere, sīvī, situs, *to leave alone, let be*], dēsinere, dēsiī, dēsitus + infin., *to cease (from), stop (doing)*

dēspondeō [dē-, *thoroughly, completely* + spondeō, spondēre, spopondī, spōnsus, *to pledge; to contract*], dēspondēre, dēspondī, dēspōnsus, *to pledge, promise; to betroth, promise in marriage*

deus, -ī, nom. pl., dī, dat., abl. pl., dīs, m., *god*

dēvorō [dē-, *down* + vorō, -āre, -āvī, -ātus, *to swallow*], -āre, -āvī, -ātus, *to devour*

dexter, dext(e)ra, dext(e)rum, *right*

dī: nom. pl. of deus

dīcō, dīcere, dīxī, dictus (see 34.14), *to say, tell*

dicta, -ōrum, n. pl., *words*

diēs, diēī, m., *day*

difficilis, -is, -e, *difficult*

digitus, -ī, m., *finger*

dīligō [dis-, *apart* + legō, legere, lēgī, lēctus, *to choose, select, pick*], dīligere, dīlēxī, dīlēctus, *to esteem, cherish, love*

diū, adv., *for a long time*

dīversus, -a, -um, *different*

dō, dare, dedī, datus, *to give*

doleō, -ēre, -uī, -itūrus, *to be sorry, be in pain*

domina, -ae, f. (see 3.10), *mistress, lady of the house*

domus, -ūs, f., *house*
    domī, *at home*
    domum, *homeward, home*

dōnō, -āre, -āvī, -ātus, *to give.*

dormiō, -īre, -īvī, -ītūrus, *to sleep*

dūcō, dūcere, dūxī, ductus (see 8.2), *to lead, take, bring; to consider*

dum, conj., *while, as long as*

duō, duae, duō, *two*

E

ē or **ex,** prep. + abl., *from, out of*

ēbrius, -a, -um, *drunk*

edō, ēsse, ēdī, ēsus, *to eat*

efferō [ex-, *out* + **ferō, ferre, tulī, lātus,** *to carry, bring*]**, efferre, extulī, ēlātus,** *to carry out, bring out*

egō, pronoun, *I*

ēheu, interj., *alas*

ēlegāns, ēlegantis, *elegant, tasteful*

enim, conj., *for*

eō, īre, iī or **īvī, itūrus,** *to go*

ēripiō [ex-, *out* + **rapiō, rapere, rapuī, raptus,** *to snatch, seize*]**, ēripere, ēripuī, ēreptus,** *to snatch from*

et, conj., *and, also*

etiam, adv., *also, even*

expellō [ex-, *out* + **pellō, pellere, pepulī, pulsus,** *to drive*]**, expellere, expulī, expulsus,** *to drive out, expel*

exspectō [ex-, *out* + **spectō, -āre, -āvī, -ātus,** *to look at, watch*]**, -āre, -āvī, -ātus,** *to look out for, wait for*

F

facilis, -is, -e, *easy*

faciō, facere, fēcī, factus, *to make, do; to consider, regard*

faveō, favēre, fāvī, fautūrus + dat., *to give favor (to), favor*

fēlīx, fēlīcis, *lucky, happy, fortunate*

ferō, ferre, tulī, lātus, *to bring, carry, bear; to say*

fidēlis, -is, -e, *faithful, devoted*

fidēs, fideī, f., *good faith, reliability, trust*

fīō, fierī, factus sum, *to become, be done, happen*

flamma, -ae, f., *flame*

fleō, flēre, flēvī, flētus, *to weep, cry; to weep for, lament*

flōs, flōris, m., *flower*

fōrtasse, adv., *perhaps*

forte, adv., *by chance*

frangō, frangere, frēgī, frāctus, *to break*

frāter, frātris, m., *brother*

frīgidus, -a, -um, *cool, cold*

frūstrā, adv., *in vain*

fugiō, fugere, fūgī, fugitūrus, *to flee; to escape*

fuī: see **sum**

fundus, -ī, m., *farm*

fūr, fūris, m., *thief*

G

gaudeō, gaudēre, gavīsus sum, *to be glad, rejoice;* + abl., *to find delight (in), take pleasure (in)*

gaudium, -ī, n., *joy, pleasure*

geminus, -a, -um, *twin, double*

gēns, gentis, f., *family, clan; nation, people;* pl., *peoples*

grātia, -ae, f., *gratitude, thanks*
    grātiās/grātēs agere + dat., *to thank*

gravis, -is, -e, *heavy, oppressive, severe*

H

habeō, -ēre, -uī, -itus, *to have, hold*

heu, interj., *alas*

hīc, adv., *here*

hic, haec, hoc, *this*

hiems, hiemis, f., *winter*

homō, hominis, m., *man*

hōra, -ae, f., *hour*

hostis, hostis, m., *enemy*
    hostēs, hostium, m. pl., *the enemy*

hūc, adv., *here, to this place*

I

iaceō, -ēre, -uī, -itūrus, *to lie, be lying down*

iam, adv., *now, already*

ibi, adv., *there*

īdem, eadem, idem, *the same*

identidem, adv., *again and again, repeatedly*

igitur, conj., *therefore*

ignis, ignis, m., *fire*

ille, illa, illud, *that; he, she, it*

illīc, adv., *there, in that place*

illūc, adv., *there, to that place*

imber, imbris, m., *rain*

in, prep. + abl., *in, on*

in, prep. + acc., *into, onto, against*

incendō, incendere, incendī, incēnsus, *to burn, set on fire, inflame*

incidō [in-, *into/onto* + **cadō, cadere, cecidī, casūrus**, *to fall*], **incidere, incidī, incāsūrus** (see 10.5), *to fall into/onto*

incipiō [in-, *in/on* + **capiō, capere, cēpī, captus**, *to take*], **incipere, incēpī, inceptus**, *to begin*

incolumis, -is, -e, *unhurt, safe and sound*

inde, adv., *from there, then*

iniciō [in-, *on* + **iaciō, iacere, iēcī, iactus**, *to throw*], **inicere, iniēcī, iniectus** + dat., *to throw/fling* (on)

inquam, inquis, inquit, perf., **inquiī**, *to say*

īnsula, -ae, f., *island*

inter, prep. + acc., *between, among*

intereā, adv. (see 36.18, 95.3, 101.7), *meanwhile*

invītus, -a, -um, *unwilling*

iocus, -ī, m., *joke, joking, jest*

ipse, ipsa, ipsum, *himself, herself, itself, themselves*

īrātus, -a, -um, *angry*

is, ea, id, *he, she, it; this, that*

ita, adv., *thus, so*

Italī, -ōrum, m. pl., *the Italians*

iter, itineris, n., *journey, route, road*

iubeō, iubēre, iussī, iussus, *to order, bid*

iūcundus, -a, -um, *pleasant, delightful*

iungō, iungere, iūnxī, iūnctus, *to join*

iuvenis, iuvenis, m., *young man*

L

labor, labōris, m., *work, toil*

laetus, -a, -um, *happy, glad*

lateō, -ēre, -uī, *to lie in hiding, hide*

lectīca, -ae, f., *litter*

lectus, -ī, m., *bed, couch*

legō, legere, lēgī, lēctus, *to read*

lepidus, -a, -um, *charming*

libenter, adv., *gladly*

licet, licēre, licuit, impersonal + dat., *(it) is allowed*

ligō, -āre, -āvī, -ātus, *to bind up*

lingua, -ae, f., *tongue*

lītus, lītoris, n., *shore*

locus, -ī, m.; m. or n. in pl., *place*

longus, -a, -um, *long, tall*
longē, adv., *far*

loquor, loquī, locūtus sum, *to speak, talk*

lūceō, lūcēre, lūxī, *to shine*

lūdō, lūdere, lūsī, lūsūrus, *to play*

lūx, lūcis, f., *light*

M

magis, adv., *more; rather, instead*

magister, magistrī, m., *master*

magistra, -ae, f., *mistress*

magnus, -a, -um, *big, great, large*

maior, maior, maius, gen., **maiōris**, *bigger*

mālō, mālle, māluī, *to prefer*

mālum, -ī, n., *apple*

malus, -a, -um, *bad, evil*
male, adv. (see 3.13, 16, 10.33, 83.1, 92.1), *badly*

maneō, manēre, mānsī, mānsūrus (see 8.15), *to remain, endure, last*

manus, -ūs, f., *hand*

mare, maris, n., *sea*

marītus, -ī, m., *husband*

māter, mātris, f., *mother*

maximus, -a, -um, *biggest, greatest*

meminī, meminisse, *to remember*

mēns, mentis, f., *mind.*

mēnsa, -ae, f., *table*

meus, -a, -um, *my, mine*

mī = mihi or vocative of meus

migrō, -āre, -āvī, -ātūrus, *to change one's residence; to go away*

mīlia, mīlium, n. pl., *thousands*

mīlle, indeclinable adjective, *a thousand*

minimus, -a, -um, *very small, smallest*

minus, adv., *less*

mīror, -ārī, -ātus sum, *to admire, wonder at*

mīrus, -a, -um, *wonderful, marvelous, strange*

miser, misera, miserum, *unhappy, miserable, wretched*; as a term describing lovers, *obsessed with erotic passion, lovesick*

mittō, mittere, mīsī, missus (see 96.4), *to send, let go*

modus, -ī, m., *way*

moenia, moenium, n. pl., *walls* (of a town or city)

molestus, -a, -um, *troublesome, annoying*

mollis, -is, -e, *soft*

mōns, montis, m., *mountain, hill*

morbus, -ī, m., *illness, sickness*

morior, morī, mortuus sum, *to die*

moror, -ārī, -ātus sum, *to delay, remain, stay*

mors, mortis, f., *death*

mōs, mōris, m., *custom*

moveō, movēre, mōvī, mōtus, *to move*

mulier, mulieris, f., *woman*

multus, -a, -um, *much*

multum, adv., *greatly, much, abundantly*

multī, -ae, -a, *many*

mūnus, mūneris, n., *gift, service*

mūtuus, -a, -um, *mutual, shared*

N

nam, conj., *for*

nārrō, -āre, -āvī, -ātus, *to tell* (a story); *to say*

nāscōr, nāscī, nātus sum, inceptive, *to be born*

nāsus, -ī, m., *nose*

nāvis, nāvis, f., *ship*

-ne: indicates a question

nē, conj. + subjunctive, *not to, so that . . . not*

nec, conj., *and . . . not*

nec . . . nec/neque . . . , *neither . . . nor*

necesse, adv. or indeclinable adjective, *necessary*

neglegēns, neglegentis, *negligent, careless, inattentive*

negō, -āre, -āvī, -ātus, *to deny*

nēmō, nēminis, m./f., *no one*

neque, conj., *and . . . not*

neque . . . neque/nec, conj., *neither . . . nor*

nēquīquam, adv., *in vain, to no purpose*

nesciō, -īre, -īvī, -ītus, *to be ignorant, not to know*

niger, nigra, nigrum, *black*

nihil, indeclinable noun, *nothing*

nīl, indeclinable noun, *nothing*

nisi, conj., *if . . . not, unless*

nōlō, nōlle, nōluī, *to be unwilling, not to wish, refuse*

nōmen, nōminis, n., *name*

nōn, adv., *not*

nōnus, -a, -um, *ninth*

nōs, pronoun, *we, us*

noster, nostra, nostrum, *our*

novus, -a, -um, *new*

nōx, noctis, f., *night*

nocte, *at night*

nūbō, nūbere, nūpsī, nūptūrus + dat., *to marry*

nūllus, -a, -um, *no, none*

numerus, -ī, m. (see 50.5), *number*

numquam, adv., *never*

nunc, adv., *now*

nūntius, -ī, m., *messenger, message*

O

ō, interj., used with vocative and in exclamations

octō, indeclinable adjective, *eight*

oculus, -ī, m., *eye*

ōlīva, -ae, f., *olive, olive tree*

omnis, -is, -e, *all, the whole, every*

onus, oneris, n., *load, burden*

oportet, oportēre, oportuit, impersonal, *(it) is fitting; one ought*

optimus, -a, -um, *best*

optō, -āre, -āvī, -ātus, *to wish for, desire*

ōrātiō, ōrātiōnis, f., *oration, speech*

ōrō, -āre, -āvī, -ātus, *to beg*

ōs, ōris, n., *mouth*

ostendō [ob-, *against* + tendō, tendere, tetendī, tentus, *to stretch/hold out, offer*], ostendere, ostendī, ostentus, *to show*

P

paene, adv., *almost*

parēns, parentis, m./f., *parent*

pāreō, -ēre, -uī, -itūrus + dat., *to obey*

parō, -āre, -āvī, -ātus, *to prepare, get ready; to purchase, buy*
  parātus, -a, -um, *ready, prepared*

pars, partis, f., *part*

parvus, -a, -um, *small*

pater, patris, m., *father*

patria, -ae, f., *nation, native land*

patrōnus, -ī, m., *patron*

paucī, -ae, -a, *few*

paulum, adv., *a little, for a little while*

pectus, pectoris, n., *chest, breast*

pecus, pecoris, n., *livestock, sheep and cattle*

per, prep. + acc., *through; along; on account of*

perdō [per-, *through* + dō, dare, dedī, datus, *to give*], perdere, perdidī, perditus, *to destroy; to lose.*

pereō [per-, *through* + eō, īre, iī or īvī, itūrus, *to go*], perīre, periī, peritūrus (see 8.2, 45.5, 76.9), *to die, perish; to come to an end; to perish (with love), be madly in love.*

pēs, pedis, m. (see 4.21), *foot*

pessimus, -a, -um, *worst*

petō, petere, petīvī, petītus, *to seek*

placeō, -ēre, -uī + dat., *to please*

plēnus, -a, -um + gen., *full (of)*

plūrēs, plūrēs, plūra, gen., plūrium, *more*

plūrimī, -ae, -a, *most, very many*

plūrimum, adv., *very much, especially, most*

plūs, adv., *more*

poena, -ae, f., *punishment, penalty*

poēta, -ae, m., *poet*

populus, -ī, m., *people*

possum, posse, potuī, *to be able; I can*

post, prep. + acc., *after*

post, adv., *after(ward), later, hereafter*

postquam, conj., *after*

postrēmus, -a, -um, *final, last*

praetereō [praeter-, *past, by* + eō, īre, iī or īvī, itūrus, *to go*], praeterīre praeteriī or praeterīvī, praeteritus, *to go past, pass by; to surpass*

pretium, -ī, n., *price*

prīmus, -a, -um, *first*

prior, prior, prius, gen., priōris, *previous*
  prius, adv., *earlier, before, previously*

proficīscor [pro-, *forward* + faciō, facere, fēcī, factus, *to make, do* + -scō, inceptive suffix], proficīscī, profectus sum, inceptive, *to set out, leave*

prōmittō [pro-, *forward* + mittō, mittere, mīsī, missus, *to send*], prōmittere, prōmīsī, prōmissus, *to promise*

prope, prep. + acc., *near*

prōvincia, -ae, f., *province*

puella, -ae, f., *girl, girlfriend, swetheart*

puer, puerī, m., *boy*

pugnō, -āre, -āvī, -ātūrus, *to fight;* + dat., *to fight with*

pulcher, pulchra, pulchrum, *beautiful, pretty, handsome*
  pulcherrimus, -a, -um, *most/very beautiful*

putō, -āre, -āvī, -ātus, *to think, consider*

Q

quaerō, quaerere, quaesīvī, quaesītus, *to seek, look for, ask*

quam, adv., *how; than; as*

quandō, adv., *when*

quantus, -a, -um, *as*
    quantum, adv., *as much as*

quārē, adv., *for which reason, therefore*

-que, enclitic conj., *and*

quī, quae, quod, relative pronoun,
    who, which, that

quī, quae, quod, interrogative adjec-
    tive, *what, which*

quīdam, quaedam, quoddam, indefi-
    nite adjective, *a certain*

quiēs, quiētis, f. (see 4.26), *rest, repose*

quīngentī, -ae, -a, *five hundred*

quis, quis, quid, interrogative pro-
    noun, *who, what*

quis, qua/quae, quid, indefinite pro-
    noun after **nē, nī, seu, sī**, *anyone, any-*
    body, somebody, anything, something

quō, adv., *where, to where*

quod: see **quī, quae, quod**

quod, conj., *because*

quoque, adv., *also*

quot, interrogative adv., *how many*

R

recipiō [**re-** *back* + **capiō, capere, cēpī,**
    captus, *to take*], **recipere, recēpī, re-**
    ceptus, *to receive*

reddō [**re-/red-**, *back* + **dō, dare, dedī,**
    datus, *to give*], **reddere, reddidī,**
    redditus, *to give back, return*

redeō [**re-**, *back* + **eō, īre, iī** or **īvī,**
    itūrus, *to go*], **redīre, rediī** or **redīvī,**
    reditūrus, *to return*

redūcō [**re-**, *back* + **dūcō, dūcere, dūxī,**
    ductus, *to lead*], **redūcere, redūxī, re-**
    ductus, *to lead back, take back*

referō [**re-**, *back* + **ferō, ferre, tulī, lā-**
    tus, *to bring*], **referre, rettulī, relā-**
    tus, *to bring back; to report; to write*
    down

reficiō [**re-**, *back* + **faciō, facere, fēcī,**
    factus, *to make*], **reficere, refēcī, re-**
    fectus, *to remake, redo, restore* (*to*
    health)

relinquō [**re-**, *back* + **linquō, linquere,**

līquī, lictus, *to leave*], **relinquere,**
    relīquī, relictus, *to leave behind*

remittō [**re-**, *back* + **mittō, mittere,**
    mīsī, missus, *to send*], **remittere,**
    remīsī, remissus, *to send back*

renovō [**re-**, *back, again* + **novō, -āre,**
    -āvī, -ātus, *to make something new*],
    -āre, -āvī, -ātus, *to renew, revive*

reportō [**re-**, *back* + **portō, -āre, -āvī,**
    -ātus, *to carry*], **-āre, -āvī, -ātus**, *to*
    bring back

rēs, reī, f., *thing, matter, affair*

respondeō [**re-**, *back* + **spondeō,**
    spondēre, spopondī, spōnsus, *to*
    give a pledge], **respondēre, respondī,**
    respōnsūrus, *to reply*

revocō [**re-**, *back* + **vocō, -āre, -āvī,**
    -ātus, *to call*], **-āre, -āvī, -ātus**, *to re-*
    call, call back

rēx, rēgis, m., *king*

rīdeō, rīdēre, rīsī, rīsus, *to laugh* (*at*),
    smile

rogō, -āre, -āvī, -ātus, *to ask*

rumpō, rumpere, rūpī, ruptus, *to*
    burst, rupture

rūs, rūris, n., *country, countryside, farm-*
    lands

S

sacculus, -ī, m. [dim.], *small bag, purse*

saepe, adv., *often*

Salvē!/Salvēte! *Greetings! Hello!*

sānctus, -a, -um, *holy, sacred; sanctified,*
    hallowed

satis, indeclinable substantive, adv.,
    enough

sciō, -īre, -īvī, -ītus, *to know*

sē, *himself, herself, oneself, itself, them-*
    selves

secundus, -a, -um (see 4.21), *second*

sed, conj., *but*

sedeō, sedēre, sēdī, sessūrus, *to sit*

semper, adv., *always*

senex, senis, m., *old man*

sentiō, sentīre, sēnsī, sēnsus, *to feel,*
    notice, realize

sepulcrum, -ī, n., *tomb*

sermō, sermōnis, m., *conversation, talk*

serviō, -īre, -īvī, -itūrus + dat., *to serve*

sī, conj., *if*

sīc, adv., *thus, so, in this way*

signum, -ī, n., *signal, sign*

silva, -ae, f., *woods, forest*

simul, adv. (see 11.14, 18), *together, at the same time*

simul ac, conj. (see 22.15, 51.6), *as soon as*

sine, prep. + abl., *without*

sinister, sinistra, sinistrum, *left*

sōl, sōlis, m., *sun*

soleō, solēre, solitus sum + infin., *to be accustomed* (to), *be in the habit* (of)

sōlus, -a, -um, *alone*

solvō, solvere, solvī, solūtus (see 36.2), *to loosen, untie; to relax, relieve*

somnus, -ī, m., *sleep*

sonitus, -ūs, m., *sound, noise*

spectō, -āre, -āvī, -ātus, *to watch, look at*

stō, stāre, stetī, statūrus, *to stand*

studium, -ī, n., *eagerness, enthusiasm*

suāvis, -is, -e, *sweet, delightful*

sub, prep. + acc., *under*

subitō, adv., *suddenly*

sum, esse, fuī, futūrus, *to be*

summus, -a, -um, *greatest, very great, the top of . . . , highest, topmost*

super, indeclinable substantive, adv., *over, above, more than enough*

surgō, surgere, surrēxī, surrēctūrus, *to get up, rise*

suus, -a, -um, *his, her, one's, its, their (own)*

T

tabellārius, -ī, m., *courier*

taceō, -ēre, -uī, -itus (see 6.3), *to be quiet/silent*

tacitus, -a, -um, *silent*

taedet, taedēre, taesum est, impersonal, *(it) bores, makes one tired/sick*

tālis, -is, -e, *such, like this, of this kind*

tam, adv., *so, as, such*

tamen, adv., *however, nevertheless*

tandem, adv., *at last, at length*

tangō, tangere, tetigī, tāctus, *to touch*

tantus, -a, -um, *so great, as great*

tantum, adv., *only; so much; so*

tegō, tegere, tēxī, tēctus, *to cover*

temptō, -āre, -āvī, -ātus, *to try*

tempus, temporis, n., *time*

teneō, tenēre, tenuī, tentus, *to hold*

tergum, -ī, n., *back*

tertius, -a, -um, *third*

tollō, tollere, sustulī, sublātus, *to lift, raise; to take away; to steal*

tot, indeclinable adjective, *so many*

tōtus, -a, -um, *all, the whole*

trādō [**trāns-**, *across* + **dō, dare, dedī, datus**, *to give*], **trādere, trādidī, trāditus**, *to hand over*

trāns, prep. + acc., *across*

trēs, trēs, tria, *three*

trīstis, -is, -e, *sad*

tū, pronoun, *you* (sing.)

tulī, see **ferō**

tum, adv., *at that moment, then*

tuus, -a, -um, *your* (sing.)

U

ubi, adv., conj., *where*

ūllus, -a, -um, *any*

umquam, adv., *ever*

unda, -ae, f., *wave*

unde, adv., *from where*

ūnus, -a, -um, *one, one alone*

urbs, urbis, f., *city*

ut, conj. + indicative, *as, when*

ut, conj. + subjunctive, *so that, that*

uterque, utraque, utrumque, *each (of two), both*

ūtor, ūtī, ūsus sum + abl., *to use*

utrum . . . an . . ., conj. (see 10.31), *whether . . . or . . .*

ūva, -ae, f., *grape, bunch of grapes*

V

valeō, -ēre, -uī, -itūrus (see 6.12, 11.17), *to be strong, be well*

    Valē!/Valēte! *Good-bye!*

varius, -a, -um, *different, various, varied*

-ve, enclitic conj., *or*

vehō, vehere, vexī, vectus, *to carry;*

pass., *to be carried, travel*
    vectus, -a, -um, *having been carried,*
      having traveled
velle: see **volō**
velut, adv., *just as*
veniō, venīre, vēnī, ventūrus, *to come*
ventus, -ī, m., *wind*
Venus, Veneris, f. (see 3.1, 45.26),
    Venus (the goddess of love)
versus, -ūs, m., *verse*
vērus, -a, -um, *true*
    vērē, adv., *truly*
vester, vestra, vestrum, *your* (pl.)
vetus, veteris, *old, ancient*
via, -ae, f., *road*
victōria, -ae, f., *victory*
videō, vidēre, vīdī, vīsus, *to see*
    videor, vidērī, vīsus sum, *to seem, be*
    seen

vigilō, -āre, -āvī, -ātūrus, *to stay awake*
vīlla, -ae, f., *country house, villa*
vincō, vincere, vīcī, victus, *to conquer;*
    to win
vīnum, -ī, n., *wine*
vir, virī, m., *man; husband*
virgō, virginis, f., *maiden*
vīta, -ae, f., *life*
vīvō, vīvere, vīxī, vīctūrus (see 5.1,
    8.10, 10.33, 107.7), *to live*
vix, adv., *scarcely, with difficulty, hardly,*
    barely
vocō, -āre, -āvī, -ātus, *to call, invite*
volō, velle, voluī, *to wish, want, be will-*
    ing
voluptās, voluptātis, f., *pleasure, delight*
vōs, pronoun, *you* (pl.)
vōx, vōcis, f., *voice*